crazy about
cakes

crazy about cakes

More than 150 Delectable Recipes for Every Occasion

Krystina Castella

STERLING

New York

STERLING
New York

An Imprint of Sterling Publishing
387 Park Avenue South
New York, NY 10016

ISBN 978-1-4027-6914-6 (paperback)
ISBN 1-4027-8929-8 (ebook)

Library of Congress Cataloging-in-Publication Data
Castella, Krystina.
  Crazy about cakes : more than 150 delectable recipes for every occasion / Krystina Castella.
    p. cm.
  Includes bibliographical references and index.
  ISBN 978-1-4027-6914-6 (pb-trade pbk. : alk. paper) 1. Cake. I. Title.
  TX771.C337 2011
  641.8'653--dc22
                            2010040169

Distributed in Canada by Sterling Publishing
c/o Canadian Manda Group, 165 Dufferin Street
Toronto, Ontario, Canada M6K 3H6
Distributed in the United Kingdom by GMC Distribution Services
Castle Place, 166 High Street, Lewes, East Sussex, England BN7 1XU
Distributed in Australia by Capricorn Link (Australia) Pty. Ltd.
P.O. Box 704, Windsor, NSW 2756, Australia

For information about custom editions, special sales, and premium and corporate purchases,
please contact Sterling Special Sales at 800-805-5489 or specialsales@sterlingpublishing.com.

Manufactured in China

2 4 6 8 10 9 7 5 3 1

www.sterlingpublishing.com

For Eve Boyl Ofstad and James K. Neill

Acknowledgments

Thank you to everyone whose help has crafted this book:

Jennifer Williams, editor

Teri Lyn Fisher, photographer

Sienna DeGovia, food stylist

Larena Faretta, pastry chef

Michela Swarthout, digital tech

Barbara Clark, project editor

Rachel Maloney, design director

Elizabeth Mihaltse, jacket art director

Jason Chow, jacket designer

Contents

Introduction

As a teenager, I loved crafts. I made greeting cards by hand, tended to the strawberries in my garden, crocheted granny squares for blankets, performed major renovations to my collectible dollhouse—and, of course, I baked! For me, "playing" was synonymous with "making," and the kitchen was the best place for fun. After I came home from school, baking was my favorite way to relax and explore. I made cupcakes, cakes, and cookies for my swim team, for bake sales, and to share at slumber parties. I would study new recipes and techniques, using my imagination to determine the best treat for upcoming birthdays, special occasions, and holidays, and I would prepare them with my own creative twist.

The first over-the-top cake I made was for my Sweet Sixteen birthday party. Most of my friends spent the hours before their parties primping to make themselves gorgeous, but I spent the day in a much more enjoyable way—by beautifying my cake. I shaped a huge golden cake that could feed more than one hundred people into the number "16." The numerals were outlined with row after row of stars piped onto the cake in a rainbow of colored frosting. Not only did the frosting match the party decorations, but it also served as an introduction to a new level of cake making. I realized that cakes are the baker's ultimate platform—at the same time as they allow us to create "look at me" desserts, they visually excite and then comfort us in a fleeting moment of tasty bliss.

After college, I turned my love of crafting and playing into a career and became an industrial designer. Today, I design products by first playfully exploring their materials and then translating those explorations into models and sketches. I've created dozens of new products this way, including furniture, toys, clothing, stationery, housewares, and soft goods.

I approach baking in exactly the same way. I develop new recipes by playing with a pantry full of ingredients, cabinets filled with baking pans, and a tool kit of decorating supplies. I particularly love the creative opportunities that sweets provide—this is one realm where it is completely acceptable to push the limits. Sometimes I want to create something healthful, sometimes I want to create something cute; at other times I want something fancy and indulgent. Taste, texture, form, and color all come together in the process of baking and decorating.

Another reason I love cakes is because of their ties to tradition and culture. Cakes are the baked treat that we are most likely to eat every day or for dessert. If there is a special occasion, holiday, or party anywhere in the world, you can bet there will be a cake made with love at the center of the celebration.

The influences for the cakes in these recipes come from far and wide, but mostly I was inspired by one of three major themes: retro-modern, ethnic fusion, and flavor fusion. In other words, I wanted to blend the past with the present, cultural influences from all four corners of the globe, and flavors to satisfy all our senses—all with a sense of fun.

RETRO-MODERN

Whether you want authentic made-from-scratch recipes for the old-fashioned cakes we all know and love or modernized interpretations that contain less fat and more natural ingredients, you'll find them in this book. For example, I have added new spices to age-old cakes such as Golden Saffron Tea Cake (page 70), White Fruitcake (page 304), and Chocolate Cherry Fruitcake (page 342). Nostalgic trifles, checkerboard cakes, sandwich cakes, and a tiered wedding cake with a lovebird topper combine retro styling and modern flavors. The proliferation of "kidults" (adults who are still part kids) in our society inspired many of the cakes, including those based on beloved characters such as Alice in Wonderland and those whose flavors are based on favorite childhood foods, such as the Peanut Sesame Raspberry Roll (page 180) and the Creamsicle Cake Pops (page 129).

ETHNIC FUSION

In these types of cakes, flavors from one cuisine are blended with a twist from another. For example, New York–style cheesecake takes a trip to Florida and discovers not only Key limes but also the Nuevo Latino influences of guava, pecans, and coconut. Global ingredients such as plantains, chayote, yucca, and beets inspired me to rethink vegetable cakes. My Italian heritage inspired the Mascarpone Cheesecake (page 118) and Zuccotto (page 132), a gelato ice cream cake. Regional flavors from the American Southwest inspired the Dulce de Leche Cheesecake (page 258) and Blue Corn Cake (page 96). And when it comes to styling, I drew on the often whimsical designs of the Japanese lunch box to create the playful Bento Birthday Bear (page 152).

FLAVOR FUSION

As I developed the recipes in this book, my friends and family couldn't believe that I was actually experimenting with such unconventional cake-baking ingredients as corn and Cheddar (for the Mac and Cheese Cupcakes, page 120), or that I was making cakes topped with eggs and sesame seeds (page 223), or that I was making croutons from Chocolate Spice Cake for Strawberry Soup (page 257). (But they were very happy with the results!) Indeed, although many of the cakes in this book are sweet, you'll find plenty of savory options and variations. My version of the classic pound cake is flavored with rosemary, olives, and sun-dried tomatoes (page 68). I also use salty and sweet combinations like bacon and chocolate, feta and apricot, and butterscotch and sea salt to fill a dinner-party array of Bundts (page 264). And I encourage everyone to experiment with unexpected contrasts in flavors, such as blueberry-chocolate (page 92) and fried dough flavored with beer (page 216). Many recipes use alcohol as a flavoring, partly because I love boozing cake up but also because alcohol offers an array of outside-the-box flavorings that are perfect to enjoy at cocktail or dessert parties.

THE HOME BAKER'S ADVANTAGE

One of the biggest benefits of baking at home is the fact that you have the ability to control the quality of your ingredients. In my recipes, I use only natural sweeteners, and I often substitute fruits or other sweet ingredients for a portion of the granulated sugar. I love to use "superfoods" like berries, pineapple, dates, and nuts and seeds, which are high in antioxidants. All-natural butter and all-purpose flour are the basis for most of my cakes, but you'll find plenty of recipes that use unsaturated fats and whole grains as well. Seasonal flavors such as summer or fall fruits don't have to be "limited edition"—many recipes can be adapted to use ingredients that are available throughout the year. And finally, when using chocolate, remember that it is not about how much you use. I recommend the highest quality you can find.

Home bakers can also control the size of their creations—after all, good things come in small packages. The craze for cupcakes has taught us to enjoy the little things in life—no more supersizing! With a focus on quality, you can have it all in a few bites of bliss. Miniature or portion-size indulgences come in every form, from German Chocolate Loaves (page 78) and Chocolate-Covered Doughnuts (page 141) to Chai Tea Cake Sandwiches (page 233), Pine Nut–Basil Financiers (page 230), and Miniature Tiered Wedding Cakes (page 191).

CAKE CRAFTING

I love the fact that, in many homes, the kitchen is the new living room, and instead of hanging out in front of the TV, people are cooking and baking. Men and women are finding happiness in the domestic arts, and a fantastic way to show off those skills is through handcrafted cakes. But the cakes we enjoy today are not the complicated creations of the past that take days to make, resplendent with spun sugar and superdetailed decorations. Artisans of all skill levels can now show off their chops with a perfectly risen sponge cake or with "accessories" like chocolate cups for Irish Cream Cakes (see page 276). My decorated cakes are not overwhelmingly complex but feature perfect details—see the recipes for the Mom Cake (page 212), the Tea with Alice cake (page 240), the Diploma Cake (page 218), and the Holiday Ginger Cakes (page 332). Crafting also extends to presentation, and this book provides ideas for serving and plating cakes in recipes and in photographs.

CAKE IS LIFE!

From baking to eating, I find the whole cake experience to be fun, but—like many people—I bake cakes for specific purposes or events. I want to make the right cake for each occasion, whether it's to serve as a simple snack, to present as a birthday gift for a friend or loved one, or to bring out as a showstopping finale to a dinner party or wedding. That's why I organized the cakes into five chapters—Everyday Cakes, Birthday Cakes, Special-Occasion Cakes, Party Cakes, and Holiday Cakes. This structure reflects how we truly *experience* cakes, and to me that is the most important part of baking.

If you want to learn more about the tools, techniques, ingredients, and how-tos of baking, take a look at the Cakes in the Know chapter. From tips on choosing the right pan to ideas for storing leftover cake, you'll find everything you need to know to expand your skills as a baker and decorator. The techniques, recipes, and design ideas in this book are here for you to re-create in your kitchen or to use as a springboard for concepts of your own. Make your cakes as simple or complex as you like. Follow the recipes exactly or experiment. Whatever approach you choose, I hope you have fun exploring all the possibilities that cake provides.

Happy baking and good eating!

—Krystina Castella

Chapter 1

Cakes in the Know

THE CAKE MAKER'S TOOL KIT

It's all about the gear. My particular obsession is collecting various pans and tools for cake making—especially the vintage items. I treasure the baking pans that I inherited from my grandmother, which are almost one hundred years old. I also scour estate sales and flea markets, where I can find really unusual tools that are no longer available. I don't draw inspiration just from antique items, though. Silicone bakeware is fairly new to the market, but I find it inspirational because it makes shaping my cakes so easy. Whatever your inspiration, using "the right stuff" is an essential part of the process.

Cake Shapes

LAYER CAKES

Most of us think of layer cakes as two or three layers, stacked on top of one another, with frosting between the layers and on the top and sides of the cake—but layer cakes are so much more. They can be any shape or size or number of layers; they can be filled or frosted with just about anything, and you may choose to leave the sides unfrosted to expose the tasty goodness.

Layer cakes can be stacked in a glass dish, as they are in a trifle (such as the Christmas Cactus Trifle on page 334), or made into sandwiches (such as the Passover Cakes on page 309). Tiered cakes

1

Contrast w/polka dots on top

Sweet 16 RAINBOW LAYERS

Accent exposed layers

(like the Quinceañera Cake, page 160) are layer cakes made by stacking layers of decreasing size on top of one another; cakes with multiple layers include Princess Cake (page 178) and Devil's Food Cake (page 76).

SHEET CAKES

These rectangular or square cakes are common party cakes because, when frosted with a smooth surface, they are ideal for decorating. They are also easy to scale up or down, depending on the size of the crowd you are expecting. Sheet cakes can be rectangular or square, filled—with cream, jam, or frosting—or not. The most common homemade size is a 9 x 13-inch rectangle.

SHAPED CAKES

Easy yet impressive, shaped cakes can be baked in special molds or pans, or formed into shapes after baking. The Day of the Dead Cake (page 317), for example, is baked in a skull-shaped pan. Cakes that are shaped after baking include the Bunny Cakes (page 300) and Mom Cake (page 212).

Shaped cakes made from dough (instead of batter) are often molded by hand and kneaded and rolled out on a floured work surface. This surface could be a cutting board, a silicone mat, or the countertop. I like to use large plastic cutting boards because they are light and easy to move around. I have a marble one, too, but I don't use it much because it is heavy.

ROLLED CAKES

Baked in a jelly-roll pan, and most often starting with a springy sponge-cake batter, rolled cakes are made by covering a large thin sheet of cake with a thin layer of frosting, filling, whipped cream, buttercream, or jam, and then rolling it into a log shape before baking. Examples of rolled cakes are the Strawberry Pistachio Yule Log Slices (page 340) and the Peanut Sesame Raspberry Roll (page 180).

INDIVIDUAL CAKES

Although cupcakes are the best-known examples, individual cakes— or single-serving cakes—come in many shapes and sizes. They are

use the egg shaped molds to make Bunnies + eggs.

Bunny + Egg cakes.

usually made in small pans, such as muffin-top pans, mini-Bundts, or mini loaf pans. Examples of individual cakes include the Salty-Sweet Savory Bundts (see page 261).

LOAF CAKES

These casual cakes are usually eaten for breakfast or snacks. Pound Cake (see page 67) is most often baked in these relatively tall, rectangular pans. Other examples of loaf cakes include the Lemon Poppy Loaves (page 228) and the Tomato Basil Cake (page 100).

RING CAKES

True to their name, these cakes are shaped like a ring, and contain a hole in the middle. In other types of cakes the center is the last part to achieve doneness during cooking. So a ring shape ensures even baking throughout by allowing heat to reach the center more quickly. Angel Food Cake (page 208) is a specific type of ring cake made in a special pan to allow for even rising of the sponge batter. Some Bundt cakes are also ring cakes, such as the Purple Rose of Cake (page 295). Other examples of ring cakes include the Cinnamon Walnut Coffee Cake (page 104) and the Pecan Cake (page 330).

Cake Pans

ROUND PANS

Readily available in diameters from 3 to 20 inches, round pans are most popular in the 8-inch, 9-inch, and 10-inch sizes. The standard depth is 2 inches, which is ideal for layer cakes. Pans that are 3 to 4 inches deep are used for single-layer or tiered cakes. Some have contoured sides (see the picture of the Chocolate Champagne Cake on page 286); others have a removable bottom, similar to a tart pan or springform pan.

SPRINGFORM PANS

Although springform pans are suitable for baking any type of cake, they are most commonly used for cheesecake. A springform pan consists of two parts: a removable base with a waffled texture, which gives it strength, and a tall ring that fits around the base and is secured with a buckle. This buckle unlocks to release the cake after baking.

Material Matters

It isn't just the shape of the pan you choose that affects how it looks—the material of the cake pan is very important for proper baking. When you choose a pan, consider its color and weight. Light-colored bakeware, including shiny metals such as aluminum or steel or cast iron coated with enamel, reflects heat. Because it does not absorb as much heat as dark pans, your cakes won't get as brown on the bottom or the edges. Stainless steel is a nonreactive metal and good for baking.

Dark-colored bakeware, including pans with nonstick coatings, absorb more heat. Nonstick pans are nice if you prefer not to heavily grease the pan. Many pans are made with reactive metals like aluminum, copper, and cast iron, which sometimes react negatively with acidic ingredients in the batter, such as lemon juice. Thick metal bakeware distributes the heat more evenly than bakeware made from thin metal. If you are concerned about browning the sides of the cake too much when baking a large cake, or one with a long baking time, your best bet is to use a thick metal pan. Earthenware and ceramics do not do a good job of retaining heat, but they are fantastic for cakes with moist ingredients and longer baking times, such as the Sweet Potato Cake (page 327). Silicone bakeware is great when it comes time to get the cakes out of the pan, but silicone's flexible nature makes the pans flop around and hard to pick up and put in the oven when they're full of batter. The solution is to always place silicone pans on top of a rigid baking sheet before filling. Transfer the sheet and pan to the oven and bake on the baking sheet as directed.

The most popular sizes for springform pans are the 9-inch and 10-inch varieties, with 3-inch-high sides. I like to make miniature cheesecakes in 4-inch-diameter springform pans. One caveat: most springform pans leak, so make sure to wrap the outside bottom and sides with foil before filling the pan with batter.

TUBE PANS

Round, with a hole in the middle, tube pans may have flat or rounded bottoms. They are available in many different diameters, with varying interior and exterior ring dimensions. The hole in the middle helps tall cakes cook more evenly. A tube cake is usually inverted before serving, to create a pleasing shape on top (see, for example, the Coffee Liqueur Bundt Cake on page 270).

ANGEL FOOD PANS

Designed specifically for angel food cake (a sponge cake made with egg whites rather than yolks; see page 208), the traditional angel food pan is a 9- or 10-inch tube pan that is 4 inches deep. It has a removable inner core and bottom, as well as cooling legs. Angel food cakes can rise to an elegant height when exposed to heat (hence the tall sides and core of the pan), yet they are very delicate and can collapse if not cooled properly (hence the legs).

BUNDT PANS

The crimped or fluted tube-shaped Bundt pan was created in the 1950s and is now an American icon. The pans allow figured cakes to pop straight out of the pan, and with only a little dusting of sugar or drizzling of glaze you have a beautiful cake. Fluted Bundt pans will need care when greasing to be sure that every nook and cranny is covered. There are dozens of Bundt shapes, from pumpkins to roses, available in several sizes.

SQUARE PANS

Square layer cakes are "in" right now—using square pans instead of round pans gives a cake a more modern look. The most common sizes for square pans are 8-inch, 9-inch, and 10-inch.

SHEET PANS

If you've ever ordered a cake at a bakery, you probably had to choose either a full

MARZIPAN ALMOND CAKE

Add tea cups to the photo for tea party

sheet (24 x 16 inches), or a half sheet (12 x 16 inches), or a quarter sheet (8 x 12 inches). Most home ovens are too small to accommodate the larger sizes, so the most common size for a homemade sheet cake is 9 x 13 inches. To make larger cakes, you can butt two smaller cakes next to each other—or, if your oven is large enough, consider purchasing larger sheet pans at a restaurant supply store.

LOAF PANS

These long, slim pans are available in a variety of sizes and lengths. Small loaf pans are typically 3 x 5¾ inches and are great to use when preparing miniature cakes as gifts. The most common larger sizes are 4 x 8 (or 4¼ x 8½) and 5 x 9 inches. Some recipes call for the extra-long 4 x 16-inch pan, which is great for baking a long family-style cake in a unique presentation. I like to line loaf pans with paper liners so the cakes are easy to remove.

JELLY-ROLL PANS

These large, flat pans look like baking sheets, except that they have taller sides—typically ¾–1 inch high. They are used to make thin sheets of cake that are suitable for rolling, or as baking sheets for pastries. The household size is 10½ x 15½ inches, although some recipes call for 11¾ x 7½, 12¼ x 9, or 17¼ x 11½-inch pans.

BAKING SHEETS

Baking sheets can be used to support other pans or to bake a hand-formed cake made out of dough. The best sheets are made from shiny aluminum; darker sheets absorb heat and may make your cakes too brown on the bottom. Purchase baking sheets about 4 inches smaller than your oven, so heat can circulate around them—12 x 15½ inches is a good size. Sheets with no lip on three sides and a raised, angled lip on the fourth side make it easy to slide cakes off—on purpose! Line baking sheets with parchment paper to diffuse the heat and allow easy cake removal.

MUFFIN TINS

Also used for cupcakes, muffin tins are commonly available in mini, medium, and large sizes. When I call for a cake to be baked in a mini muffin tin, that means I have tested the recipe using tins that have cavities about 1¾–2 inches in diameter and about ¾–1 inch deep. Standard or medium cupcakes were baked in a tin that has cavities about 2¾–3 inches in diameter and 1⅛–1½ inches deep; large muffin tins have cavities that are about 2–2½ inches deep. Although you can bake cupcakes directly in the tin—and some recipes specify this—most people prefer to use paper or foil liners so that the cakes are easy to remove and hold. Liners are available in standard sizes, as well as in different heights, which can vary the size and shape of the cupcake. You can also find figured muffin tins that have patterns molded into the metal.

SPECIALTY PANS

There are hundreds of specialty cake pans on the market, for everything from miniature bite-size treats to larger-than-life extravaganzas. The shapes range from very simple stars and hearts to incredibly complex castles and storybook characters. You can find geometric shapes (pyramids, hexagons, or domes), religious shapes (crosses), numbers, and seasonal shapes (snowflakes). Two-part pans are used to create teddy bears and other shapes that are designed to stand upright.

pumpkin cakes

— make in shaped pans or use small Bundt pans

You don't have to bake your cake in a pan. You can bake cakes in drinking glasses, coffee mugs, earthenware bowls, or baking dishes. Paper cups can also be used for baking, because most are lined with a wax coating that does not melt—although if you are unsure, line the inside of the cup with parchment paper or aluminum foil. Cakes stored in a baking dish will give your presentation a homemade feeling. I have seen some people try to pass off a store-bought cake as home-made by transferring it to a cake plate, but I have never seen someone transfer a cake to a baking dish. This is a sure sign that it is homemade! Pretty baking dishes are perfect for sheet cakes or single-layer cakes (such as the Chocolate Cherry Fruitcake on page 342) that you plan to transport to a party or give as a gift. In addition, disposable baking pans are very useful for giving and transporting cakes. They can also be placed inside a cake pan and used instead of parchment paper to prevent sticking and to diffuse the heat.

Cake-Making Tools

As an industrial designer, I love my tools. I have five toolboxes: one for woodworking, another for metalwork, one for sculpting, a fourth for sewing, and the fifth one is filled with cake-making and decorating supplies. But no matter what I'm making, I've found that the secret to success doesn't have anything to do with purchasing tons of tools; rather, it lies in having the best basic tools for the job. Following is a list to get you started.

MEASURING CUPS

To achieve the most accurate measurements, use 2-cup glass measuring cups with spouts for liquid ingredients (use 2-quart cups for dividing batter between pans). Use cup sets in graduated (typically ¼-, ⅓-, ½-, and 1-cup) sizes for dry ingredients. Spoon the dry ingredients into the cups and remove any excess ingredients by running a knife over the top of the cup to level.

MEASURING SPOONS

Household teaspoons and tablespoons usually are designed for aesthetics and are not accurate for cooking or baking. To be sure you have the correct volume, use a set of measuring spoons in graduated sizes.

MIXING BOWLS

Although I have many choices when it comes to mixing bowls, my antique Pyrex bowls with '60s-style patterns on the side are sturdy and versatile and make me happy, so I use them all the time. For most home cooks, a good starter set consists of three bowls—one with a 3-quart capacity, one with a 2-quart capacity, and another with a 1½-quart capacity. The larger bowls are useful for whipping eggs, creaming, and combining dry ingredients, and the smaller bowl is good for melting chocolate and combining mix-ins such as chips, nuts, and dried fruits. An array of 1-cup bowls to hold chopped ingredients and small mixtures is also handy. Plastic and melamine bowls are light, durable, nonreactive, and quiet when using an electric hand mixer and can be put in the microwave. Purchase bowls with a spout for pouring, if possible; bowls with lids are also useful for transporting ingredients or mixtures to places where you need to complete your preparation on-site. Stainless steel bowls are good for mixing and folding, but they might be noisy when using an electric hand mixer and can't be put in the microwave. Heavy-duty ceramic bowls are designed not to chip when using a hand mixer, but many are purely decorative, so make sure they're meant for cooking before you purchase them.

ELECTRIC MIXERS

An electric mixer is the best way to beat eggs to various stages of consistency and is also the best way to cream ingredients. If you're using a handheld electric mixer, you'll notice that the beaters on older models have a post running down the middle of each beater, whereas newer mixers have convex, curved wires with open centers that allow for better movement of the batter. Buy a handheld mixer that has a good range of power and speeds and both whisk-style and standard beater attachments. Hand mixers are available in cordless and corded models.

If you're in the market for a stand mixer, you already know that its main advantage is that you don't need to hold the bowl steady as you mix; it locks in place. Stand mixers also come with many different attachments—for whisking, kneading dough, and making ice cream.

FOOD PROCESSOR OR BLENDER

I use my food processor all the time to grind nuts, blend sauces, and form dough into a ball. A blender can sometimes be used as a food processor to whip or purée relatively small amounts of liquids.

PASTRY BLENDER

This hand tool has several parallel U-shaped wires attached to a handle. It is used to blend shortening and flour together until the mixture forms crumbs, usually about the size of coarsely ground meal.

SPATULAS, WHISKS, WOODEN SPOONS

Stock your tool kit with whisks, wooden spoons, and rubber spatulas of varying sizes. Use whisks for beating ingredients, wooden spoons for folding, and rubber spatulas for scraping the bowl and mixing frosting.

CAKE LEVELER

If you bake a lot of cakes, you may want to invest in a cake leveler, which cuts a cake horizontally into equal thicknesses. Most cake levelers are adjustable, so you may be able to create several layers out of a single cake. A sharp, long, serrated knife can also be used for creating layers.

COOKIE CUTTERS

Cookie cutters aren't just for cookies; I often use them to cut cakes into shapes after baking. Metal cutters are usually sharpest, but when shape matters, plastic cookie cutters will also do. Metal cutters rust if not dried properly, so be sure to place them in an oven on low heat (200°F) for 10 minutes to dry out after washing.

DOUGHNUT CUTTER

This metal tool is made of two 1-inch-high rings, one inside the other. Doughnut cutters are available with plain or fluted edges. Convertible cutters allow you to take out the center ring to make round filled doughnuts. To use the cutter, first dip it in flour, then press it into the dough.

ZESTERS AND GRATERS

Used to remove the zest from citrus fruits, a zester or a microplane grater allows you to remove only the thin outer layer of the peel and not the bitter white pith. A box grater can be used for large ingredients, such as carrots and potatoes, but many of them have a side with small holes for zesting as well.

OVEN

All ovens bake differently and vary in accuracy, so get to know your oven intimately by testing a variety of recipes. Is the oven hotter or cooler than the thermometer indicates? Does the air circulate well, or is the oven hotter at the edges? Once you know your oven, adjust the timing, baking temperature, and placement of cakes accordingly.

If you are using a convection oven, a good general rule is to bake your cake for slightly less time and/or at a slightly lower temperature than you would if you were using a conventional oven. Due to increased air circulation around the pans, cakes baked in a convection oven have less moisture loss, and the sugars in fruits and vegetables caramelize more quickly. Either bake your cake at the same temperature you would use in a conventional oven, but for a shorter time (about 25–30 percent), or bake your cake for the same amount of time at a lower temperature (about 25 degrees cooler). The recipe directions in this book assume that you are using a conventional oven.

OVEN THERMOMETER

I lived in a rental house for ten years, and the oven in that house had no temperature gauge on it whatsoever. I got used to measuring its temperature with an oven thermometer, and even now that I have a digital oven, I always like to check its accuracy with an oven thermometer. The time of day and altitude can also affect oven temperature.

CANDY AND FRYING THERMOMETERS

A candy thermometer is used to measure the temperature of sugar mixtures, sauces, and frostings at their various stages of cooking. A frying thermometer measures the temperature of oil for frying doughnuts and other fried cakes. Some thermometers can be used for both candy making and deep-frying; others are designed for either purpose. Purchase one that clips onto the side of the saucepan.

COOLING RACKS

Although some cakes should be cooled partially or completely in the pan, others may continue to brown slightly and get soggy if left in a hot pan. These should be placed on a rack to cool. Cooling racks are essentially metal grids or bars on legs. They allow air to circulate around the entire cake so it cools evenly. If you have a small kitchen, look for stackable cooling racks.

DOUBLE BOILER

A double boiler is good for items that need to be heated very slowly or gently over low heat. Delicate foods are placed in the top pan and water is placed in the bottom pan. Make sure that the water in the bottom does not touch the top pan, or it may boil over and contaminate the ingredients. If you don't have a double boiler, you can fashion one by placing a large heatproof mixing bowl over a medium saucepan filled partially with water. Melting chocolate and blending delicate sauces are usually best done over simmering water in a double boiler (not in the microwave) because you can keep an eye on the ingredients, heat them gradually, stir them gently, and remove them immediately from the heat when they're done. Look for a double boiler in which the top saucepan is not too deep—about 3 inches for a 2-quart saucepan.

DEEP FRYER

If you don't have a special appliance for deep-frying, a heavy-bottomed pot or saucepan will do the job nicely. Just remember to keep a lid handy in case of an unexpected fire. Also, choose a large pot with short handles to lessen the chance that you might accidentally tip it over; deep sides will lessen grease splatters.

SIFTERS

Most people, including me, hate sifting, but sometimes you just have to "go there." Sifting gets rid of lumps in dry ingredients like flour and confectioners' sugar that can cause clumps in your cake or frosting. When directed to do so in recipes, sift flour before measuring. If you don't have a sifter, you can use a handheld sieve. Small sifters are good for dusting cakes with confectioners' sugar or cocoa powder.

PLASTIC WRAP

Use plastic wrap whenever you want to retain moisture; for example, you should cover dough with plastic wrap when you put it in the refrigerator or freezer to chill.

PARCHMENT PAPER

Lining your pans with parchment paper prevents sticking and encourages even baking by absorbing and distributing the heat. It also prevents the bottoms of your cakes from burning. Some people like to butter the paper before filling the pan to further prevent sticking, especially for batters that are low in fat. I also put paper on baking sheets when I prepare pastries.

PASTRY BRUSH

A pastry brush is used to distribute sauces and syrups evenly over cakes. Invest in an all-natural, high-quality boar-bristle or silicone brush so you don't risk getting hairs on the cake. You will know it is a high-quality brush by the price—good brushes are not cheap. Good

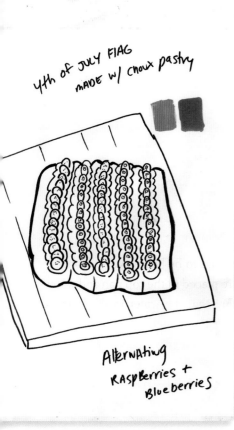

4th of JULY FLAG made w/ choux pastry

Alternating Raspberries + Blueberries

brushes can handle anything from thick syrups to light egg washes; they are lightweight and easy to grip. Dedicate your brush for use with baked goods only—unless you want your cake to taste like barbecue sauce or garlic!

ROLLING PIN
If you splurge on one tool, make it a heavy marble rolling pin: it's worth every penny. It makes rolling out dough much easier than it is with a wooden rolling pin.

RULER
A ruler is good to have on hand for marking a cake before cutting it into layers and for ensuring that decorations are evenly spaced.

TIMER
Baking time is always going to be inexact. It will depend on the moisture in the ingredients, how many pans are in the oven at the same time and thus how much room there is for air to circulate, and how accurate your oven's temperature is. Buy a kitchen timer but carry it with you when you are baking. You don't want the timer on your stove or oven to beep while you're too far away to hear it!

THE CAKE DECORATOR'S TOOL KIT

Beautiful cakes tempt us through our eyes. We love looking at them, hate cutting into them, and adore eating them. Millions of people around the globe decorate cakes as an outlet for their creativity. Some find cake decorating fun and relaxing; others are very serious about it as an art—the art of edible sculpture. To most decorators, the process of decorating is just as important as the look of the final cake.

To me, the appeal of decorating lies partly in its impermanence. As an industrial designer, I create mass-produced products out of plastic, metal, wood, and fabric. I always try to lengthen the life cycle and improve the sustainability of my designs, but with cake, the pressure is off. I make it, I eat it—and it is gone.

Today, sugar craft—the fancy term for candy making and cake decorating—is a large industry, and cake decoration is a major sector

wedding cake

top with love birds

give the cake a retro 60's feel!

make it 7 layers tall

shape: rounded square

of it. Cake decorating appeals to everyone from pastry chefs to graffiti artists to stay-at-home moms. Classes are taught at community colleges, cooking schools, gourmet shops, and hobby stores. Well-known cake decorators have their own recognizable styles, and up-and-comers subscribe to magazines, attend workshops, and practice to develop their skills. Some decorators build life-size figures out of cake, others focus on daintily decorated half-inch cubes. Below is a crash course on the basics of the craft.

Types of Decoration

FROSTING AND ICING

Although these terms are often used interchangeably, frosting is usually thick enough to spread on a cake and icing is generally thin enough to be drizzled or poured over it. Both are made primarily with confectioners' sugar mixed with liquid and flavorings. Sometimes, eggs and butter are added. Some are cooked; others are not. There are hundreds of different types of frostings and icings, including thick and fluffy Chocolate Frosting (page 351), smooth Lemon Icing (page 358), and hard Royal Icing (see page 355).

BUTTERCREAM

Sinfully rich and fluffy, buttercream is made from butter, eggs, and sugar. Some buttercreams are cooked; others aren't. The bases for buttercream include whole eggs, egg whites, yolks, and custards, and they can be flavored with melted chocolate, extracts, liquor, zests, and fruits.

GLAZES

Glazes—similar to icings, but thinner—are shiny toppings and fillings that are brushed, poured, drizzled, or dripped onto cakes. Thin glazes soak into the cake for additional flavor. Fresh fruits, jams, and preserves can be made into fruit glazes by straining out the seeds and thick chunks of pulp. Jellies can be made into glazes by heating them and mixing with other ingredients. Chocolate glazes are made by combining melted chocolate with cream and butter or corn syrup until the mixture reaches a pourable consistency. Caramel glazes (such as the one that goes on the Caramel Apple Cake, page 319) form a shell on the top of a cake that can range in consistency from gooey to hard. Egg-wash glazes are brushed on cakes, creating a shiny finish and allowing the cake to brown evenly.

JAMS, PRESERVES, FRUIT PURÉES, AND FRUIT CURDS
Jams and preserves can be used straight from the jar for fillings, and fresh fruit, either alone or with a bit of sugar, makes a fine filling when puréed. Curds, usually made from citrus fruits (see the Key Lime Cheesecake on page 115), also incorporate butter, eggs, and sugar, and have a rich, creamy texture.

GANACHE
Chocolate ganache, made from melted chocolate and heated cream, is poured over cakes to create a smooth surface and always makes an impressive topping. When combined with butter, it makes a delicious Chocolate Buttercream filling (see page 360).

PASTRY CREAM
This rich, delicate custard is made with milk, eggs, sugar, and flour and can be used to fill cakes, doughnuts, pastries, and many other desserts. It can be flavored with vanilla, lemon, chocolate, raspberry, orange, and many other flavors. The Princess Cake (page 178) uses pastry cream in between the layers.

WHIPPED CREAM AND NONDAIRY TOPPING
A generous amount of whipped cream adds a sweet, luscious finish to cakes and can also be used to fill, frost, and moisten them. Whipped cream is made by beating air into cream that contains more than 30 percent milk fat. You can sweeten it by adding flavorings or sugar. Nondairy topping is made from coconut or palm oil and is sweeter than whipped cream. It is good for those who are lactose intolerant.

MERINGUE
Made from sugar and egg whites beaten until they are very stiff, meringues are frequently used as frostings and fillings. Meringue can be left out to dry for a period of time, resulting in a crunchy outer layer and a soft interior, or toasted quickly under the broiler or with a

Espresso "cup" cakes

←— Find fun cups at party store

use my favorite color combination to brighten

kitchen torch to achieve a light brown finish. The s'mores on page 245 are topped with meringue.

MARZIPAN

Marzipan is a pliable confection used to fill and cover cakes. Made with finely ground almonds, sugar, and egg whites, it is very dense and sweet. It can be rolled out into sheets, cut to size, and then wrapped around cakes, or it can be artistically sculpted into shapes ranging from simple to elaborate, including fruits, animals, and fanciful characters (see the Almond Marzipan Cake, page 234). It is also available premade in many supermarkets and cake-decorating shops.

FONDANT

Fondant is a pliable, moldable confection made from sugar, water, and cream of tartar. After it is cooked to the soft-ball stage, it can be rolled out into sheets and cut into pieces and used to top and fill cakes. When done well, is quite impressive and professional—see the Wedding Cupcakes on page 194. Fondant can also be sculpted into shapes and used for cake decoration. It requires some skill to make: the sugar mixture must be heated and cooled in a precise way to prevent crystals from forming. Otherwise, the fondant becomes flat and gritty. It is also available premade in cake-decorating stores. Pieces of fondant can be attached together by dipping them in water, pressing them together, and allowing them to dry.

Decorating Tools

TURNTABLE
A turntable is helpful to rotate the cake while filling or topping it. There are cake-decorating turntables that elevate the cake, but lazy Susans work just fine.

ACETATE
This clear plastic film is used for shaping melted chocolate. Pipe a pattern on the acetate, let it dry, and it can be transferred to the cake. It works much better than parchment or wax paper because the chocolate does not stick to it and it can be easily rolled, allowing the chocolate to dry in a curved shape. Large 12 x 18-inch sheets of acetate are available at cake-decorating and candy-supply stores. I usually cut them down into smaller, more manageable sheets. Clear report covers, available at office-supply stores, are also made of acetate (and very cheap), so in a pinch you can use them.

CORRUGATED CARDBOARD
Instead of decorating a cake on a serving plate, sometimes it is easier to place it on a very stiff piece of cardboard (use a piece the same size as the cake or slightly larger), decorate, and then, using a large spatula, transfer the cake to a serving plate. Cardboard also works well when you are planning on transporting your cake in a cake keeper or if you want to box it for gift-giving.

Cake decorating stores sell food-safe corrugated-cardboard rounds and squares in every size imaginable. I always have a selection on hand just in case I get the impulse to bake a tiered cake! If you do not have precut cardboard rounds or squares on hand, you can use a utility knife to cut the shapes out of a clean corrugated box. After cutting, wrap the cardboard in aluminum foil.

ICING SPATULAS
Most of the time, I use a simple butter knife or rubber spatula to apply frosting and icing in a textured pattern, but if I want a smooth surface, a flexible icing spatula with a thin, straight edge makes frostings and fillings so much easier to apply. Choose a stainless steel spatula with a

blade that is six or eight inches long and has a rounded tip. For more detailed icing, an offset spatula works well, too.

SMOOTHERS, EDGERS, AND DECORATING COMBS

These tools, which come in a variety of sizes, allow you to sculpt textures, patterns, and intricate designs in the icing on the sides and tops of cakes. Smoothers are broad plastic scrapers used to create a smooth finish on buttercream frostings. Edgers and decorating combs create patterns, such as straight lines or cross-hatching, as you draw them across the cake. The tines of a fork or the edges of a serrated knife also can be used for this purpose. A fondant smoother—a flat plastic tool with a handle—is used to press and smooth fondant and marzipan on the tops and sides of cakes. The advantage of using this tool as opposed to your hands is that it has a large flat surface and eliminates the chance of leaving fingerprints.

FOOD COLORING

Liquid, gel, or powdered food coloring can be added to batter, frosting, icing, fondant—you name it—to create almost any color in the rainbow. Liquid food coloring is available at most grocery stores and is best used with white or light frostings or batters. To create light colors, add a few drops; to make deep colors, add several drops. Adding liquid food coloring will thin a frosting or icing, so you may need to add more confectioners' sugar to reach the desired consistency.

Gel and paste food colorings are highly concentrated; you need only a little bit to create dark or bright colors. You can find these products online or in specialty stores. If you want to make black or dark-colored frosting, start with chocolate frosting and add coloring gels. Powdered food coloring can be brushed on to create deep colors. Combine powders with water or lemon extract to use for painting. You can purchase powdered food coloring in metallic, iridescent, and deep colors.

CUTTERS AND STAMPS

After rolling out marzipan or fondant, you can cut it into a variety of shapes using small cookie cutters. Dip the cutter in confectioners' sugar or flour if it sticks to the topping. Cutters can also be used to press outlines into frosting or icing that can be filled with sugar or other topping ingredients. Cookie stamps are a great way to press patterns into marzipan or fondant. If you can't find cookie stamps you like, you can use the rubber stamps available in stationery stores, which provide many more options. You can also have your own rubber stamps custom-made by a local office supply store.

CANDY MOLDS, COOKIE MOLDS, AND ICE CUBE TRAYS

These molds are all great for shaping chocolate. Just pour the melted chocolate in the mold and let it cool, and it snaps right out. That's how I made the white chocolate leaves in the Magic Peppermint White Forest Cake (page 337). I particularly like springerle molds—used in the preparation of traditional German anise-flavored cookies—which have especially intricate details. Freezer trays that form ice cubes into interesting shapes are available in both hard plastic and silicone. There are many more types of shapes available in hard plastic, but I like silicone better because it is more flexible.

PASTRY BAGS

Pastry bags are cone-shaped bags used to extrude—or pipe—icing, frosting, whipped cream, meringue, and pastry dough through a shaped tip. A coupler holds the tip to the bag. They are made out of reusable or disposable materials such as plastic, canvas, parchment paper, or nylon. Bigger is better: 10-inch and 12-inch bags are the most common, but as you learn to control the bags you may want to get larger ones. It is nice to have several pastry bags at your disposal, so you can separate the different colors without stopping to refill.

A mechanical pastry bag has a stainless steel or silicone barrel to hold the frosting or icing and usually comes with a number of interchangeable tips. Many people find mechanical bags easier to control than a conventional pastry bag. To use one, place the frosting in the barrel and crank the handle to press the mixture to the tip.

You can also use homemade tools, such as recycled squirt bottles and airtight plastic bags with a corner cut off, to pipe frosting. The latter is excellent for drizzling chocolate.

In many stores, you can buy disposable, ready-made tubes of icing and frosting with the piping tip built into the tube. You can cut the tip to vary the line thickness, and throw it away when finished. These tubes are available in a variety of colors and consistencies. They present a simple way to create small decorations and to write on cakes for home bakers who don't have a large selection of equipment on hand.

PASTRY TIPS

Pastry tips are sold in sets. I have one set that includes more than one hundred tips, but I really only use the same few over and over. Large tips are good for thick mixtures like meringue and pastry dough, small tips are good for delicate writing, and medium-size tips are best for borders. Round tips extrude a smooth line and are used to outline shapes, to fill and pipe designs, for writing, beads, dots, balls, stems, vines, flower centers, lattice, or cornelli lace. Serrated tips extrude textured lines and are used to create stars, zigzags, textured borders, shells, ropes, and rosettes. To get started, you need just a few round and star-shaped tips in large, medium, and small sizes.

STENCILS

Plastic stencils are available in a variety of patterns. You can use them to create a design in sifted sugar on the top of a cake, or to outline shapes for cutting. Paper doilies make good stencils, or you can make

your own stencil with paper and scissors or chipboard and a utility knife.

EDIBLE PATTERN TRANSFERS
At most cake-decorating supply stores, a multitude of nicely designed patterns are available to transfer directly onto cakes and candy. For those who prefer not to create their own custom-designed transfers (see page 56), these add an elegant touch.

INGREDIENTS

Remember chemistry class, when you put certain elements together and—poof!—magic (or, in my case, an explosion) took place? Cake making is the same. It relies heavily on the chemistry of certain ingredients to achieve the desired results. Understanding a little about the properties of each ingredient will help you not only to improvise in the kitchen, but also to make better cakes—and to prevent explosions!

Flours, Meals, and Oats

ALL-PURPOSE FLOUR
For most of the recipes in this book, I used unbleached all-purpose flour—that is, for all except the white or brightly colored cakes, for which I used bleached flour. When added to batter, the high protein (gluten) levels in all-purpose flour make cakes more sturdy. That's why all-purpose flour is good for dense cakes, such as pound cakes.

CAKE FLOUR
Because it has less protein than all-purpose flour, cake flour makes softer, lighter, more airy cakes. It is available in bleached or unbleached forms. Both forms can be used interchangeably, but bleached flour produces a cake that's brighter in color.

WHOLE WHEAT FLOUR
Whole wheat flour lends cakes an earthy flavor. Strain it through a sieve to soften it up a bit before baking.

WHOLE WHEAT PASTRY FLOUR

Ground from whole wheat flour, whole wheat pastry flour is softer and finer, and has more nutrients, than white flour. It gives cakes and pastries a "natural" flavor.

SEMOLINA

Semolina, or coarsely ground durum wheat, contains the wheat kernel that flavors cakes and also gives them a crispy texture. When added to cakes, semolina is almost always combined with flour. It produces a rich wheat flavor.

SPECIALTY FLOURS

Flours made from plants or grains other than wheat can be added to cakes, but they cannot be directly substituted for wheat flours. Yucca flour—also known as manioc flour or cassava flour—is made from yucca root that is dried, shredded, and pounded into flour. It is used as a mainstay in many Latin American recipes. If used alone, it is a gluten-free ingredient, although in cakes it is often combined with other flours. It can be found at many Hispanic groceries. Potato flour is made from cooked, dried, and ground potatoes and should not be confused with potato starch, which is made only from the starch of a potato. Potato flour is an important part of Jewish cooking and the Passover meal because it contains no leavening agents. If used alone, it is a gluten-free ingredient, although in cakes it is often combined with other flours.

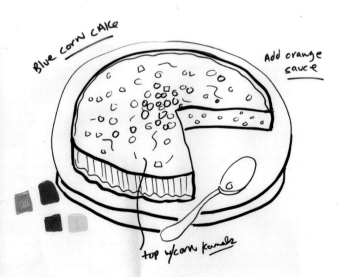

Blue corn cake

Add orange sauce

top w/corn kernels

CORNMEAL, POLENTA, CORN FLOUR

Cornmeal is a grain ground from yellow, white, or blue corn. It is available in fine, medium, and coarse consistencies (I prefer fine or medium grinds). Polenta is made by boiling cornmeal; corn flour is more powdery in texture than cornmeal and looks similar to all-purpose flour.

OATS

In cakes, it's best to use uncooked old-fashioned rolled oats, not instant or quick-cooking oats, which produce mushy results. Steel-cut oats can also be used, but they are less absorbent than rolled oats and give the cake a crunchy texture.

Binders

EGGS

Eggs contribute in several ways to cakes. They add moisture (because of their high water content) and some fat (from the yolks), but their primary role is to give cakes their tender texture. As eggs are heated, their proteins bind themselves to each other and to other ingredients. When you beat eggs (or the yolks or whites alone), bubbles form. These bubbles trap air, which helps distribute the oven's heat evenly throughout the cake. If you don't beat eggs long enough—at least 2 minutes, for most recipes—the result will be a flat cake. On the other hand, if the eggs are overbeaten—longer than about 5 minutes—they become too stiff, and you must start over. Eggs come in a variety of sizes, from peewee to jumbo, but all the recipes in this book call for large eggs. Eggs combine better at room temperature, but they are easier to crack when they are cold.

SHORTENINGS

Fats—including butter, vegetable shortening, margarine, and oil—are called shortenings because they coat flour and keep its strands of gluten short, which in turn prevents the cake from getting too tough. I prefer butter over other shortenings because to me it contributes the most flavor, and I also prefer to use unsalted instead of salted butter because I like to control the amount of salt in a recipe. All the recipes in this book call for unsalted butter.

MILK

To achieve the richest flavor, all the recipes in this book that call for milk were developed using whole milk, not skim or low-fat milk. However, if you prefer to use milk with a lower fat content, feel free to experiment with it. I also like to use buttermilk, which has a high fat content and adds a buttery rich, tangy flavor to baked goods. Evaporated milk is a dense milk that has about 60 percent of the water removed and gives cakes a heightened milk flavor. Sweetened condensed milk is a very thick and creamy milk to which sugar has been added; it is often used for cake sauces.

CREAM

Heavy cream and heavy whipping cream are creams that contain 36 percent or more fat and double in volume when they are whipped. Whipping cream and light whipping cream have between 30 and 36 percent fat and can also be whipped. I use them all interchangeably, with only slight differences in the resulting texture and fullness. Light cream, half-and-half, coffee cream, and table cream are all names for creams with 18 to 30 percent fat; they cannot be whipped. Nondairy whipped topping traditionally contains no dairy products and is good for those who are lactose intolerant, but recently some major brands have begun adding milk and cream to their nondairy toppings for marketing purposes, so check the label.

CHEESE

The most common type of cheese used in baking is cream cheese. It is soft and smooth, gives cheesecake a wonderful texture, adds tang to frostings, and makes a tasty filling for coffee cakes. Always use dense softened blocks of cream cheese, not whipped cream cheese, which has too much air. Other cheeses you will use for recipes in this book are mascarpone, a soft Italian cheese with a delicate flavor; queso fresco, a mild, soft, unaged Spanish cheese; and my all-time favorite, sharp Cheddar cheese.

Leavening Agents

YEAST

Yeast is a cluster of tiny living cells that convert to carbon dioxide in the presence of sugar, thereby leavening the dough. Active dry yeast and quick-rising yeast are the two most common forms used for cakes. (Fresh yeast is also available, but it has a very short shelf life.) Quick-rising yeast has lower moisture content and more active cells per package, which helps it act faster. But I call for active dry yeast in my recipes because I find that it has more flavor than quick-rising yeast.

When preparing a cake, proof the yeast by combining it with sugar and a warm liquid—if it is foamy in 10 minutes, it is suitable for use.

Do not add yeast to liquid that is boiling, or you can kill it. The liquid should be warm to the touch. If you don't use it often, purchase yeast in small packets instead of jars or large containers to prolong its shelf life.

CREAM OF TARTAR

Cream of tartar is also known as potassium bitartrate—an acid salt that is a by-product of wine making. It is sometimes added to egg whites to stabilize them during whipping.

BAKING POWDER AND BAKING SODA

These ingredients, when mixed with liquid, cause a chemical reaction that releases carbon dioxide, which makes cakes rise. Baking soda contains sodium bicarbonate, which is activated immediately when it comes into contact with an acidic ingredient like buttermilk or sour cream. When using baking soda, you will need to bake the cake right away because carbon dioxide dissipates quickly. Baking soda is unstable at high temperatures and good for recipes with short baking times.

Baking powder contains sodium bicarbonate and cream of tartar. It is commonly labeled double-acting because the two ingredients react with acids at different times. Baking soda acts when the ingredients are first combined, and the cream of tartar reacts over a long period of time during baking. Baking soda and baking powder are often mistaken for each other, but they are not interchangeable. They leaven differently, and their flavors are different, too. Baking soda is bitter, so if you add too much it will destroy the taste of the cake.

Sweeteners

SUGAR

In addition to sweetening, sugar absorbs liquid, making cakes soft and light. Creaming butter and sugar together incorporates air, creating tiny air bubbles. These bubbles expand in the oven during baking to help the cake rise.

There are five types of sugar commonly used in cakes:

- Granulated sugar is standard white table sugar. It has a medium-grain texture and is a good all-around sugar for cakes.

- Superfine sugar, also known as castor sugar, has a fine-grain texture and is good for delicate cakes and meringues.

- Brown sugar is white sugar combined with molasses. It is available in both dark and light versions, depending on how much molasses flavor you want. Always pack brown sugar firmly into the measuring cup to get an accurate measure.

- Confectioners' sugar, or powdered sugar, is sugar that is ground to a powder and combined with cornstarch. It is sometimes used for baking when you want an extremely fine texture. It is more often used in icing to produce a silky-smooth surface.

- Crystal, or coarse, sugar has extra-large granules and is used for decorating.

HONEY

Honey, available in many varieties, is both a flavoring and a preservative. I use clover honey, the most popular type of honey, but you may choose to vary the flavor with sage honey, orange-blossom honey, or one of the many other kinds available. If you are the type of person who doesn't eat an entire cake in a few sittings but rather slowly rations it out over the course of a week, add honey to your cake to prolong its shelf life.

MOLASSES

Molasses can be used alone as a hearty sweetener, or in combination with sugar or other sweeteners to add a rich, rustic flavor. Molasses is what lends gingerbread its distinctive flavor. The recipes in this book call for unsulfured molasses—the finest quality available—which is made from the clarified and concentrated juice of sun-ripened sugar cane.

MAPLE SYRUP

A natural sugar derived from black, red, or sugar maple trees, maple syrup is available in various grades. Grade A is light and has a mild flavor; grade B is darker and has sharper flavor. Although I will use only

Substituting Honey for Sugar

Honey can be used as a substitute for sugar in many recipes to modify the flavor, keep cakes moister longer, or reduce the "sugar high" experienced after eating cake. My recommendation is to experiment by cutting the amount of sugar called for in a recipe by half and substituting honey for the remainder. Keep notes as you bake, and once you see how the recipe behaves, you can take away more sugar and add more honey the next time you bake. Keep the following properties of honey in mind as you experiment:

- Honey is sweeter than sugar, so use less of it. If the recipe calls for 1 cup of sugar or less, substitute a scant measurement in the same volume of honey. If the recipe calls for more than 1 cup of sugar, reduce the quantity of honey to two-thirds of the volume of sugar.
- Honey is heavy: 12 ounces of honey weighs about the same as 8 ounces of water. So avoid using it as a substitute in light, airy sponge cakes (they will have a hard time rising). On the other hand, honey works very well in pound and butter cakes.
- Honey is a liquid: reduce the other liquids in the recipe by 1/4 cup for each cup of honey used.
- Honey is acidic: add 1/2 teaspoon of baking soda for each cup of honey used.
- Honey encourages baked goods to brown: reduce the oven temperature by 25 degrees and watch the oven toward the end of the baking time to avoid blackened cakes.
- Honey is best when bought locally.
- Honey should be not served to babies less than one year old.
- Honey can act as an allergen for some people.
- Honey is better for diabetics than sugar, but diabetics must still consume it in moderation.

grade A on my pancakes, I use grade B for baking because I want the maple flavor to really stand out.

CORN SYRUP

Made from cornstarch, corn syrup consists primarily of glucose. It is used as a sweetener, thickener, and preservative in cakes and icings. It prevents crystallization and stabilizes the cake as it bakes. Light corn syrup, which contains small quantities of salt and vanilla, is clear and colorless has a light, sweet flavor. Dark corn syrup has a medium-brown color and contains refiners' syrup (a type of molasses). It has a much more assertive flavor. Both can be used interchangeably in recipes, resulting in the same texture but different flavors.

AGAVE NECTAR

Agave nectar is rapidly becoming the sweetener of choice for vegan baking and for those looking to lower their glycemic index. It is a good substitute for honey, maple syrup, corn syrup, granulated sugar, and brown sugar. Agave nectar has a more neutral flavor than honey or maple syrup, and works well in cakes with delicate flavors. Like corn syrup, agave nectar will not crystallize; like honey, agave nectar may cause baked goods to brown too quickly, so lower the oven temperature by 25 degrees and keep an eye on the cake during baking.

AGAVE SUBSTITUTION CHART

    1 cup honey = 1 cup agave nectar
    1 cup maple syrup = 1 cup agave nectar
    1 cup corn syrup = ½ cup agave nectar; increase other
        liquids in recipe by ½ cup
    1 cup granulated sugar = ⅔ cup agave nectar; reduce other
        liquids in recipe by ⅓ cup
    1 cup brown sugar = ⅔ cup agave nectar; reduce other
        liquids in recipe by ¼ cup

Flavorings

SALT

Salt boosts flavors—it even increases sweetness—and it also strengthens the gluten in wheat and slows down all those chemical reactions created by leavening agents. Most of the time, I use common table salt in cakes, but when I want to boost the salt flavor I use kosher salt or sea salt.

SPICES

Even though I prefer to buy many ingredients in bulk, large jars of spices are never worth it for me. I prefer to invest in variety of spices, and because they lose their potency quickly, I would rather buy only the quantity that I need.

EXTRACTS

Like spices, extracts can lose their flavor over time—although some people say that vanilla extract improves with age if stored properly. Flavor loss occurs because many extracts include alcohol, which evaporates. Recommended storage time is up to one year. Purchase small amounts of extracts, then store them in a cool, dark place. Make sure to close bottles of extract tightly. For better flavor, purchase pure

CARROT CAKE

Oversized carrot w/ white chocolate flowers

extracts—those that are derived from plants, nuts, or beans—whenever possible. Artificial extracts are chemical compounds that mimic the flavor of natural ingredients.

LIQUOR, LIQUEUR, SPIRITS, WINE, AND BEER

Many types of alcohol can be used to flavor cakes. My favorite is rum—light, golden, and dark, all of which enrich the flavors of cakes, fillings, and frostings. I also like nut-based liqueurs like amaretto and fruit-based liqueurs like Kirsch. Coffee and Irish cream–flavored liqueurs go well with both vanilla and chocolate cake. Champagne, wine, and beer can also be used in cakes to add subtle flavors. There is a misconception that alcohol burns off during baking: in truth, only some of it burns off with heat. The shorter the baking time, the more alcohol remains. For example, miniature cupcakes that bake for 10–15 minutes will retain more alcohol then a large Bundt cake that bakes for 45–50 minutes. Alcohol in boiled icings or sauces will retain less potency than alcohol added to uncooked icings, sauces, and fillings. If you don't have a well-stocked bar, the best thing to do is to purchase small (airline-size) bottles to use as flavorings.

COFFEE

Coffee adds a delicious flavoring to cakes and provides a stay-awake jolt that many diners crave after a rich meal. It accents vanilla- and chocolate-based cakes perfectly but also goes well with fruity flavors, such as raspberry and orange, and nutty flavors, including almonds and hazelnuts. When thinking about coffee, think strength. Dissolve instant-coffee granules in a couple of tablespoons of hot water, or prepare double-strength espresso for small batters and triple-strength drip coffee for high-volume batters. And if you don't mind a coarser cake, add finely ground espresso beans for an intense coffee flavor.

COCOA AND CHOCOLATE

Ah, chocolate—my favorite ingredient! Chocolate comes in many forms, including solid and powdered. Powdered chocolate for baking is sold in two varieties: unsweetened cocoa powder and Dutch-process cocoa powder. Unsweetened cocoa powder is bitter but has a nice deep chocolate flavor. It is an acid, and when it is used in recipes that have baking soda, an alkali, their interaction causes the cake to rise. Dutch-process cocoa powder is treated with an alkali to neutralize its acids. It is used in some recipes that have a more delicate flavor. Cocoa powder can be sifted and added to other dry ingredients or mixed with a small amount of boiling water and added to liquid ingredients.

Solid chocolates include bittersweet, semisweet, milk, German sweet, unsweetened, and white.

Bittersweet chocolate generally has a strong bitter chocolate taste and contains less sugar than semisweet chocolate. The best bittersweet chocolate contains 65 percent or more chocolate liquor: the higher the percentage, the more flavorful the chocolate. The most popular chocolate chips are made from semisweet chocolate and usually contain less cocoa butter than bittersweet chocolate, so they are better able to retain their shape during baking.

Milk chocolate is made from either condensed milk or a milk-and-sugar mixture. It contains less chocolate liquor than bittersweet or semisweet chocolate. The better the milk chocolate, the higher the percentage of chocolate liquor.

German sweet chocolate was created in 1852 by a man named Samuel German, from whom—rather than the country of Germany—it derives its name. It is a chocolate blend that is sweeter than semisweet chocolate and contains chocolate liquor, sugar, cocoa, flavorings, and lecithin.

Unsweetened chocolate is chocolate in its rawest form, with no sugar added. It has a strong bitter taste that is sweetened by the sugar in the baked goods.

Rich and creamy white chocolate does not contain chocolate liquor, so officially it should not be classified as chocolate. But high-quality brands of white chocolate contain many ingredients found in other chocolates, such as cocoa butter, sugar, milk solids, vanilla, and lecithin. White chocolate is extremely delicate, so always melt it over very low heat.

Couverture is a high-quality chocolate found in specialty stores.

It contains extra cocoa butter and is used for coating cakes and pastries, to which it gives a smooth finish and glossy sheen.

Fruits and Vegetables

DRIED FRUITS
Dried fruits, such as raisins, currants, and apricots, add flavor and a chewy texture to cake. If the recipe calls for softening, place the dried fruit in boiling water or liquid for 5 minutes before using.

FRESH FRUITS AND VEGETABLES
Fresh fruits and vegetables, such as carrots, zucchini, apple, and bananas, not only add flavor and texture to cakes but also keep them moist and soft for a long time. Shredded, grated, or mashed potatoes, sweet potatoes, yucca, and yams are often used as a starch in cakes. In many cases, fruits and vegetables of the same type can be substituted for others with similar textures if you are willing to tolerate a substantial flavor variation. Berries can be substituted for other berries (some sweet and some tart); squashes can be substituted for other squashes; root vegetables for other root vegetables, and so on.

CANDIED FRUITS
Candied fruits—like pineapple, red and green cherries, oranges, and currants—are much sweeter and a bit softer than dried fruits. Traditionally used inside fruitcakes, they also make festive decorative toppings.

To candy your own fruits, cut large fruits into small pieces or slices (cut cherries in half). Combine 1 cup sugar, ¼ cup honey, and 1 cup water in a heavy saucepan. Boil, stirring constantly, until the mixture reaches 235°F on a candy thermometer. Lower the heat and drop ½ cup cut-up fruit into the liquid. Cook over low heat for 5–10 minutes, or until the fruit is soft and the rind is transparent. Drain and let cool on wax paper.

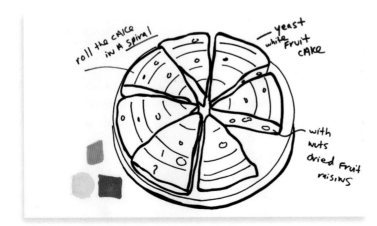

Coconut Know-How

HOW TO MAKE COCONUT CURLS

Preheat the oven to 350°F. Using a hammer and an ice pick, pierce two of the black "eyes" on the top of a fresh coconut. Release the milk and save it for another use. Place the whole coconut on a baking sheet and bake for 30–40 minutes, or until the coconut begins to crack. Set it aside to cool for 1 hour. Wrap the cooled coconut in a clean kitchen towel and break it into pieces with the hammer. Remove the shell and, using a vegetable peeler, remove the dark skin. Use the peeler to shave long or short curls from the flesh. Store the curls in damp paper towels until ready to use or toast as directed below.

TWO WAYS TO TOAST COCONUT

1. Place fresh coconut curls on a cookie sheet and bake at 325°F for 7–10 minutes, or until golden. Stir a few times during baking.

2. Place a little butter in a skillet. Add fresh coconut curls and sauté for 5–7 minutes, or until golden.

HOW TO TINT COCONUT

Combine a few drops of water and a few drops of food coloring in a small plastic container. Add fresh coconut curls. Cover and shake well until the coconut is colored.

COCONUT

Coconut comes in many forms—fresh, dried, sweetened, unsweetened, shredded, flaked, and desiccated. Fresh coconut can be shredded with a peeler or in a food processor, or it can be shaped into large curls. Unsweetened coconut allows you to control the sugar in the recipe. Sweetened coconut is soaked in corn syrup and is therefore sweeter and moister than unsweetened coconut. Flaked and shredded coconut can be used interchangeably—only the textures are different. Flaked coconut makes a smooth cake; shredded coconut makes a coarser cake. I like to use large coconut flakes as a garnish. Desiccated coconut is usually unsweetened, dried, and very finely ground. Toasting coconut dramatically changes the flavor by bringing out the fruit's natural oils. Tinting coconut with food coloring is common in cake decorating.

PUMPKIN

Pumpkin purée is the form of pumpkin most often used for baking. Most people prefer canned pumpkin purée because it is quick and easy to use in recipes—and, boy, was I glad I know how to make my own purée when, in 2009, there was a big canned-pumpkin shortage in

America! I use sugar pumpkins, which are smaller and sweeter than the pumpkins from which you carve your jack-o'-lantern. To make your own, slice a pumpkin in half and remove the seeds. Reserve the seeds for roasting if you like. Bake at 375°F for 1½ hours. Remove the pumpkin and cool. Scoop the flesh into a food processor or blender and purée until smooth.

SEASONAL FRUITS

These days, most fruits are available throughout the year, regardless of whether they're in season or not—although you may pay dearly for them and they are not always of great quality. I love to bake with fresh fruits of the season—strawberries, the first fruits of spring; peaches, the fruits of summer; and cranberries, the delicacies of the fall. I also love to create unique flavor combinations with fruits out of season—there is nothing like adding blueberries to apple cake in the fall or pomegranates to an apricot cake in the summer. I stock up on seasonal fruits when they are fresh, available, and cost-effective, and either freeze or can them to use when they are hard to find. When I can't find a particular fruit for a recipe, I substitute a similar fruit—for example, if I can't find kumquats, I use bitter oranges.

CITRUS FRUITS

When a citrus fruit requires both zesting and juicing, zest it first, then squeeze the juice. Using a microplane zester or a grater with very small holes, zest only the colored part of the peel. Try not to zest any white pith. Then slice the fruit in half and extract as much juice as possible. Strain the seeds before using.

Nuts and Seeds

Nuts and seeds are high in fat. When they are exposed to heat, whether during baking or toasting, they release their oils, thus intensifying their wonderful flavors—but they can also burn quickly. Mixing nuts into a batter protects them, but when they are placed on top of a cake they toast much more rapidly than the cake bakes, so they may burn. Covering the cake with foil after the nuts and seeds are slightly toasted will help prevent this. Nuts go rancid quickly, so keep them in the freezer to prevent spoiling.

The way that nuts and seeds are prepared also affects the flavor and texture of a cake. Whether nuts are left whole, sliced, chopped, or ground makes a big difference—each technique exposes a different amount of surface area. The smaller the pieces of nut, the more flavor they contribute. When nuts are ground, as they are in the Opera Cake (page 253) or in marzipan (page 354), they are used as a paste. A little sugar or flour should always be added to the nuts to help make grinding easier and absorb the oils.

To measure nuts accurately, always follow the format called for in the recipe. For example, if a recipe calls for a cup of chopped walnuts, measure them after the walnuts are chopped, not while they are still whole or halved. There are many more nuts in a cup once they are chopped, ground, or slivered.

ESSENTIAL TECHNIQUES

Baking is all about planning. Most of a baker's time is spent organizing ingredients and prepping the batter—after all, once the batter is in the pan and in the oven, it does its own thing, and the baker's only responsibility is to take it out when it is ready and cool the cake properly. The order in which the techniques are listed in this section reflects the order in which most of the recipe instructions are given.

Before You Begin: Get Ready for Cake

READ THE RECIPE

It may sound obvious, but you would be surprised how infrequently people read a recipe all the way through before starting to prepare it. Reading a recipe prevents surprises. It helps ensure that you have all the ingredients and equipment on hand, and alerts you to any steps that take extra time, such as allowing dough to rise or sauces to chill.

ASSEMBLE THE INGREDIENTS

Do a quick check and make sure you have enough of all of the ingredients on hand. If you don't, you may want to bake another cake for which you do have the ingredients on hand, or you may want to improvise and substitute similar ingredients for the ones you're

Fund-Raising with Cakes

CAKEWALK

I attended my first cakewalk on a visit to my niece's school in Portland, Oregon. By the time the night was over, our family had won six cakes! The cakewalk is a raffle-type game played at fund-raisers or carnivals. Members of the organization that wishes to raise funds donate dozens of cakes. To play, guests each buy a ticket that has a number on it. Numbered squares are laid in a path on the floor, and each person stands on the square that has his or her number on it. As music plays, the ticket holders walk around the path; when the music stops, they stop. A number is called and the person standing on the square with that number wins a cake. Many rounds are played and cakes are given out after each round.

The game is based on a form of dance called the cakewalk, practiced by African Americans in the southern United States prior to Emancipation. Dance competitions were held on plantations in which prizes, including cakes, were given to the best dancers. The style of dance varied by region: some dancers walked a straight chalk line carrying buckets of water on their heads; others emulated the wild dancing of the native Seminole Indians, which featured lots of jumping and gyrating.

BAKE SALES AND CAKE STALLS

Bake sales (called cake stalls in England) are a common fund-raising tool. I used to prepare cupcakes to raise money for my swim team when I was in grade school. In addition to clubs and athletic organizations, bake sales are found at town halls on Election Day, at church festivals, or in any setting in which a group needs to raise funds. Traditionally, people donate homemade baked goods, such as cakes, cookies, cupcakes, and pies, but it is becoming more common for some people to bake at home and others to donate store-bought items. There are also companies that produce cakes for bake sales—people order from a brochure, and the cakes are delivered in time for the event.

LAMINGTON DRIVES

Lamington drives are a favorite fund-raising tool in Australia and New Zealand. These incredibly popular events—named after the Lamington, a small sponge cake covered with a thin chocolate-and-coconut coating—follow a slightly different procedure from our traditional bake sales. In the United States, every member of the fund-raising organization is responsible for contributing a baked treat to the sale. In a Lamington drive, however, members of the organization take orders for cakes. When all the orders are in, the members gather to prepare the Lamingtons together. Sometimes the group bakes one large cake from scratch and cuts it into small pieces to make individual cakes. Alternatively, the group might order a plain sponge or pound cake from a bakery, then cut it into pieces. The pieces are then dipped in chocolate, rolled in coconut, plated, and delivered to the donors.

High-Altitude Baking

Because there is less air pressure at higher eleva-tions, altitude affects baking in several ways. Baking times differ, depending on how far above sea level your kitchen is. With less air pressure weighing them down, leaveners tend to work too quickly at high altitudes, so by the time your cake is done all the air has escaped, leaving the cake flat. At high altitudes, the amount of leaveners used in a recipe should be adjusted downward, by 10–25 percent at 5,000–7,000 feet above sea level, or downward even more if your kitchen is higher than that. Egg whites are usually beaten only to the soft-peak stage at high altitudes to keep them from deflating. Sugar is also adjusted downward, by 1–3 tablespoons per cup at 5,000 feet. Flour tends to be drier at high altitudes, so the amount of liquids in a recipe is adjusted upward, by 2–3 tablespoons for each cup at 5,000 feet and 3–4 tablespoons at 7,000 feet. In addition, those at high altitudes should increase oven temperature about 20 degrees and decrease baking times by 10–20 percent, allowing the cake to cook faster, before the gases escape. For more information, visit your local agricultural office or cooperative extension Web site.

missing. If you really want a specific cake, you may have to make a quick trip to the market. If some ingredients need to be softened, or melted and cooled, bring them to the proper temperature while you collect your equipment.

SET OUT THE TOOLS
Gather the tools and equipment you will need for the recipe. Set out the baking pan or pans, measuring cups and spoons, bowls, mixers, and cooling racks, as well as decorating tools like pastry bags and icing spatulas.

PREHEAT THE OVEN
Unless a recipe specifies otherwise, adjust the oven racks so that they are as close to the middle as possible. Turn on the oven and preheat it for 7–10 minutes to the specified temperature. This is very important, because if the oven is not at temperature when you begin baking, the timing will be off—or, worse, the ingredients will not react properly with one another and the cake will not bake properly.

CHOOSE THE CORRECT PAN
All the recipes in this book were developed using specific pan sizes. Using a pan that's too small and filling it too close to the top could cause the batter to overflow as the cake rises. Using a pan that's

Scaling Cake Recipes

Many of the recipes in this book call for batter from a classic cake, such as Devil's Food Cake, that appears in another section of the book. Sometimes, you'll need more or less batter for the second cake than the original recipe yields. If you need less batter, I would advise against trying to scale the original recipe down and instead use the extra batter to bake a small "auxiliary" cake or a few cupcakes. (I freeze these to have on hand for gift giving, impromptu parties, or bribes.) If you prefer to reduce the recipe, then divide it by half or into thirds. (Single eggs should be beaten or separated before they are divided.)

If, on the other hand, you need more batter than the original recipe yields, first take a look at how many pans you can fit in your oven. When I need to use more pans than will fit into my oven, I prepare the batter in batches. That way I can reuse the pans, and I don't have to worry about eggs deflating or baking powder or baking soda activating too soon. Use pans of the same size and capacity, so that the batter comes up to the same depth in the pan. This ensures that the cakes will all have the same baking time. If your pans are larger than the ones specified in the recipe, you may need to increase the baking time, but do not increase the oven temperature.

For large events, requiring a big cake made with lots of batter, I like to use square or rectangular pans because the resulting cakes are easy to connect and make into one big festive shape.

too large may result in a flatter cake. If you do not have a pan that's called for in the recipe, consult the chart on page 39 to find out the correct pan's volume, then search your cabinets for a pan (or two) that matches its volume. Alternatively, increase or decrease the amount of batter so that it fits in your pan. It is best to use all the batter in a recipe rather than using a portion of it and storing the rest, because most leaveners begin their reacting process once they are mixed with other ingredients. If you have leftover batter, I recommend using it to prepare cupcakes or a smaller cake in addition to the main cake.

First Steps

PREPARE THE PAN

Preparing the pan is very important: it prevents the cake from sticking and facilitates easy removal. For most recipes, I like to butter and flour the pans (or use cocoa powder instead of flour on chocolate cakes) and leave it at that. Butter tastes good, but it does make a darker crust than some other greasing agents. Some people prefer to not grease pans when baking sponge cakes or angel food cakes, to allow the cake to rise freely and prevent it from slipping, but I have never had a problem with slippage. Clarified butter has no taste and shortening does not burn easily, so they can also be used for greasing. Cooking spray made from vegetable oil is very popular because it is quick and easy and great for lowfat recipes. However, do not use cooking spray on nonstick pans, which tend to be darker and retain more heat. If you do, you may end up with a very dark crust. Lining the pan with parchment paper makes the cake easier to remove. Cut the paper to size and then butter it (if called for in the recipe). Buttering the paper works best with spongy or foamy cakes.

To butter and flour a pan, hold a tablespoon or two of butter in a piece of wax paper. Generously coat the bottom and sides of the pan with butter. If you are using a decorative pan, such as a Bundt or fluted pan, be sure to apply the butter generously to the grooves. If a recipe tells you to flour a pan, add two tablespoons of flour to the buttered pan and shake it until the butter is coated with flour. Invert the pan and tap it to knock out any extra flour. If you need a floured work surface, knock the flour out onto whatever surface you plan to use.

To line a round pan with parchment paper, hold the pan right side up on a sheet of the paper and trace the outline of the bottom of the pan onto the paper with a pencil. Cut the paper slightly smaller than the circle. Butter the pan, then place the paper in the bottom of the pan and butter and flour as directed.

Some cakes (mostly cheesecakes, custard, and pudding cakes) require indirect heat and more moisture in the oven and are best baked in a water bath. Without it, cheesecakes tend to crack out of dryness and custards tend to be rubbery. To prepare a water bath, choose a roasting pan that is at least two inches larger than your cake pan. If your roaster has a rack, use it—this will diffuse more heat. If using a springform pan, cover the outside of the pan (on the sides and bottom) with two or three layers of foil in a crisscross overlap. This will prevent water from leaking into the pan. Place the smaller pan in the roasting pan without the rack, fill the roaster with water until it comes about ½–⅔ of the way up the sides of the smaller pan, then remove the smaller pan and place the roaster in the oven. Preheat the oven with the water-filled roaster in it.

Standard Pan Sizes and Their Capacities

This chart shows the approximate capacity, in volume, of various baking pans. Some recipes call for filling the pan two-thirds to three-quarters of the way to the top with batter; others call for less batter so that the cake comes out in thinner, easy-to-stack layers. If you bake in a smaller or larger pan than is called for in the recipe, adjust the baking time accordingly.

For example, when you divide batter among 24 mini muffin cups instead of two 8-inch round pans, your baking time will be shorter because the cakes are smaller. But when you bake the same amount of batter in one large Bundt pan, your baking time will be longer because the cake is deeper. Usually, the deeper the cake, the longer the baking time.

PAN SIZES   **APPROXIMATE VOLUME**

MUFFIN TINS

Extra mini
(1¾-inch diameter x ¾-inch depth) . . . . . 2 tablespoons

Mini (2-inch diameter x 1-inch depth) . . . ¼ cup

Medium
(2¾-inch diameter x 1⅛-inch depth) . . . . ⅓ cup

Large (3½-diameter x 2-inch depth) . . . . . ¾ cup

Extra large
(4-inch diameter x 2-inch depth) . . . . 1 cup

Medium muffin top
(2¾-inch diameter x ½-inch depth) . . . . . ¼ cup

Large muffin top
(4-inch diameter x ½-inch depth) . . . . ½ cup

NOVELTY PANS

Baba molds (3½-inch diameter) . . . . ¾ cup

Brownie bar pans (2-inch) . . . . 2 tablespoons

Dome (1¾-inch diameter) . . . . 2 tablespoons

Dome (3-inch diameter) . . . . ¾ cup

Dome (6-inch diameter) . . . . 5 cups

Flower (2-inch) . . . . 2 tablespoons

Flower (4½-inch) . . . . 1 cup

Heart (1¾-inch) . . . . 2 tablespoons

Heart (4-inch) . . . . ¾ cup

Oval tart (2½ x 3-inch) . . . . ¼ cup

Pumpkin (3½-inch) . . . . ½ cup per cavity

Shortcake pan (3½-inch) . . . . ⅔ cup

Skull (7-inch) . . . . 6 cups

Star (1¾-inch) . . . . 2 tablespoons

Star (4-inch) . . . . ¾ cup

LOAF PANS

2½ x 4-inch . . . . 1¼ cups

3 x 5½ . . . . 2 cups

4½ x 6-inch . . . . 3 cups

3½ x 8-inch . . . . 3½ cups

4 x 8-inch . . . . 4 cups

4¼ x 8½-inch . . . . 5 cups

4½ x 8½-inch . . . . 6 cups

5 x 9-inch . . . . 8 cups

5 x 10-inch . . . . 10 cups

4 x 16-inch . . . . 13 cups

ROUND PANS
(STANDARD DEPTH = 2 INCHES)

4-inch . . . . 1½ cups

5-inch . . . . 2¾ cups

6-inch . . . . 3¾ cups

7-inch	5 ¼ cups
8-inch	6 cups
9-inch	8 cups
10-inch	11 cups
12-inch	15½ cups
7-inch, 3 inches deep	5¾ cups
8-inch, 3 inches deep	8 cups

SPRINGFORM PANS

4-inch	3 cups
8-inch	8 cups
9½-inch	10 cups
10-inch	12 cups

SQUARE PANS

4 x 4-inch	3 ½ cups
5 x 5-inch	5 cups
6 x 6-inch	6 cups
8 x 8-inch	8 cups
9 x 9-inch	10 cups
10 x 10-inch	12 cups

BUNDT PANS

3½-inch	¾ cup
8-inch	7½ cups
9-inch	9 cups
10-inch	12 cups

TUBE AND ANGEL FOOD PANS

8-inch tube, 3 inches deep	9 cups
9-inch tube, 3 inches deep	10 cups
9-inch angel food, 4 inches deep	12 cups
10-inch tube, 4 inches deep	16 cups
12-inch ring, 3 inches deep	12 cups

RECTANGULAR PANS

7 x 11-inch	6 cups
8 x 12-inch	9 cups
9 x 13-inch	4 cups

JELLY-ROLL PANS

7½ x 11¾-inch	4 cups
9 x 12¼-inch	5 cups
10½ x 15-inch	10 cups
11½ x 17¼-inch	13 cups

When the smaller pan is filled with batter and ready to go in the oven, gently lower it into the heated water bath. When the cake is done, carefully remove the smaller pan from the water bath without getting water on the cake.

To prepare a double boiler, add water to the lower pan, but take care that the bottom surface of the top pan does not touch the water. Double boilers are ideal for delicate frostings, icings, sauces, jams, and melting chocolate. The point of using it is to heat the ingredients as gently as possible over the lowest heat possible. Consistent stirring and constant supervision are usually required.

PREPARE THE INGREDIENTS

Butter and cream cheese are easier to beat, and combine better with other ingredients, if they are at room temperature. So remove them, and any other ingredients, from the refrigerator 20–30 minutes before you need them—but be aware of the room temperature. I have walked back into the kitchen after 20 minutes on a hot day to find a pool of butter on the counter.

Then you can separate the eggs. You'll find this task is much easier while the eggs are cold. To separate, crack the egg on a flat surface, not the rim of a bowl. Pull apart the egg and hold it over an empty bowl. Let the whites but not the yolks drop into the bowl. Slide the yolk back and forth between the shells, being careful not to drop any yolk into the bowl. Even the tiniest bit of yolk in the whites will prevent them from foaming properly. If you are using egg whites, let them come to room temperature first: they will be fuller after you beat them than if you use them cold.

The next step is measuring all the ingredients. To achieve the most accurate measurements, use glass cups with pour spouts for liquids and measuring cups for dry ingredients. Prepare the ingredients as directed in the recipe. For example, if the recipe calls for sifted flour, sift it first, then measure it. Scoop the dry ingredient into the cup, then scrape off the excess with a knife to level it. Use measuring spoons, instead of household flatware, for correct teaspoon and tablespoon measurements and level the tops, too.

Now you're ready to get out all of the other ingredients and prep them as needed. Zest the citrus, chop or grind the nuts and/or chocolate, plump the dried fruits, and so on.

Batter Basics

MIX DRY INGREDIENTS

I like to mix flour, leaveners, and spices or other dry flavorings first and set them aside while I cream the butter and sugar or whip the eggs. Be sure to mix dry ingredients thoroughly so that the leavenings and flavorings are evenly distributed.

CREAM BUTTER AND SUGAR

When the butter is at room temperature, cut it into small pieces and put it and the sugar (and any other ingredients) in a bowl that's large enough for the batter. If you're using a hand mixer with standard beaters, beat for at least 2 minutes, or until light and fluffy. The mixture will change in color from bright yellow to cream or pale ivory. The consistency should be similar to that of whipped cream.

BEAT THE EGGS

If the recipe calls for beating egg whites until they are foamy, use your mixer's whisk attachment and, if directed, a little cream of tartar. Beat on medium speed for about one minute, or until the cream of tartar dissolves and the egg whites have foamy bubbles.

If you are to beat the whites until soft peaks form, follow the steps for foamy egg whites, but increase the mixer speed to medium-high and beat for about 2–3 minutes, until they look opaque but are still moist. The egg whites should form soft, limp peaks when lifted with the beater.

If you are to beat the whites until stiff peaks form, continue to beat for 1–2 minutes longer than the soft-peak stage, until the whites look glossy and form firm peaks when lifted with the beater.

If you are to beat whole eggs with sugar until the mixture reaches the ribbon stage, use your mixer's standard attachment and beat the ingredients on medium-high speed until the mixture has increased in volume. It will change in color from bright yellow to light yellow. There will also be concentric rings in the batter around the beater. When the beaters are lifted, the batter will fall back into the bowl like a ribbon.

COMBINE THE WET AND DRY INGREDIENTS

Folding is a technique used to combine two ingredients of different densities, such as a heavy batter and very light, airy egg whites. To fold, add the lighter ingredient to the heavier one a little at a time, remembering that the goal is to prevent the trapped air in the lighter ingredient from deflating. Use a rubber spatula to gently lift the heaver mixture over the lighter one, blending continuously until just combined. Once the ingredients are combined, stop.

stack 3 layers high

← easter cake

use the flower plate

To stir wet and dry ingredients together, I like to gradually add the flour mixture to the wet mixture before I add chunky ingredients like chocolate chips or nuts. Overmixing toughens gluten, resulting in a tougher cake, so the batter needs to be mixed only until blended.

Yeast cakes need to be kneaded, because as soon as flour is moistened, gluten begins to form, and kneading allows the gluten to strengthen and interact with yeast so the dough will rise. Kneading is a workout, and most dough requires 8–10 minutes of kneading, depending on the recipe. Most people rarely knead for long enough, which means that the dough will not rise properly. If you're "lazy," you may want to knead dough in a bread maker or food processor or stand mixer: that's okay; it will still work. To knead by hand, gather the dough into a ball and transfer it to a flour-coated work surface. Spread the dough a bit by pressing it down, then fold it over toward you and push it away with your palms. Repeat these motions gently for 8–10 minutes, or until the dough is elastic and smooth.

FILL THE PANS

Once you've mixed the batter, the final step is to put it in the pan. If you're using only one pan, this is easy enough, but how do you divide batter evenly among several pans? Pour it into a measuring cup and check to be sure the same amount goes into each pan. Pour the batter from a bit of a height and allow it to fold over on itself. This will trap air bubbles and make a fluffy cake.

If you are making a marble cake, you probably started with a light-colored batter, which you then divided in half. Then you added additional ingredients or flavorings to one of the halves to darken it. Marble cakes can also be made by swirling batter with jam or dulce de leche, or two batters of a similar consistency. To create a marble effect, pour or spoon the darker batter or ingredient over the lighter one in the pan, then run a knife through the two in a swirling motion.

Heating and Cooling

Always place cakes in the middle of the oven to bake. If you like, you can check the cakes halfway through the baking time. If you're using two pans, and one pan is baking faster than the other, rotate the pans.

Most baking times are expressed as a range. Check your cake for doneness before the shorter amount of time has transpired. Insert a cake tester, knife, toothpick, or chopstick into the center of the cake. If it comes out sticky, or if the batter is still somewhat liquid, continue baking. If the tester comes out clean, or if there are loose crumbs attached, your cake is done. When baking a layer cake or a sheet cake, you should not find that the cake is getting too brown on top before it is cooked in the middle. For cakes baked in taller pans with longer baking times, check the cake when it is about two-thirds of the way through the shorter baking time. If the top is getting too brown, cover the cake loosely with foil.

Dense cakes can be removed from the pan within 5 minutes of baking; lighter chiffon or sponge cakes are more temperamental and need to "settle" and cool down for about 15–20 minutes before being removed. Otherwise, they could break apart, stick to the pan, or sink. Cool the cake in the pan on a wire cooling rack for the time specified in the recipe. The wire rack allows air to circulate and the pan to cool evenly, preventing deflation and sogginess. To remove the cake from the pan, loosen it by running a knife around the edge of the cake. Using potholders, hold the pan and a plate together, with the plate inverted on top of the pan, then flip both over so that the cake is inverted onto the plate. Lift the pan off the cake. If you used parchment paper, peel it off and discard it. Then invert the plate onto the cooling rack so that the cake lands right side up, and let it cool completely. To keep a cheesecake from cracking while it cools, leave it in the oven (be sure to turn the oven off!) with the oven door slightly ajar so it cools as slowly as possible.

Constructing and Assembling

Everything I need to know about constructing and decorating cakes I learned through practice, although I did get some good tips in art school. I studied both architecture and graphic design before I settled on industrial design as a major at the Rhode Island School of Design.

Deep-Frying

Frying dough or batter in oil or clarified butter makes cakes that are crisp on the outside and moist on the inside. The oil holds in moisture and prevents the dough or batter from drying out.

Always add enough oil to the pot (see page 39 for guidelines on choosing the correct pot) to allow the batter or dough to move freely. Heat the fat gradually over a low flame, monitoring the temperature with a deep-fat or candy thermometer, to 365°F (or whatever temperature is specified in the recipe). Test the oil with a small piece of bread or a little batter. Do not allow the oil to smoke, as that means it is too hot and the outside of the cake will brown quicker than the inside will cook.

Add the first batch of room-temperature batter or dough to the oil, making sure that the spoonfuls are of roughly equal size so that the cakes will cook evenly. Rotate or turn the cakes with a slotted spoon until they are browned on all sides; then lift them from the oil with a slotted spoon, so that the oil can drain back into the pot. Transfer the fried cakes to plates or a pan lined with paper towels; then place the plates or pan in the oven on low heat to keep them warm. Remove any little dough pieces floating in the oil. Bring the oil to the correct temperature again and fry the next batch.

Learning about the relationships between forms, precision crafting, model making, and color are all key to successful design, no matter what the medium.

LAYER CAKES

To cut a single cake into layers, place the baked cake on a lazy Susan or a cutting board covered with wax paper. If you want to create two layers, use a ruler to find the midpoint of the cake and mark it with a toothpick. Then rotate the cake and mark it at the same height five more times around the perimeter, using equally spaced toothpicks. Cut the cake horizontally at toothpick height with a long serrated knife, using a sawing motion while rotating the cake. Then remove the toothpicks. If you want to create three or more layers, use the

Baking Contests

My husband, Brian, and I are both teachers at the same college and have long breaks several times a year. In the spring and summer, we jump in our car and take a road trip across the United States. We are gone for weeks at a time. We stop at dozens of towns that host state and county fairs, most of which feature baking contests designed to highlight locally grown ingredients. Even though I don't enter these competitions, I always have my eye on that blue ribbon, and I think that someday I'll have to enter one. I have never won a blue ribbon for anything . . . although if there had been baking contests in my school instead of spelling bees and debate teams, I think I would have had a chance!

Many classic American cakes have originated in recipe contests, including Lane cake, pineapple upside-down cake, and German chocolate cake. All were developed by home bakers, not professional pastry chefs.

Today, contests have exploded in popularity and are held for myriad reasons. Some are sponsored by food or housewares companies or by food growers to promote products, foods, or brands. They're a good way to get the word out and advertise. Other contests are sponsored by publishers, TV shows, or bloggers who collect recipes for publication. Some contests simply promote the idea of home baking to keep regional recipes alive, or to promote locally grown or organic ingredients. And even more contests are directed at the next generation of bakers and a new audience—kids.

People bring unique ideas and enthusiasm to these contests, as well as different skill levels. Most contests have separate categories for food professionals on the one hand and home cooks on the other. Some contests have separate categories for various types of foods or baked goods. Some contests ask entrants to improvise or improve upon a given recipe, and others require only that you use a given ingredient. The judging sheet is filled with criteria and usually includes taste, freshness, appearance, creativity, and popular appeal. You can find yearly listings and deadlines for baking contests online. If you have limited time or want the big prize, forget the small fairs and the blue ribbons and go for the Pillsbury Bake-Off. The grand prize in this contest: a cool million dollars.

same measuring, marking, and cutting technique at different heights. When all the layers are cut, look at the layers and choose the order of assembly. Save most even layers for the top and bottom of the cake and the others for the middle layers.

To level a domed cake, first remove it from the pan. Set it on a plate, and then place the plate in a larger baking pan. The sides of the pan should come up to the topmost straight edge of the cake, just under the slope of the dome. Lay a long serrated knife flat against the top of the pan, with the blade facing the cake. Slowly cut the cake dome off, making sure to keep your knife level as you gently saw back and forth. Eat or save the domed top for later.

To construct a three- or four-layer cake, you can simply stack the layers one on top of the other and frost. But if you're baking a tiered cake with more than four layers, then you'll want to use cardboard platforms and ⅜- or ½-inch-diameter wooden dowels (found in craft or hardware stores) to hold the construction in place. After all the cake layers are baked and cooled, cut pieces of stiff corrugated cardboard to the same size as the cake layers (you don't need cardboard for the bottom layer). You'll need four dowels per layer; if they're too tall, saw them to the height of each layer (you don't need dowels for the top layer). Place the bottom layer of cake on a serving tray and, using the smaller tier as a guide, insert the dowels as supports about ½ inch in from the edge of the smaller tier. Top with the next tier's cardboard and place the next layer on it. Insert the dowels as you did on the bottom tier. Continue until all the layers are assembled. Frost from the top down.

To layer a cake with pillars (found in craft stores and cake-decorating stores), bake all the cake layers and choose decorative plates to uses as bases. Choose three or four pillars for each layer, making sure that they are longer than the height of each layer (you don't need pillars for the top layer). Place the bottom layer on its decorative plate or serving tray and insert the pillars as supports. Top with the next tier's plate and place the cake on top. Insert more pillars. Continue until all the layers are assembled. Frost from the top down.

ICE CREAM CAKES

Bake the cake in the same pan you will assemble it in, or bake it in a pan of a similar size. (Springform pans make it easy to assemble ice cream cakes.) Remove the cake from the pans and, if necessary, level the top. Cut the cake into layers and freeze, placing wax paper between each layer, so the cake hardens. It is very important that the layers be frozen when they are assembled.

Cut a sheet a of parchment paper to fit the pan. Make the sheet big enough so that it covers the bottom and continues up the long sides of the pan, with a 2–3-inch overhang on both sides.

Soften the ice cream, but do not let it melt. If you will be mixing in any ingredients, soften it in a bowl.

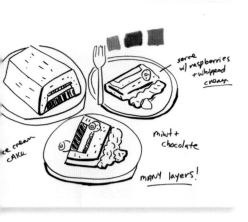

serve w/ raspberries + whipped cream

mint + chocolate

ice cream cake

many layers!

Spread a layer of softened ice cream in the pan 1½ inches thick. Place one layer of cake over the ice cream and press down. Add additional fillings, then spread another layer of ice cream over the cake. Press a second layer of cake over the ice cream. Cover and freeze for 3–4 hours, or until the cake is completely hard. Let the cake sit for a few minutes at room temperature and then, using the parchment-paper overhangs, remove it from the pan. Invert the cake to serve, making sure that the ice cream is the top layer, and remove the paper.

If you wish to frost your cake, do so at least 30 minutes before you plan to serve it. Frost the cake and add the toppings of your choice, then return it to the freezer for 30 minutes to 1 hour. Let it sit for a few minutes at room temperature before serving.

ROLLED CAKES

Cakes are easier to roll when they are thin and while they are still warm. Bake the cake in a jelly-roll pan lined with parchment paper. Place a piece of wax paper slightly longer than the cake on a work surface. Invert the cake and parchment paper onto the surface while still warm (but not hot). Remove the parchment paper and test-roll the warm cake, being careful not to crack it. Trim away the edges if they get in the way. If your cake is stiff and you need to make it more flexible, score a few lengthwise slits on the bottom side of the cake, cutting halfway through. Unroll the cake and cool completely.

Spread the filling on the cake, leaving a one-inch margin around the edges. Roll the cake away from you. Place it on a serving plate seam side down. Wrap it in plastic wrap and refrigerate for 2 hours to set the filling. Bring the cake to room temperature before serving. Cut the cake into slices using a serrated knife.

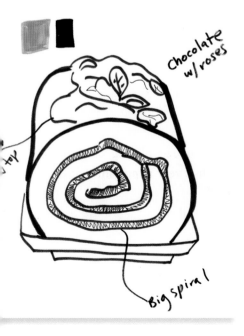

chocolate w/ roses

top

Big spiral

Piping Techniques

How to Use a Pastry Bag

1. Choose your tip shape and place the tip on the bag, securing it with a coupler. Different shaped tips will require you to hold the bag straight or at an angle.

2. Fill the bag one-half to two-thirds full with frosting. Fold over the edges to prevent the frosting from drying and hardening.

3. Tightly squeeze the sides of the bag until the frosting emerges from the tip onto the cake. Control the flow of the frosting to create the desired shape.

4. Practice, practice, practice.

BOLD SHAPES Frost the entire cake with thick frosting. With a large tip, make bold shapes like circles or spirals.

DELICATE DESIGNS Frost the entire cake with thin frosting. Use a small writing tip to create detailed delicate designs such as lines, spirals, and circles.

STARS Choose a star-shaped tip in the size that best suits your design. Holding the piping bag upright, gently squeeze the bag to release the frosting and form a star. Pull the bag away quickly to make a neat point on the star.

TWISTED ROPES Choose a rope-shaped tip in the size your design requires. Hold the piping bag at a slight angle and pipe a continuous line with even pressure, twisting the bag as you pipe.

TRAIL Insert a small round tip into your pastry bag. Hold the bag at a 45-degree angle against the cake. Apply pressure to form the icing into a dot. Then move the tip from left to right (or right to left if you're a lefty), starting and stopping at consistent intervals to create a line of dots.

SHELLS Use a star tip, and press the tip on the surface of the cake at your starting point. Gently squeeze the bag and lift it up, then down, returning to the surface of the cake every 1/2 to 1 inch and pulling the tip off to release the frosting from the tip. Start your next shell where you left off and continue until you have finished the cake.

DOTS Use a pastry bag with a writing tip and hold the bag over the area you wish to decorate. Press out the frosting so it forms a dot. Release the pressure on the bag and detach the tip from the dot. To reduce the points from the dots, flatten the points with a damp paintbrush. For a playful design, make large dots with a large tip, and over-pipe them with smaller dots using a small tip.

LINES, LOOPS, ZIGZAGS, AND TRELLISES The smaller the hole on a writing tip, the finer the line. Choose a tip to match the line size you would like to make. Rest the tip on the cake at your starting point. Hold the bag at an angle and pipe out a little frosting, lifting the bag slightly above the surface as you continue. Do not pull on the line, or it will break. When you reach the end of the line, release the pressure. Create loops, zigzags, and curves with your lines. You can also create a grid or trellis by overlapping lines.

OVERPIPING To create more elaborate textures, pipe one design over another using different techniques. Use a larger tip for the first piping and a smaller one for the overpiping. Choose two different colors of icing to create detailed designs.

STITCHING If you would like your piping to look like embroidery or stitching, use a small writing tip. Hold the tip against the cake. Press some frosting out of the pastry bag while you are moving your hand and lifting it slightly, then press the tip against the cake again. Repeat, moving your hand up and down to create stitches.

WORDS Words are created like doodling. To create cursive writing, use a small writing tip to pipe a continuous flow of frosting. To create individual letters, start piping at the beginning of each letter and pull the tip away from the cake at the end of each letter.

FLOWERS Place a petal tip into your piping bag. Pipe about five flat petals in a circle so they overlap each other. Pipe different colored dots in the centers of the flowers.

TO MAKE A ROSE Using a flat tip, first pipe a dot as the base. Starting at the center, add petals that stand straight up, making a circle around the center in overlapping segments as you go. To make different shaped roses, vary the size of the segments, making them small in the center and large toward the perimeter.

TO MAKE A PANSY Using a flat tip, first pipe a dot as the base. Use a flat tip and make the petals flush with the surface of the base. Add dots to the center.

LEAVES It is nice to add leaves to your flowers because it will make them look more like flowers. Hold the bag at a 45-degree angle to the cake. Without moving the tip, squeeze the bag and allow the frosting to fan out. Lessen your pressure as you pull the tip away to a point.

Filling and Frosting

LAYER CAKES

Determine how much frosting and filling you will need for the top, the sides, and the layers in between (see the chart on page 52). Divide the frosting and filling appropriately in small bowls. To fill, set the bottom layer on a serving plate or cardboard round. Mound the filling on it and spread evenly with an icing spatula to the edges. Top with the next layer of cake, making sure to align the edges of the cake, and spread with more filling. Continue until all the layers are stacked.

To frost, you should first cover the top and sides of the cake with a "crumb coat"—a thin layer of frosting that covers loose crumbs and prepares a smooth surface for the rest of the frosting. Remove any large lumps or crumbs and clean the spatula. Let the frosting set for about 20 minutes on the counter or in the refrigerator to harden. Mound additional frosting in the center of the top layer and spread it evenly to cover. Place four overlapping strips of wax paper under the cake to cover the plate. Then spread the frosting over the sides, turning the plate as needed. If desired, use a cake comb to make ripples in the frosting on the sides. Remove the wax paper and serve.

CUPCAKES

For thin icings and glazes, turn the cupcake over and dip it into the topping mixture, then flip it over and let sit to dry. Spread thicker frostings with the back of a spoon, or an icing spatula, or pipe it on with a pastry bag.

SHEET CAKES

Unlike layer cakes, sheet cakes should be frosted on the sides first. After you've frosted the sides, dollop the remaining frosting on top of the cake in four quadrants and spread it evenly.

ICINGS

Since icing is thinner than frosting, it is easier to drizzle it onto a cake. Work slowly and steadily from a height about six inches above the cake. Drizzle the icing directly from a spoon, or squeeze it from a pastry bag with a round tip.

GLAZES

Put the cake on a cooling rack with a baking sheet underneath. Pour on the glaze, starting in the center of the cake, and let it drip over the sides into the pan. If you miss some spots, spoon on the glaze to fill them.

WHIPPED CREAM

Use a cream with 30–40 percent milk-fat content and sweeten it according to the recipe instructions. Whip cream on medium speed with your electric mixer's whisk attachment until soft peaks form. Do not overwhip. Spread the cream over the cake with a rubber spatula and refrigerate until ready to serve.

Decorating

STENCILING

Stenciling is an easy and quick method for topping cakes. You simply dust confectioners' sugar or cocoa powder through a stencil onto a frosted or unfrosted cake. Appropriate stencils include paper cutouts, patterned doilies, or even fresh flowers, the outlines of which will remain after the flowers are removed.

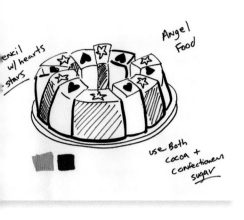

Stencil w/ hearts + stars

Angel Food

use Both cocoa + confectioners sugar

Here's how to make and use a stencil:

1. Cut a circle (or rectangle or square) a little larger than the cake from a piece of poster board.

2. Draw a pattern on the poster board and cut it out with a utility knife. You can also fold the circle into quarters or eighths and cut out shapes as if you were creating a paper snowflake.

3. Put confectioners' sugar or cocoa powder in a fine-mesh sieve. Place the stencil on the unfrosted cake and sift the sugar or cocoa powder lightly over the stencil. Carefully lift the stencil straight up to reveal the pattern. To stencil a frosted cake, first refrigerate the cake for about 45 minutes, or until the frosting hardens, and then place the stencil over the frosting.

MARZIPAN AND FONDANT

To cover your cake with marzipan or fondant, first chill the cake on a plate or piece of corrugated cardboard for 1 hour to create a sturdy base. After it has chilled, cover the cake with a glaze or an icing (see page 52) to create a smooth surface. Meanwhile, roll out the marzipan or fondant first to a ½-inch thickness on a work surface dusted with confectioners' sugar, and then rotate and roll again. Continue to roll and rotate until the marzipan or fondant reaches a ⅛–1/16-inch thickness, using the chart on page 54 to determine the size you'll need. Loop the marzipan or fondant over your rolling pin and transfer it to the cake, centering it carefully. Press the fondant or marzipan onto the cake and smooth it, working from the center out to the edges and from the top down over the sides. Smooth with your hands or a fondant-smoothing tool, and use a pastry wheel (or mini pizza cutter) to trim the edges where the fondant or marzipan meets the plate. Cover the cake with plastic wrap so the fondant or marzipan doesn't dry out.

To create decorative elements such as flowers, bows, or dots with marzipan or fondant, roll it out to the desired thickness (leftover scraps from trimming can be rerolled if desired), and then use cookie

How Much Fondant Do You Need?

This chart assumes that one-layer cakes are 2 inches high and two-layer cakes are 4 inches high.

IF YOUR CAKE DIAMETER IS DIAMETER	YOUR FONDANT SHOULD WEIGH	ROLL FONDANT TO
6 inches round (1 layer)	12 ounces	12 inches
8 inches round (1 layer)	16 ounces	14 inches
10 inches round (1 layer)	20 ounces	16 inches
12 inches round (1 layer)	32 ounces	18 inches
6 inches round (2 layers)	18 ounces	14 inches
8 inches round (2 layers)	24 ounces	18 inches
10 inches round (2 layers)	36 ounces	10 inches
12 inches round (2 layers)	48 ounces	22 inches
6 inches square (2 layers)	24 ounces	16 inches
8 inches square (2 layers)	36 ounces	18 inches
10 inches square (2 layers)	48 ounces	22 inches
7 x 11 sheet	30 ounces	13 x 16 inches
9 x 13 sheet	40 ounces	14 x 18 inches

cutters or a utility knife to cut out shapes. You can also press stamps into uncut marzipan or fondant to emboss textures and patterns on it, then form the embossed material into the desired shapes. Wet the shapes with a little water to attach them to the fondant- or marzipan-covered cake, or press the shapes directly into wet frosting—that is, frosting that hasn't had a chance to dry out in the air.

Fondant and marzipan also make a great canvas for painting decorative elements onto cakes. First, draw your design, in actual size, on parchment paper. After covering the cake with marzipan or fondant, cut out your design and use the drawing as a template, pressing its outline onto the surface of the cake. Then use a paintbrush or a pastry bag to paint or pipe Royal Icing (page 355) into the outline. Let the icing dry (leave plenty of time for this—at least 3 or 4 hours). Then use food coloring diluted with water or edible markers to paint over the icing. Blend colors, add highlights and shading, and add cross-hatching or patterns if you wish.

Frosting Color Wheel and Palettes

Use this color wheel—a chart for mixing food coloring—to create color schemes that will help give your cakes an occasion-specific look.

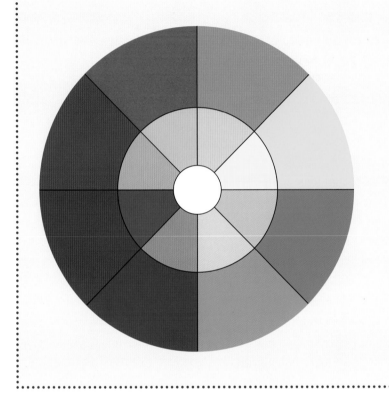

Color Key

- Red and yellow make orange
- Yellow and blue make green
- Blue and green make turquoise
- More blue and less red make purple
- More red and less blue make violet
- Blue and orange or red and green make brown
- Red and white make pink
- Orange and white make peach
- Yellow and white make lemon
- Green and white make mint
- Turquoise and white make sea green
- Blue and white make light blue
- Purple and white make lavender
- Brown and white make light brown
- To make black frosting, start off with chocolate frosting and add black coloring gel

EDIBLE TRANSFERS

If you want to decorate a cake with images that contain tons of writing (like a diploma) or lots of minute, crisp photographic details, an edible icing photo transfer is easier than decorating freehand—especially if your artistic skills aren't the best—and it also ensures accuracy. Individual photo transfers can be custom-ordered online or at cake-decorating shops. If you get hooked, you may even want to invest in an edible-icing printer. It works just as an ink-jet printer does, except that the inks are edible.

Premade edible transfers are available in sizes up to 8½ x 11 inches, so they work well for 8-inch cakes (alternatively, use several

icing
heat transfer

classy
looking

GraduAtioN CAke!

transfers on a larger cake). Many cake-decorating supply stores that make edible transfers also scan, size, and enhance your own artwork and print it on the transfer. All you need to do is give them your digital original or a color photocopy of your artwork. If you have small designs and order the 8½ x 11-inch size, you can fit several designs on one page and then cut them out yourself. Freeze the transfer for 20 minutes so it hardens and peels off easily from the backing. Place the transfer on a cake that has already been covered first with a layer of marzipan or fondant and then with a thin coating of Royal Icing (page 355). Make sure the icing is moist before you apply the transfer.

CHOCOLATE

Chocolate should be tempered for ease of shaping before you use it to decorate cakes. Tempering changes the crystal structure of the chocolate, providing stability and giving it a nice sheen and a crispy snap. Here's the method I prefer:

1. Chop the chocolate and put in the top of a double boiler. Be very careful to keep water or any moisture away from the chocolate, or it will not temper properly.

2. Melt the chocolate over low heat while stirring with a rubber spatula. Bring the chocolate to 110°F (measure with a candy thermometer). Remove from heat and let cool to 80°F.

3. Heat the chocolate again until it reaches 91°F (this will be quick). The chocolate should be tempered at this point; to test it, spread a thin layer on a plate or dip a knife into it, and let it cool. It should be hard, not sticky, and shiny, not streaked.

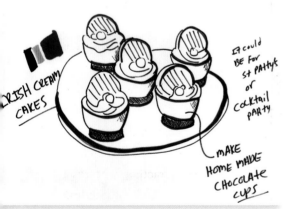

IRISH CREAM
CAKES

It could
BE For
St PAtty's
or
cocktail
PArty

MAKE
HOME MADE
CHOCOLATE
cups

Once it's tempered, you can pipe chocolate directly onto cakes. Let it cool to set. You can also pour tempered chocolate into candy or silicone molds. Let it harden before you remove it from the molds and place it on cakes.

SERVING

A cake's seductive nature is enhanced with flawless presentation. Serving plates, cake pedestals, cutting tools, and dessert plates have been made since the earliest cakes were served, and you can find many of these artifacts preserved in museums—including cake plates from the Roman Empire, Victorian cake pedestals, seventeenth-century cake dishes used in Japanese tea ceremonies, and cake plates designed by Frank Lloyd Wright and Charles Lewis Tiffany.

Living on a modest budget, I scour flea markets, estate sales, and thrift stores for unique yet attractive cake stands, plates, and servers that will enhance any cake's appeal. My homespun collection includes cake stands and monogrammed serving sets (with other people's initials) that I've found at reasonable prices and that I love to use.

Presenting a Whole Cake

The plate on which you choose to serve your cake will have a huge impact on its presentation. Think about the colors of the cake, its frosting, filling, and decorations, and then consider how a plate's color and material will affect the cake's appearance.

A plate with contrasting colors or materials, or with seasonal colors or materials, will have a dramatic effect. White or cream-colored plates are best if you can't decide on a color, since they allow the cake to stand out. Choose a plate with a texture or detailing around the rim for an added dimension, and consider picking up this design detail when you pipe the icing. Colored transparent-glass plates can pick up colors in the cake to highlight them but not be distracting, whereas a clear glass plate will fade away and make your cake stand out. Sterling silver plates have a classic, elegant richness. When serving multiple whole cakes, large trays that hold individual cake plates of contrasting colors make a graphic, classy presentation.

Presenting Small and Individual Cakes

Individual cakes provide excellent opportunities for presentation and plating. Let the shape of the cakes dictate the composition.

For example, you could place thick triangular cakes on their edges. Cut a square cake into rectangles, and then cut the rectangles into triangles, and serve one piece inverted and the other upright.

Unfrosted cakes and those that won't stick together can be placed on top of one another to create a pyramid or tower. They can also be placed in paper wrappers and stacked.

You could also line up individual cakes on a long, narrow plate. Spacing the cakes varies the aesthetic: cakes that are far apart seem monumental; cakes that are close together seem more cozy.

Wax paper bags are good wrappers for snack cakes, and foil makes a good wrapper for individual cakes. If the cakes are hidden in a lunch box, unwrapping them is like opening a gift.

Plating and Garnishing

Whole cakes often look more beautiful than sliced cakes, because once a cake is cut—depending on the skill of the cutter—it sometimes gets messy. Use the guidelines on the next few pages to cut your cake into pieces that will look pretty on a plate; then add other graphic elements to make individual servings as intriguing as the whole. For example, ice cream, sauces, fruit, whipped cream, and chocolate are all good visual companions for a plated slice of cake. The intersection between the slice and these other elements is also important. Drizzling a sauce over the cake gives a more casual impression than setting the cake in a pool of sauce, for example. Several decorative elements can be used together—such as marzipan flowers and sauce—and then you can highlight the colors of the cake by drawing on it with frosting and setting it in a pool of sauce.

ROUND AND RING-SHAPED CAKES

These cakes, as well as shapes like ovals, flowers, or hexagons, are best cut in wedges. To create equal-size slices, mark your cake by scoring it lightly with a knife before cutting. If you make a few different cakes of the same shape but different flavors—for example, a chocolate Bundt cake, a vanilla Bundt cake, and an orange Bundt cake—they can be cut and the slices rearranged so that each single cake comprises slices of varying flavors.

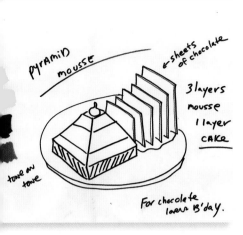

pyramid mousse

sheets of chocolate

3 layers mousse
1 layer cake

tone on tone

For chocolate lovers B'day.

SQUARE, RECTANGULAR, AND SHEET CAKES

These rectilinear cakes can be cut into squares, small rectangles, long rectangles, diamonds, or even triangles, and each shape will have a different effect on the presentation. For best results, follow a cake-cutting chart, or make scores in the cake before cutting begins. You can also frost with more than one kind of frosting, so that you end up with squares in a variety of colors, which can be rearranged to form a mosaic; diamond-shaped slices can be rearranged into a star. Sheet cakes can also be cut with cookie cutters in an almost infinite number of shapes, or use a stencil template to cut out a character, word, or shape. Form a cake "tower" by cutting, stacking, and rearranging slices in a vertical configuration.

GENERAL GUIDELINES

When you serve your cake, remember that the plate and its garnishes become part of the whole composition. Take advantage of the opportunity provided by the intersection between cake and plate to enhance a design detail. For example, you can create a transition between the cake and the plate that is smooth, minimal, or high-lighted. A smooth transition might involve choosing a plate with slightly contrasting or similar color as the cake. A minimal transition might involve creating a simple line of sauce that mimics a line on the plate. A highlighted transition might involve adding a heavily piped detail to the cake slice, creating a strong visual separation between cake and plate.

Select plates with designs that are visible around the rim. Plates with images or patterns in the center don't do much to accent the style of large cakes or slices, since the cake sits on top of the image or pattern. However, the image or graphic on the plate can be unveiled and a hidden surprise exposed if you are good at eating all the crumbs.

You can also play with the shapes of the slices on the plate to create a sculptural landscape. A triangular watermelon slice, a square slice of cake, and a round dome of ice cream create a strong graphic composition. Repeat the shape of the cake in a sauce on the plate, or contrast it with another shape. Dust confectioners' sugar or cocoa

Coconut cakes

use teri's silver dishes

try to find purple or pink orchids

in a pattern on the plate. Create color contrast by using both. Put chocolate, caramel, or another sauce in a pastry bag fitted with a thin tip (or in a squirt bottle) to create detailed lines on the plate, or draw a thick line with a large pastry tip. Edible flowers, leaves, chocolate, and candies can highlight a pattern on the plate. Fruit, such as papaya slices or coconut or cantaloupe halves, can be made into a miniature plate for ice cream or cake.

Equipment for Presentation

CAKE SERVERS
Cake servers not only look elegant; they make serving multilayer cakes much easier. Dipping a cake server in a tall glass of hot water also helps to keep it from getting gooped up as you cut the slices. Transferring the cake to the plate gracefully is easiest with a cake server. Tongs can also be used to lift small cakes or slices.

PEDESTALS AND CAKE KEEPERS
Pedestals convert even the simplest cake into an immediate showstopper. Elevating a cake is a surefire way to make it look more impressive. Presenting a cake in a cake keeper under an opaque or transparent dome also offers unveiling opportunities, and storing leftover cake under a dome will help keep it fresh. If the cake needs to be refrigerated, move the shelves in the fridge before putting the cake in the keeper to make sure you have enough room for its height. Multitiered cake pedestals are good for serving several different small cakes and individual cakes or cupcakes.

CAKE PLATES AND PLATTERS
There are many pedestal options available for serving round cakes, but not many for square or sheet cakes. A square cake looks good on a square plate and a round cake on a round plate, but you can also switch it up a bit graphically and put a round cake on a square plate and vice versa. To convert a standard plate into a low cake pedestal, attach small drawer knobs on the four corners on the underside of the plate to elevate it slightly. A plate placed on top of a charger also creates contrast.

make sure the chocolate is extra smooth

pile with fruit figs + dates

put on a nice cake server

CAKE BARS like CANDY BARS

serve w/ whipped cream

make a graphic display on tray

SHAPED PLATES

Plates that mimic natural shapes—such as flowers or stars—can add to the fun of serving cake, especially when you add an element like a sauce, ice cream, or whipped cream. Each one of these items can be arranged to create a graphic narrative on the plate. Play around with small cakes on big stands and vice versa. Plates with compartments offer fun opportunities for dividing the cake, sauce, and ice cream graphically.

BOWLS AND BASKETS

In addition to plates and platters, baskets and bowls make lovely—and often appropriate—serving utensils. Place small cakes in a large bowl or basket, either unwrapped or wrapped in parchment or paper muffin cups.

ETHNIC DISHWARE

Pattern, shape, and material can transport your mind to a faraway place and heighten the cake-eating experience. Blue corn cake, for example, works well on a rustic southwestern ceramic plate; zuccotto looks good on an Italian patterned ceramic plate. Bamboo steamers make great serving plates for steamed Asian cakes or rice cakes. A carved wooden tray highlights African cakes. A bowl filled with sugar syrup is perfect for some Indian cakes. French dishware with illustrations around the rim sets a traditional Provençal tone for canelés.

PAPER PLATES AND NAPKINS

Glass, china, or even plastic dessert plates are nicer for a small crowd, but paper plates simplify cleanup—and they are easy to customize to a particular theme—if you are hosting a large crowd. You can shape the plate by cutting it or punching holes around the rim; you can glue it with graphics or stack together plates of varying sizes. Cakes that are not too rich or buttery can be served on patterned paper napkins. Look for napkins adorned with patterns that reflect your theme—Hawaiian prints for pineapple upside-down cake, French toile for financiers, and Mexican prints for skull cakes. Paper muffin cups are available in a variety of prints and patterns, and can also

VALewtiwes chocolates

make some w/nuts

truffles w/ raspBerry cream inside

be used for serving small individual cakes or slices. Doilies offer a kind of retro "grandma" aesthetic.

NATURAL PLATES

Banana leaves, corn husks, and coconut slices are examples of natural materials that can be easily used as disposable plates or as liners for other dishware.

CUSTOM DISPLAY

If you want to get really crafty, you can build a custom display that fits your cake's theme out of foam core. Consider creating a carousel for a carnival-themed novelty cake, or a temple for a Passover cake.

SHARING AND PRESERVING

If you want to bring the most talked-about dish to a party, bring the cake. A homemade cake is always admired, and a treat for most people who don't bake. If you really want to be a star, try making a cake that has unique flavors and decorations and an unusual presentation. Giving cakes to friends and family who live far away is a great way to share a birthday, baby shower, or holiday. Following are some tips to ensure that your cakes arrive at their destination safely.

Transporting Cakes

Transporting cakes that aren't covered with icing or thick frosting is a cinch. Bundt cakes and pound cakes dusted with confectioners' sugar, cakes topped with fondant or marzipan, and lightly iced cakes covered with glazes that harden are the easiest to transport. These can be kept in the baking pan or placed on a serving plate, then covered with foil before leaving your kitchen. Preparing the cake in a paper liner or disposable metal pan means you don't have to worry about getting your pan back, though you may wish to bring a serving plate to whatever event you're attending.

If you don't have a cake carrier or if you need a custom-size box, purchase a clean box with a lid that is an inch or two larger than the cake. Since cake sizes are almost infinitely variable and boxes are sometimes hard to find, I often buy the box first and then bake the cake to fit the box. Your local bakery or supermarket may be willing to sell you a box—any box will do, so you can also pick one up from a shipping or packing store.

If the cake is not in a paper liner and is iced or frosted, spread some frosting to use as "glue" in the center of a sturdy piece of cardboard that's the size of the bottom of the box. Place the cake on top. This will keep the cardboard from shifting within the box and lessen the chance of the cake smashing against the sides. For heavier cakes, use two or three layers of cardboard. Place double-stick tape on the bottom of the box and set the cardboard and the cake in the box. If you're transporting tiered cakes, whether on pillars or stacked, transport the layers individually, in separate boxes. Once you arrive at your destination, assemble the cake and add final frosting details, toppers, and garnishes.

If it is hot outside, keep the cake in the car with the air-conditioning on. Try not to stop short. At the event, you can lift ether the cake from the box or tear the box apart and slide it out. You may also want to pack a kit of extra icing and any tools you might need to touch up the cake.

Shipping Cakes

The best cakes for mailing are somewhat dense, such as the White Fruitcake (page 304) or Pumpkin Rum Cakes (page 322). If you're going to ship a cake, make one with a topping that hardens, such as fondant, marzipan, or tempered chocolate. I like to pack cakes for mailing in the clear plastic, snap-close cake and cupcake containers that supermarkets use for their own baked goods. (When I purchase cakes and muffins, I save the containers. When I don't have any on hand, I ask the person at the bakery counter if he or she will sell them. Every time, the answer has been yes.) Bake a cake that is slightly smaller than the size of the box. You have the option to send the cake as is or preserve it by freezing it and mailing it on dry ice. If you freeze it, freeze the cake in the container. To ship the frozen cake, purchase a corrugated cardboard box that is at least two inches bigger then your cake all around—bottom, top, and sides. When you're ready to ship, put about two inches of cushioning material (cornstarch peanuts or popcorn) in the bottom of the box. Place the plastic container holding the cake in the center, and add more cushioning material around the sides and top. If necessary, add packets of dry ice, which are available at many supermarkets. Seal the box with packing tape. Ship frozen cakes via overnight mail; unfrozen cakes may be shipped via Priority Mail.

Storing Cakes

The shelf life of a cake and the best method for storing it really depend on the cake's ingredients. A cake—like cheesecake—that contains perishable ingredients, such as custard and whipped cream, or a cake topped with frosting made from raw eggs or milk should be refrigerated. Sponge cakes, pound cakes, fruitcakes, chiffon cakes, and coffee cakes, on the other hand, will stay fresh at room temperature in a cake keeper or wrapped in plastic. Cakes with moist ingredients and fresh fruits can lose their freshness quickly; these should be placed in a cake keeper, wrapped in plastic, or stored in the refrigerator. Fried cakes are not recommended for storing and should be consumed within a few hours.

If you plan to freeze a cake, I find that it's best to do so before frosting it. Wrap the cake layers in plastic and freeze the frosting separately in a plastic container. If the cake is already frosted, refrigerate it so the frosting can harden. Then seal the cake completely in an airtight container or an inner layer of wax paper and an outer layer of aluminum foil. Thaw it at room temperature, which will take between 2 and 6 hours, depending on the temperature of the room and the size of the cake. If you wrap the cake in wax paper and foil, allow the cake to thaw halfway, then remove the layers and continue thawing.

Cakes will keep in the freezer for up to 3 months. If you are honoring the tradition of eating a piece of your wedding cake on your first anniversary, keep your expectations low. My husband and I learned this the hard way. Instead of indulging in a piece of the cake at our anniversary picnic, we wound up burying it at an improvisational

wedding FAVORS

package
Fondau t
cAKes in
Boxer

get the
Boxes 1st.
then mAke the
cAKes to size.

ritual ceremony in the woods. Our cake topper marks the spot, which we visit every few years.

Giving Cakes

As many people have discovered, cake makes a wonderful gift, especially if you're presenting it at a party. Here are a few suggestions for making the moment special:

- Set small individual cakes in paper wrappers and place snugly in a box. A keepsake wooden box, a box that is designed to reinforce the style of the cake, or a stack of boxes, each holding a different cake, will make a lasting impression on the recipient.

- Wrap individual unfrosted cakes in parchment, origami paper, or gift wrap.

- Bake the cake in new or vintage bakeware; present the cake and the baking dish together as a gift.

- Bring the cake to the party on a pedestal or in a cake carrier, and offer the pedestal or carrier as part of the gift. Prepare a recipe from a book and give the book along with the cake.

Everyday Cakes

GOLDEN CAKES

The bright, fluffy, creamy golden cakes in this section run the gamut from the light-as-a-feather sponge cakes to bready spice cakes to an ultradense pound cake. Yellow cakes get their color from the ingredients—butter, eggs, and vanilla—and sometimes from lemon and saffron. Enjoy them as a simple plain slice with tea or alongside fresh fruit, or give them a flavor makeover by adding mix-ins such as chocolate chips, dried fruit, or even sun-dried tomatoes and olives.

Pound Cake

Makes about 6 cups batter, enough for one 4½ x 8½-inch loaf

Old-fashioned pound cake recipes are easy to remember: they call for one pound each of flour, eggs, sugar, and butter. They are a bit dense for today's tastes, so this recipe is a lightened-up yet still substantial version that hits the spot any time of day. If you like to experiment with savory cakes, try adding herbs and vegetables to this one and reducing the sugar to ¾ cup—it is an excellent recipe to use as a base.

2 cups all-purpose flour
1 teaspoon baking powder
½ teaspoon salt
½ pound (2 sticks) unsalted butter, at room temperature
1⅔ cups granulated sugar
5 large eggs
1½ teaspoons vanilla extract
¼ cup whole milk
1½ cups Vanilla Frosting (page 367)

1. Preheat the oven to 350°F. Butter and flour a 4½ x 8½-inch loaf pan or line the pan with a paper liner.

2. Combine the flour, baking powder, and salt in a mixing bowl.

3. Beat the butter and sugar in a large mixing bowl with an electric mixer on medium speed until creamy. Add the eggs one at a time, beating well after each addition. Beat in the vanilla.

4. Gradually add the flour mixture, alternating with the milk, on low speed until blended.

5. Pour the batter into the pan and bake for 55–70 minutes, or until a knife inserted in the center comes out clean. Cool in the pan for 10 minutes, then transfer to a rack to cool completely. Spoon on the frosting.

Variations

Chocolate Swirl Pound Cake: Melt 3 ounces semisweet chocolate in a double boiler. Divide the batter in half and add the chocolate to one batch. Transfer the batters to the pan and swirl together with a knife. Top with Vanilla Icing (page 358).

Lemon Pound Cake: Add ¼ cup freshly squeezed lemon juice and 1 teaspoon grated lemon zest with the milk. Top with Lemon Icing (page 358).

Sun-Dried Tomato Pound Cake: Reduce the sugar to ¾ cup. Add ⅓ cup finely chopped sun-dried tomatoes and ¼ teaspoon ground white pepper with the milk. Dust with confectioners' sugar.

Rosemary Pound Cake: Reduce the sugar to ¾ cup. Add 1½ tablespoons fresh chopped rosemary with the dry ingredients.

Olive Pound Cake: Reduce the sugar to ¾ cup. Add ½ cup chopped black or green olives with the milk. Dust with confectioners' sugar.

Cherry Pound Cake: Add ¼ cup cherry juice and 1 cup chopped cherries with the milk. Top with Cherry Icing (page 358).

Ginger Pound Cake: Add 2 teaspoons grated fresh ginger with the milk. Serve with Chocolate Sauce (page 352) and Half-Whipped Cream (page 358) on the side.

Golden Yellow Cake

Makes about 8 cups batter, enough for one 8-inch three-layer cake

3 cups all-purpose flour

4 teaspoons baking powder

½ teaspoon salt

½ pound (2 sticks) unsalted butter, at room temperature

2 cups granulated sugar

4 large eggs, separated

2 teaspoons vanilla extract

1 cup whole milk

4½ cups Vanilla Buttercream (page 356)

I have been making this quick and easy butter cake for years. It is very flavorful, and it also makes a sturdy cake for my decorating adventures, which is why several other recipes in this book call for this batter. Here, I present it as a three-layer cake filled and topped with vanilla buttercream.

1. Preheat the oven to 350°F. Butter and flour three 8-inch round pans.

2. Combine the flour, baking powder, and salt in a mixing bowl.

3. Cream the butter and sugar in a large mixing bowl with an electric mixer on medium speed until fluffy. Add the egg yolks and beat well. Beat in the vanilla.

4. Gradually add the flour mixture, alternating with the milk, on low speed until blended. Set aside.

5. In a clean bowl with clean beaters, beat the egg whites until stiff peaks form. Gently fold the egg whites into the batter with a rubber spatula.

6. Divide the batter among the pans. Bake for 20–25 minutes, or until a knife inserted in the center comes out clean. Transfer to a rack to cool completely.

7. Place one cooled layer on a serving plate and top with one-fourth of the buttercream. Place a second layer on top and spread with another one-fourth of the buttercream. Top with the third layer, and use the remaining buttercream on the sides and top of the cake.

Variations

Golden Chocolate-Chip Cake: Add 1 cup mini chocolate chips to the batter before folding in the egg whites. Top with Dark Chocolate Frosting (page 351).

Espresso Cake: Reduce the milk to ½ cup. Add ¾ cup double-strength brewed espresso and 2 tablespoons ground espresso beans with the milk. Top with Coffee Frosting (page 351).

Layered Pudding Cake: Cut each baked layer in half horizontally, making six layers. Prepare a double batch of your choice of Pastry Cream (page 358) and divide it among six bowls, coloring each with a different food coloring. Spread the pastry cream between the layers. Top the cake with confectioners' sugar.

Lemon Cake: Replace the vanilla extract with ¼ cup freshly squeezed lemon juice.

Golden Saffron Tea Cake

Makes one 10-inch round cake

The appeal of this yeast cake is that it highlights the pure goodness of simplicity. You can count on it to give you a hearty golden cake that is lower in fat than a rich butter cake. Serve plain, or with jam. The saffron gives this cake its golden color; the anise variation tastes great with a spot of tea.

1½ cups lukewarm whole milk
1 packet (¼ ounce) active dry yeast
1 tablespoon granulated sugar
⅛ teaspoon saffron threads
3¾ cups bread flour
1 tablespoon cold unsalted butter
1 tablespoon clover honey
1 large egg, lightly beaten
2 large egg whites, lightly beaten

1. Line a baking sheet with parchment paper.

2. Combine the milk, yeast, and sugar in a small bowl and let sit for 5 minutes. Add the saffron and let sit 5 minutes longer.

3. Put the flour in a food processor and pulse in the butter until the mixture resembles coarse meal. Pulse in the honey and egg, then add the yeast mixture and pulse until mixed.

4. Dust a work surface with flour. Turn out the dough on the surface and knead until smooth, about 8–10 minutes. Place in a bowl greased with butter and cover loosely. Let rise for 1 hour, or until doubled in volume.

5. Punch down the dough, form into a 10-inch round, and place on the prepared baking sheet. Cover loosely and let rise for 30 minutes.

6. Preheat the oven to 400°F. Brush the dough with the egg whites, covering the entire surface. Prick holes

in the dough with a fork and bake for 20–25 minutes, or until lightly browned. Transfer to a rack to cool completely.

Variation

Anisette Cake: Omit the saffron. Add 1 tablespoon anisette liqueur and 1 teaspoon grated orange zest with the milk. Top with Orange Icing (page 358).

Sponge Cupcakes

Makes about 7½ cups batter, enough for 18 cupcakes

Soft and springy sponge cakes are equally good plain or topped with confectioners' sugar. I like to make these in a cupcake pan and watch the batter pop out of the paper liners, leaving a crimped pattern on the edge of the cake. To make this as a layer cake, see the variation following.

¾ pound (3 sticks) unsalted butter, at room temperature

1½ cups granulated sugar

6 large eggs, separated

1 teaspoon vanilla extract

3 cups self-rising flour

¼ teaspoon cream of tartar

2 tablespoons confectioners' sugar for dusting

1. Preheat the oven to 350°F. Arrange the oven racks so that one of them is at the highest possible position. Line 18 medium muffin cups (see page 39) with paper or foil liners that are taller than the muffin cups.

2. Beat the butter and sugar in a large mixing bowl with an electric mixer on medium speed until pale and creamy.

3. Beat in the egg yolks and vanilla, then gradually beat in the flour on low speed. Set aside.

4. In a clean bowl with clean beaters, beat the egg whites and cream of tartar until stiff peaks form. Gradually fold the egg whites into the batter with a rubber spatula.

5. Divide the batter among the liners and bake on the top rack for 15–20 minutes, or until golden brown and a knife inserted in the center comes out clean. Cool in the pans for 10 minutes, then transfer to a rack to cool completely. Dust with confectioners' sugar.

Variations

Chocolate Sponge Cupcakes: Reduce the flour to 2½ cups and add ½ cup unsweetened cocoa powder with the flour and 2 ounces melted and cooled bittersweet chocolate to the butter mixture.

Layered Sponge Cake: Bake the cake in two buttered and floured 8-inch cake pans for 25–30 minutes. Top with Vanilla Buttercream (page 356).

American Buttermilk Sheet Cake

Makes about 9 cups batter, enough for one 8 x 12-inch cake

3½ cups cake flour

1½ tablespoons baking powder

1 teaspoon salt

¾ cup (1½ sticks) unsalted butter, at room temperature

1½ cups granulated sugar

1⅓ cups buttermilk

4 large eggs, separated

1 tablespoon vanilla extract

3 cups Vanilla Frosting (page 357)

The all-American sheet cake gets its tang from buttermilk, but you can also use yogurt or sour cream to achieve a different kind of zing. The surface of this cake is perfect for decorating.

1. Preheat the oven to 350°F. Butter and flour an 8 x 12-inch pan.

2. Combine the flour, baking powder, and salt in a mixing bowl.

3. Beat the butter and sugar in a large mixing bowl with an electric mixer on medium speed until fluffy.

4. Gradually add the flour mixture, alternating with the buttermilk, on low speed until blended. Beat in the egg yolks and vanilla; set aside.

5. In a clean bowl with clean beaters, beat the egg whites until stiff peaks form. Gently fold the egg whites into the batter with a rubber spatula.

6. Spread the batter into the pan and bake for 30–35 minutes, or until a tester inserted in the center comes out clean. Cool in the pan for 5 minutes, then transfer to a rack to cool completely.

7. Top with vanilla frosting.

Variation

Chocolate Buttermilk Sheet Cake: Reduce the flour to 3 cups and add ⅔ cup unsweetened cocoa powder. Top with Chocolate Ganache (page 351).

Cake

2 cups sifted cake flour

2½ teaspoons baking powder

½ teaspoon salt

⅓ cup vegetable oil

1⅓ cups granulated sugar

4 large egg yolks

1 teaspoon grated lemon zest

⅓ cup freshly squeezed lemon juice

¼ cup whole milk

1 teaspoon vanilla extract

8 large egg whites

1 teaspoon cream of tartar

Meringue Topping

3 large egg whites

¼ teaspoon cream of tartar

1 cup granulated sugar

¼ cup water

¼ teaspoon salt

1 teaspoon freshly squeezed lemon juice

Filling

4 cups Lemon Filling (page 354)

Lemon Chiffon Cake

Makes about 7 cups batter, enough for one 3½ x 8-inch three-layer cake

If you get a craving for lemon meringue, this is the cake to bake. The chiffon is lightened by mixing meringue into the batter, and after baking you can cover the entire cake with meringue, or cover only the top and leave the sides exposed. To toast the meringue, use a kitchen torch after you've assembled the cake.

1. To make the cake, preheat the oven to 325°F. Butter and flour two 3½ x 8-inch loaf pans.

2. Combine the flour, baking powder, and salt in a mixing bowl.

3. Combine the oil, 1 cup of the sugar, and egg yolks in a large mixing bowl. Beat with an electric mixer on medium speed until the sugar is dissolved. Beat in the lemon zest, lemon juice, milk, and vanilla. Add the flour in three stages until combined.

4. In a clean bowl with clean beaters, beat the egg whites until foamy. Add the cream of tartar and remaining ⅓ cup of sugar and beat until stiff peaks form. Gently fold the egg whites into the batter with a rubber spatula.

5. Divide the batter between the pans and bake for 20–25 minutes, or until the cake springs back when touched and a tester inserted in the center comes out clean. Transfer to a wire rack to cool completely.

6. To make the topping, in a clean bowl with clean beaters, beat the egg whites and cream of tartar until stiff peaks form; set aside.

7. Heat the sugar, water, and salt in a saucepan over medium heat, stirring occasionally, until the mixture boils. Continue to cook for 2–3 more minutes, or until a candy thermometer reaches 238°F.

8. Pour the syrup very slowly over the egg whites and beat at high speed until stiff peaks form. Stir in the lemon juice.

9. Cut each loaf horizontally into three layers. Place one layer on a serving plate and top with one-fourth of the filling. Place a second layer on top and spread with another one-fourth of the filling. Top with the third layer and add a dollop of meringue. Repeat with the second loaf, filling, and meringue.

White Cake

Makes about 10 cups batter, enough for one 8-inch three-layer cake

This cake is not quite golden because it has no egg yolks, but, because it contains butter, it isn't completely white, either. This is the best recipe to use when ultrawhite cakes are desired for decorating (as in the Day of the Dead Cakes on page 317) or when adding bright food colorings (as in the Sweet Sixteen cake on page 167). It also contains a bit less fat due to the elimination of the egg yolks.

3½ cups bleached cake flour

1½ tablespoons baking powder

1 teaspoon salt

9 large egg whites

1⅓ cups (2⅔ sticks) unsalted butter, at room temperature

2¼ cups granulated sugar

2 teaspoons vanilla extract

1½ cups whole milk

3 cups Vanilla Custard (page 356), chilled

3 cups Seven-Minute Frosting (page 178)

1. Preheat the oven to 350°F. Butter and flour three 9-inch round pans.

2. Combine the flour, baking powder, and salt in a mixing bowl.

3. In a clean bowl with clean beaters, beat the egg whites until fluffy, set aside.

4. Beat the butter and sugar in a large bowl with an electric mixer on medium speed until fluffy. Beat in the vanilla, and milk.

5. Add the egg whites on low speed, then gradually add the flour mixture, beating for about 1 minute.

6. Divide the batter among the pans and bake for 30–35 minutes, or until a tester inserted in the center comes out clean. Cool in the pan for 10 minutes, then transfer to a rack to cool completely.

7. Place one cooled layer on a serving plate and top with one-half of the custard. Place a second layer on top and spread with the remaining custard. Top with the remaining layer and spread the frosting on the top and sides of the cake.

CHOCOLATE CAKES

Love chocolate? This section is for you! From the bittersweet chocolate of devil's food cake to the ultrasweet German chocolate cake, I love it all. Chocolate is the most popular flavor of cake in America, so it's obvious I'm not alone in my enthusiasm. These are cakes to eat slowly, so you can savor each tasty bite.

Devil's Food Cake

Makes about 14 cups batter, enough for one 9-inch three-layer cake

In my house, devil's food cake rarely lasts more than a few hours, so I feel completely comfortable frosting this cake—my favorite of all time—with chocolate cream cheese frosting and leaving it on the counter under a cake keeper. If you think this cake will last longer than one day at your house, though, you can either refrigerate it or top it with regular Chocolate Frosting (page 351) and leave it at room temperature. My secret ingredient? Apple juice, which gives the chocolate a hard-to-pinpoint fruity flavor boost.

1. To make the cake, preheat the oven to 375°F. Butter and flour three 9-inch round pans.

2. Melt the chocolate in a double boiler; set aside to cool.

3. Combine the flour, cocoa powder, and salt with the baking soda and baking powder in a mixing bowl.

4. Beat the butter and sugar in a large mixing bowl with an electric mixer on medium speed until fluffy. Add the eggs one at a time, beating well after each addition. Stir in the melted chocolate.

5. Gradually add the flour mixture, alternating with the buttermilk, on low speed until blended. Add the apple juice and vanilla.

6. Pour the batter into the pans and bake for 30–35 minutes, or until a knife inserted in the center comes out clean. Cool in the pans for 5 minutes, then transfer to a rack to cool completely.

Cake

5 ounces bittersweet chocolate

3½ cups all-purpose flour

¼ cup unsweetened cocoa powder

1 teaspoon baking soda

2 teaspoons baking powder

¼ teaspoon salt

¾ pound (3 sticks) unsalted butter, at room temperature

3 cups firmly packed light brown sugar

5 large eggs

¾ cup buttermilk

1½ cups unsweetened apple juice

1½ tablespoons vanilla extract

Chocolate Cream Cheese Frosting

Makes about 4 cups

2 boxes (8 ounces each) cream cheese, at room temperature

½ cup (1 stick) unsalted butter, at room temperature

1 tablespoon vanilla extract

⅔ cup unsweetened cocoa powder

⅛ teaspoon salt

4½ cups confectioners' sugar

¼ cup unsweetened apple juice

7. To make the frosting, beat the cream cheese, butter, and vanilla in a large mixing bowl with an electric mixer on medium speed until fluffy. Add the cocoa powder and salt on low speed until blended.

8. Gradually add the confectioners' sugar, alternating with the apple juice, on low speed until the frosting is thick and spreadable.

9. Place one cooled layer on a serving plate and top with one-fourth of the frosting. Place a second layer on top and spread with another one-fourth of the frosting. Top with the remaining layer and spread the remaining frosting on the sides and top of the cake, swirling with a large icing spatula.

Variation

Orange Devil's Food Cake: Replace the apple juice in the cake and frosting with orange juice. Add ½ teaspoon finely grated orange zest to each batter.

German Chocolate Loaves

Makes about 7½ cups batter, enough for eight 2½ x 4-inch cakes

German chocolate cake has what I call flavor harmony: the pecans, coconut, and chocolate all blend together to create a one-of-a-kind taste sensation. German sweet chocolate, or sweetened dark chocolate—the invention of a man named Samuel German—was specially developed to add an extra cocoa punch to baked goods; the pecans and coconut are flavors from the American South, where this cake originated. These messy but totally delicious loaves are the sloppy Joes of cakes.

1. To make the filling, combine the evaporated milk, sugar, butter, egg yolks, and vanilla in a large saucepan. Stir constantly over medium heat for 12 minutes, or until thickened and golden brown. Remove from the heat and stir in the coconut and

Coconut Pecan Filling

12 ounces evaporated milk

1½ cups granulated sugar

¾ cup (1½ sticks) unsalted butter, at room temperature

4 large egg yolks

1½ teaspoons vanilla extract

2⅔ cups sweetened flaked coconut

1½ cups chopped pecans

German Chocolate Frosting

Makes about 4½ cups

1 pint heavy cream

1 cup granulated sugar

6 ounces German sweet chocolate, coarsely chopped (about 1 cup)

½ cup (1 stick) unsalted butter, at room temperature

1 tablespoon vanilla extract

Pinch salt

Cake

2 cups all-purpose flour

1 teaspoon baking soda

¼ teaspoon salt

4 ounces German sweet chocolate, coarsely chopped (about ⅔ cup)

¾ cup (1½ sticks) unsalted butter, at room temperature

1½ cups granulated sugar

3 large eggs

1 teaspoon vanilla extract

1 cup buttermilk

½ cup pecan halves for garnish

pecans. Cool to room temperature for 30 minutes, or until thick.

2. To make the frosting, bring the cream and sugar to a simmer in a small saucepan, stirring constantly. Turn the heat to low and cook for 4–5 minutes, until the sugar is dissolved. Remove from the heat. Add the chocolate and butter and stir until melted. Stir in the vanilla and salt. Let cool for 30 minutes.

3. To make the cake, preheat the oven to 350°F. Butter and flour eight 2½ x 4-inch loaf pans.

4. Combine the flour, baking soda, and salt in a mixing bowl.

5. Melt the chocolate and butter in a double boiler. Transfer to a large mixing bowl and cool slightly. Stir in the sugar until blended. Add the eggs, one at a time,

beating with an electric mixer on medium speed after each addition. Beat in the vanilla.

6. Gradually add the flour mixture, alternating with the buttermilk, on low speed until blended.

7. Pour the batter into the pans and bake for 25–30 minutes, or until a tester inserted in the center comes out clean. Transfer to a rack to cool completely.

8. Cut the cooled loaves in half horizontally and spread ⅔ of the filling on the bottom halves. Spoon the frosting over the top halves, and add the remaining filling on top of the frosting. Place the top halves on the bottom halves, and top each loaf with a pecan half.

Chocolate Chip Sour Cream Cake

Makes about 8 cups batter, enough for one 8-inch cake

This is my favorite chocolate cake to linger over with a cup of coffee. The sour cream gives it a rich, tangy "smack," but if you prefer an equally rich yet milder flavor, try the mayonnaise variation. It is slightly retro and simply decadent.

1. Preheat the oven to 350°F. Butter and flour an 8-inch round fluted pan.

2. Place the butter and chocolate in a large mixing bowl. Pour the boiling water over and stir until melted. Stir in the vanilla and sugar and let cool. Add the sour cream and use an electric mixer on low speed to blend.

3. Combine the flour, baking soda, and baking powder in a mixing bowl.

4. Gradually add the flour mixture to the butter mixture on low speed until smooth. Add the chips and set aside.

5. In a clean bowl with clean beaters, beat the egg whites until stiff peaks form. Gently fold the egg whites into the batter with a rubber spatula.

---

5 tablespoons (⅔ stick) unsalted butter, at room temperature

3 ounces unsweetened chocolate, coarsely chopped (about ½ cup)

1 cup boiling water

1 teaspoon vanilla extract

1½ cups granulated sugar

½ cup sour cream

2 cups all-purpose flour

1 teaspoon baking soda

1 teaspoon baking powder

1½ cups chocolate chips

3 large egg whites

1 tablespoon unsweetened cocoa powder for dusting

6. Pour the batter into the pan and bake for 50–60 minutes, or until a tester inserted in the center comes out clean. Cool in the pan for 15 minutes, then transfer to a rack to cool completely. Dust with the cocoa powder before serving.

Variation

Chocolate Mayonnaise Cake: Replace the sour cream with mayonnaise. Omit the chocolate chips. Top with Chocolate Glaze (page 351) instead of cocoa powder.

Chocolate Sponge Roll

Makes about 4 cups batter, enough for one 11-inch rolled cake

Like many sponge cakes, this one is lower in fat than cakes made with a lot of butter. The form and design of the cake also help cut the calories—the tight roll requires a very thin layer of cream cheese filling. For a thick roll, prepare the cake in a 7 x 11-inch (very small) jelly-roll pan. The pattern baked into the top of the cake is a subtle decorative touch.

1. Preheat the oven to 350°F. Line a 7 x 11-inch jelly-roll pan with parchment paper, then lightly butter and flour the paper.

2. Combine the flour, cocoa powder, and salt in a mixing bowl.

3. Beat the egg yolks and 1⅓ cup of the sugar in a large mixing bowl with an electric mixer on medium speed until thick. The mixture should reach the ribbon stage. Beat in the vanilla and set aside.

4. In a clean bowl with clean beaters, beat the egg whites until stiff peaks form. Gently fold half the egg whites into the batter with a rubber spatula, then fold in the remaining egg whites.

5. Dust the flour mixture over the batter and fold in a little at a time until fully integrated.

Cake
1 cup cake flour
¼ cup Dutch-process cocoa powder
⅛ teaspoon salt
8 large eggs, separated
3 large egg yolks
1⅓ cups granulated sugar
1 teaspoon vanilla extract
2 ounces unsweetened dark (at least 60% cacao) chocolate, melted

Cream Cheese Filling
Makes about 2 cups
6 ounces reduced-fat cream cheese
1 teaspoon freshly squeezed lemon juice
½ teaspoon vanilla extract
2½ cups confectioners' sugar

Chocolate Sponge Roll, Golden Sponge Roll.

6. Remove ½ cup of the batter and add it to the melted chocolate. Set aside.

7. Spread the remaining batter in the pan. Then, dipping a skewer into the reserved darker batter, drizzle straight lines from short side to short side, about 2 inches apart, over the lighter cake in the pan. Spread out smaller lines in a V shape from the center.

8. Bake the cake for 20–25 minutes, then test with your finger to see if it springs back. If so, test with a skewer to see if it is done. Remove from the pan and transfer to a rack to cool completely. Peel off the parchment.

9. To make the filling, combine the cream cheese, lemon juice, and vanilla in a medium mixing bowl with an electric mixer on medium speed. Gradually add the confectioners' sugar on low speed until the filling reaches spreading consistency.

10. Place the cooled cake decorated side facedown on a plate and spread with a thin layer of filling, stopping about ¼ inch from the edge. Starting from the long side and working away from you, roll the cake tightly. Place on a serving plate, seam side down.

Variation

Golden Sponge Roll: Increase the flour to 1⅓ cup and the vanilla to 1 teaspoon. Omit the cocoa powder. Replace the dark chocolate with ½ ounce milk chocolate.

White Chocolate Cake

6 ounces white chocolate, chopped

3½ cups all-purpose flour

½ teaspoon baking soda

½ teaspoon baking powder

½ teaspoon salt

½ pound (2 sticks) unsalted butter, at room temperature

2 cups granulated sugar

½ cup firmly packed light brown sugar

2 tablespoons vanilla extract

6 large eggs

1 cup buttermilk

White Chocolate Sour Cream Frosting

Makes about 3½ cups

12 ounces white chocolate

2 tablespoons unsalted butter

2 teaspoons vanilla extract

1 container (16 ounces) sour cream

White Chocolate Cake with White Chocolate Sour Cream Frosting

Makes about 10 cups batter, enough for one 9-inch two-layer cake

I can't really write a chapter on chocolate cakes without including my all-time favorite white chocolate cake recipe. Some people say that white chocolate isn't really chocolate, but if it says chocolate on the label, that is good enough for me.

1. To make the cake, preheat the oven to 350°F. Butter and flour two 9-inch round pans.

2. Melt the chocolate in a double boiler, stirring constantly. Set aside to cool.

3. Combine the flour, baking soda, baking powder, and salt in a mixing bowl.

4. Beat the butter, both sugars, and vanilla in a large mixing bowl with an electric mixer on medium speed until creamy. Add the eggs one at a time, beating well after each addition. Blend in the chocolate.

5. Gradually add the flour mixture, alternating with the buttermilk, on low speed until blended.

6. Divide the batter between the pans and bake for 30–35 minutes, or until a knife inserted in the center comes out clean. Cool in the pans for 10 minutes, then transfer to a rack to cool completely.

7. To make the frosting, melt the chocolate and butter in a double boiler. Remove from heat and let cool for 5 minutes. Stir in the vanilla and sour cream, then let cool completely.

8. Place one cooled layer on a serving plate and top with one-third of the frosting. Top with the remaining layer and spread the remaining frosting on the sides and top of the cake.

Variation

Milk Chocolate Pudding Cake: Replace the white chocolate with milk chocolate. Use Chocolate Pastry Cream (page 358) between the layers and frost the top and sides with Milk Chocolate Frosting (page 351).

FRUIT CAKES

One of life's pleasures is the sweet freshness of fruit in season—and another is slicing up your favorite fruits and baking their flavors into cakes. Unlike holiday fruitcakes made with dried and candied fruits, the cakes you will find here are all made with fresh fruit. I love the fact that fruit is so versatile, and many of these recipes can be customized by substituting a similar fruit for the one I call for. You can even keep your taste buds tantalized throughout the year by using homemade fruit preserves in your cake creations. Here you will also find twists on classic flavor combinations, such as pears and sour cream, fruit shortcakes, and an upside-down cake made with stone fruit. Whether you grow the fruit yourself or visit local farmers markets, be sure to use the freshest fruit you can buy.

Pear Sour Cream Cake

Makes one 12-inch cake

Each cake has its unique temptation, and this one is all about the cinnamon-spiked pear-and-sour-cream topping. The sturdy yeast cake (based on a classic French savarin, a traditional yeast cake soaked in Kirsch or rum), can also be made without the topping and eaten with your favorite jam or Lemon Icing (page 358).

1. To make the cake, butter and flour a 12-inch round tart pan.

2. Combine the yeast, sugar, and water in a small bowl. Let stand for 10 minutes, or until foamy.

3. Combine the flour and salt in a mixing bowl.

4. Beat the eggs, butter, and pear nectar in a large mixing bowl

Cake

1 packet (¼ ounce) active dry yeast

¼ cup granulated sugar

¼ cup warm water

1⅔ cups all-purpose flour

1 teaspoon salt

3 large eggs

½ cup (1 stick) unsalted butter, at room temperature

¼ cup pear nectar

with an electric mixer on medium speed until creamy. Stir in the flour mixture and the yeast mixture on low speed.

5. Dust a work surface with flour. Turn out the dough and knead until smooth, about 10 minutes. Cover loosely with plastic and let sit for 1 hour, or until doubled in size. Punch down the dough and transfer to the pan. Cover again and let rise for 45 minutes, or until doubled in size.

6. To make the topping, melt the butter in a medium skillet. Add the pears and brown lightly. Stir in the pear nectar, cornstarch, and ½ teaspoon cinnamon and mix until thickened slightly. Combine the remaining cinnamon with the sugar and set aside.

7. Preheat the oven to 375°F. Bake the cake for 20 minutes, or until lightly browned. Top with the pear topping, sour cream, and cinnamon sugar, then continue to bake for an additional 15–20 minutes, or until a tester inserted in the center comes out clean. Let cool in the pan for 20 minutes, then remove to cool completely.

Strawberry-Rhubarb Jam Cake

Makes one 7 x 11-inch cake

When I was ten years old and in the Junior Garden Club, there was a blue ribbon given monthly for the best home-grown flowers, fruits, and vegetables. The only flower prize I ever won was for daisies (maybe that's why the daisy is my favorite flower even today), but I won a ribbon every year for my strawberries and rhubarb, which is still my favorite jam combination—and it tastes much better in cake than on toast!

1. To make the rhubarb, preheat the oven to 350°F. Put the rhubarb in a 9 x 13-inch baking pan and mix in the ginger, nutmeg, and sugar. Spread in a single layer over the pan. Pour in the pineapple juice and spread the rhubarb evenly in the pan. Cover with foil and bake for 20–25 minutes. Remove the foil, stir the rhubarb, and continue to bake for

Jam Cake

2⅓ cups all-purpose flour

1 teaspoon baking powder

½ teaspoon baking soda

½ teaspoon salt

½ cup (1 stick) unsalted butter, at
    room temperature

1½ cups granulated sugar

3 large eggs

1¼ cups whole milk

1 teaspoon vanilla extract

1½ cups strawberry-rhubarb jam

Garnish

1½ cups Half-Whipped Cream
    (page 359)

an additional 10–15 minutes, or until the rhubarb is tender. Set aside to cool, leaving the oven on.

2. While the rhubarb bakes, make the cake. Butter and flour a 7 x 11-inch baking pan.

3. Combine the flour, baking powder, baking soda, and salt in a mixing bowl.

4. Beat the butter and sugar in a large mixing bowl with an electric mixer on medium speed until light and fluffy. Add the eggs one at a time, beating well after each addition.

5. Gradually add the flour mixture, alternating with the milk, on low speed until blended. Add the vanilla.

6. Spread the batter into the pan. Stir in ¾ cup of the jam and half the rhubarb, and swirl with a knife to marbleize the batter. Bake for 35–40 minutes, or until a tester inserted in the center comes out clean. Cool in the pan.

7. Place the cooled cake on a serving plate. Top with the remaining jam and rhubarb, then serve with whipped cream.

Plantain Cake

Makes about 9 cups batter, or enough for one 8 x 12-inch cake

5 large very ripe plantains, peeled and sliced lengthwise

2¼ cups all-purpose flour

1 tablespoon baking powder

½ teaspoon salt

½ cup (1 stick) unsalted butter, at room temperature

¾ cup firmly packed light brown sugar

½ cup granulated sugar

2 large eggs

2 tablespoons golden rum

Juice of 2 limes

1 teaspoon vanilla extract

¾ cup Rum Syrup (page 355)

Brown sugar for sprinkling

I picked up the idea for this recipe in Miami at a tiny Caribbean take-out place. All the regulars were ordering plantain cake, so I had to try it. It was delicious! My taste buds analyzed the flavors, and this is the cake I re-created from my memory. I could not resist roasting the plantains, which intensifies their sweetness, and I dressed up the finished product with rum sauce.

Plantains look like large bananas. They are very sweet and are best used when they are ultraripe, or when they turn black in color. If you can't find black plantains at your supermarket, try a Latin American grocery, or buy the yellow ones and ripen them for a few days in a dark place.

1. Preheat the oven to 350°F. Line a rimmed baking sheet with foil. Butter and flour an 8 x 12-inch pan.

2. Prick the plantains on all sides with a fork and roast for 35–40 minutes, or until soft. Cool on a rack. Purée three of the roasted plantains in a blender; you should have 1½ cups.

3. Combine the flour, baking powder, and salt in a mixing bowl.

4. Beat the butter and both sugars in a large mixing bowl with an electric mixer on medium speed until light and fluffy. Add the puréed plantains and mix until well blended. Add the eggs one at a time, beating well after each addition.

5. Gradually add the flour mixture on low speed until incorporated. Beat in the rum, lime juice, and vanilla on medium speed for 1–2 minutes.

6. Transfer the batter to the 8 x 12-inch pan and bake for 25–30 minutes, or until a knife inserted in the center comes out clean. Let cool in the pan and then slice into squares to serve.

7. Slice the remaining plantains and arrange on dessert plates next to slices of cake. Drizzle with rum syrup and sprinkle with brown sugar.

Tropical Fruit Salad

2 tablespoons firmly packed light
   brown sugar
¼ teaspoon salt
2 tablespoons freshly squeezed lime
   juice
1 cup peeled cubed mango
1 cup peeled cubed papaya
¼ cup peeled cubed limes
¼ cup apricot nectar

Cakes

1 cup all-purpose flour
1 teaspoon baking powder
¼ teaspoon baking soda
¼ teaspoon salt
¼ teaspoon ground cinnamon
4 tablespoons (½ stick) unsalted
   butter, at room temperature
½ cup firmly packed light brown
   sugar
¼ cup canola oil
1 tablespoon clover honey
1 teaspoon of vanilla
1 tablespoon grated lime zest
½ teaspoon lemongrass powder
¼ teaspoon ground cardamom
1 tablespoon fresh lime juice
3 large eggs
½ cup peeled cubed mango
½ cup peeled cubed papaya
¼ cup chopped macadamia nuts

Variation

Plantain Walnut Cake with Coconut Frosting: Add 1 cup chopped walnuts after you add the rum. Top with Coconut Frosting (page 352) and chopped walnuts.

Tropical Fruit Cakes

Makes about 5¼ cups batter, enough for eight 3½-inch shortcakes

The appeal of these cakes, which draw on the kaleidoscope of tropical flavors from the Caribbean and Southeast Asia, is their simple yet fruity-fresh taste—perfect for a light sun-drenched snack. Baked in a shortcake pan—similar to a large muffin tin, except with a well in the center—they are filled with tropical fruit salad.

1. To make the fruit salad, toss the brown sugar, salt, lime juice, mango, papaya, limes, and apricot nectar in a large mixing bowl. Cover and refrigerate for 3 hours.

2. Preheat the oven to 350°F. Butter and flour eight 2 x 3½-inch shortcake pans.

3. Combine the flour, baking powder, baking soda, and salt with the cinnamon in a mixing bowl.

4. Beat the butter and brown sugar in a large mixing bowl with an electric mixer on medium speed until creamy, then beat in the oil, honey, vanilla, lemongrass powder, cardamom, and lime zest and juice.

5. Add the eggs one at a time, beating well after each addition. Add the flour mixture on low speed and blend until smooth. Fold in the mango, papaya, and macadamia nuts.

6. Pour the batter into the pans and bake for 25–30

Topping

2⅓ tablespoons Cinnamon Sugar
(page 352)

minutes, or until a knife inserted in the center comes out clean. Transfer to a rack to cool completely.

7. Spoon the fruit salad into the well in the shortcakes. Sprinkle cinnamon sugar over each.

Cake

1¼ cups all-purpose flour

½ cup unsweetened cocoa powder

1½ teaspoons baking powder

¼ teaspoon salt

1 teaspoon ground cinnamon

½ teaspoon ground ginger

½ cup (1 stick) unsalted butter, at room temperature

½ cup firmly packed light brown sugar

2 large eggs

1 teaspoon vanilla extract

1 teaspoon grated lime zest

2 teaspoons freshly squeezed lime juice

½ cup plain yogurt

2 cups fresh blueberries

Berry Icing

Makes about 2½ cups

4 cups confectioners' sugar

½ cup (1 stick) unsalted butter, at room temperature

4 teaspoons freshly squeezed lemon juice

1 tablespoon grated lemon zest

½ cup fresh blueberries

Chocolate-Blueberry-Lime Yogurt Cake

Makes one 8-inch Bundt cake

Chocolate rounds out the sweetness of the berries in this fruity cake. Try it with different types of berries, such as raspberries, blackberries, or gooseberries.

1. To make the cake, preheat the oven to 350°F. Butter and flour an 8-inch Bundt pan.

2. Combine the flour, cocoa powder, baking powder, salt, cinnamon, and ginger in a mixing bowl.

3. Beat the butter and sugar in a large mixing bowl with an electric mixer on medium speed until fluffy. Beat in eggs, vanilla, lime zest, and lime juice. Add the flour mixture, alternating with the yogurt, and blend. Using a wooden spoon, stir in the blueberries.

4. Pour the batter into the pan and bake for 40–45 minutes, or until tester inserted into the center comes out clean. Let cool in the pan for 20 minutes, then transfer to a rack to cool completely.

5. To make the icing, combine the sugar, butter, and lemon juice until blended. Stir in the lemon zest and ¼ cup crushed blueberries.

6. Place the cake on a serving plate. Spread with the icing and top with the remaining blueberries.

Peach Upside-Down Cake

Makes one 8-inch round cake

If you think "pineapple" when you hear upside-down cake, it's time to expand your horizons! Summer's classic stone fruit is ideal in this cake—or try it with plums, cherries, or apricots. If you don't have a cast-iron skillet, be sure the skillet you use is oven-proof.

Topping

½ cup (1 stick) unsalted butter

¾ cup firmly packed light brown sugar

8 fresh peaches, pitted and halved

Cake

1¾ cups all-purpose flour

1½ teaspoons baking powder

½ teaspoon baking soda

½ teaspoon salt

½ cup (1 stick) unsalted butter, at room temperature

¾ cup granulated sugar

2 large eggs

1½ teaspoons vanilla extract

¾ cup buttermilk

1 cup peeled chopped fresh peaches (about 2 medium)

1. Preheat the oven to 375°F.

2. To make the topping, melt the butter in an 8-inch cast-iron skillet. Add the sugar and cook, stirring, for 3 minutes, or until the sugar is dissolved and begins to caramelize. Remove the skillet from the heat and arrange the peaches, cut side down, in a circular pattern. Set aside.

3. To make the cake, combine the flour, baking powder, baking soda, and salt in a mixing bowl.

4. Beat the butter and sugar in a large mixing bowl with an electric mixer on medium speed until fluffy. Beat in the

Front: Peach Upside-Down Cake; back: Plum Upside-Down Cake.

eggs, one at a time, for 2–3 minutes, and then add the vanilla.

5. Gradually add the flour mixture, alternating with the buttermilk, on low speed until blended. Fold in the chopped peaches.

6. Spoon the batter over the peaches in the skillet. Bake for 40–50 minutes, or until a knife inserted in the center comes out clean. Cool in the pan for 20 minutes.

7. Run a knife around the inside edge of the skillet to loosen the cake. Set a serving plate over the skillet and, holding both together, carefully turn the plate and skillet upside down. Replace any fruit that sticks to the skillet.

Variations

Plum Upside-Down Cake: Replace the peaches in the topping with 10 unpeeled fresh plums and the peaches in the cake with 3 peeled fresh plums.

Cherry Upside-Down Cake: Replace the peaches in the topping with 1½ cups halved pitted fresh cherries, spreading them out to make a single layer. In the batter, replace the chopped peaches with 1 cup diced cherries.

Apricot Upside-Down Cake: Replace the peaches in the topping with 10 unpeeled fresh apricots and the peaches in the cake with 3 peeled fresh apricots.

Date Poke Cake

Makes about 8 cups batter, enough for one 8 x 8-inch cake

A poke cake is exactly that—a cake with large holes poked all the way to the base. When you pour on the topping, it seeps into the holes, adding moisture and flavor to the cake. This cake is topped with toasted coconut for even more flavor.

1. To make the cake, preheat the oven to 350°F. Butter and flour an 8 x 8-inch square pan.

Cake

1½ cups warm unsweetened apple
  juice
1 cup dried dates, pitted and
  chopped
1 teaspoon baking soda
1 teaspoon baking powder
½ teaspoon salt
6 tablespoons (¾ stick) unsalted
  butter, at room temperature
1¼ cups granulated sugar
1¾ cups all-purpose flour
2 large eggs
1 teaspoon vanilla extract
1 cup shelled walnuts, chopped

Coconut Topping
Makes about 2 cups
1 cup sweetened flaked coconut
⅔ cup firmly packed light brown
  sugar
6 tablespoons (¾ stick) unsalted
  butter
¼ cup heavy cream

2. Combine the apple juice and dates in a small bowl and let stand for 20 minutes.

3. Mix the flour, baking soda, baking powder, and salt in a mixing bowl.

4. Cream the butter and sugar in a large mixing bowl with an electric mixer on medium speed until fluffy. Beat in the eggs and vanilla.

5. Gradually add the flour mixture on low speed until blended. Using a wooden spoon, stir in the dates and apple juice.

6. Transfer the batter to the pan and bake for 30–35 minutes, or until a knife inserted in the center comes out clean. Turn off the oven but leave the cake inside.

7. To make the topping, mix the coconut, sugar, butter, and cream in a small saucepan. Cook over medium heat for 3–5 minutes, or until the butter melts.

8. Using a chopstick, poke 16 holes in the cake, 1½ inches apart. Make the holes deep enough so that the chopstick almost touches the bottom of the pan. Pour the topping over the cake.

9. Heat the oven to 450°F. Brown the cake for 3–5 minutes, or until the topping is toasted. Cool in the pan.

VEGETABLE CAKES

Okay, I recognize that cakes made with vegetables don't sound like the sweetest of the crop, and it's true that some of these cakes are savory—but you will be surprised at just how sweet and candy-like tomatoes and corn can be when baked in a cake. No one ever questions using carrots in cakes (see page 176), so I invite you to use other root vegetables and flours—including potatoes, beets, and yucca—the same way. The results are dense, rich, healthful, and delicious. Best of all, in addition to being delicious desserts, these cakes all work really well when served alongside the main course—meaning that you don't have to wait for dessert in order to have cake.

Blue Corn Cake
Makes about 8 cups batter, enough for one 10-inch cake

After a hard day backpacking up and down the Grand Canyon during a family vacation in the Southwest, the first thing I craved was a slice of the hearty blue corn cake that I had first tasted earlier on my trip. I could see why the Navajo people found this violet-colored cornmeal cake nourishing not only for the body but also for the soul. It is both sweet and savory, rich and dense. So before I left Arizona I bought a ten-pound bag of finely ground blue cornmeal, and when I returned home I set to work to re-create the cake that is so popular throughout the region. I began by experimenting with my Italian grandmother's polenta cake recipe, and ended up with this substantial cake, which makes a hearty side dish for a light meal.

1. To make the cake, preheat the oven to 325°F. Butter and flour a 10-inch round fluted tart pan.

2. Combine both cornmeals, the flour, baking powder, and salt in a large mixing bowl. Mix well and set aside.

3. Combine the butter, milk, honey, eggs, and zest in a medium mixing bowl and beat with an electric mixer on medium speed. Stir into the flour mixture, mixing until blended. Fold in ½ cup corn kernals.

Cake
1 cup blue cornmeal

1 cup yellow cornmeal

1 cup all-purpose flour

½ cup cooked fresh corn kernels (I used yellow and Triple Play sweet corn)

2 teaspoons baking powder

1 teaspoon salt

½ cup (1 stick) unsalted butter, melted and cooled slightly

1¼ cups warm whole milk

¾ cup clover honey

3 large eggs

1 teaspoon grated orange zest

Honey Orange Syrup
Makes about ⅔ cup

2 tablespoons clover honey

¼ cup sweetened condensed milk

1 tablespoon grated orange zest

¼ cup orange juice

Garnish
½ cup cooked fresh corn kernels

2 teaspoons grated orange zest

Top: Tomato Basil Cake; middle: Jalapeño Cake; bottom: Beet-Potato Pound Cake.

4. Pour the batter into the pan and bake for 25–30 minutes, or until a knife inserted in the center comes out clean. Cool in the pan for 30 minutes, then transfer to a rack to cool completely.

5. To make the syrup, whisk the honey, condensed milk, orange zest, and orange juice in a small saucepan over medium heat. When the mixture begins to boil, remove it from the heat and let cool. Pour the syrup over the cake, or serve it alongside as a sauce. Garnish with corn kernels and orange zest.

Variation

Polenta Cake: Increase the flour to 1½ cups and replace both cornmeals with 1 cup polenta. Add 1 teaspoon fennel seeds, ¼ cup golden raisins, and 1 cup chopped almonds to the cornmeal mixture.

Jalapeño Cake with Molasses Sauce

Makes about 4 cups batter, enough for two 3 x 5½-inch loaves

This cornbread-like pound cake gets its bite from jalapeños; remove the seeds to reduce the heat, if you like. It is great on its own or with the traditional southern molasses sauce. Make the sauce quickly while the cake is cooling slightly; the cake and sauce taste best warm.

1. Preheat the oven to 375°F. Butter and flour two 3 x 5½-inch loaf pans.

2. Combine the cornmeal, flour, salt, sugar, baking powder, and baking soda in a mixing bowl and set aside.

3. Combine the sour cream, milk, eggs, and butter in a large mixing bowl and beat with an electric mixer on medium speed. Finely chop half the jalapeños and add them to the sour cream mixture. Add the cornmeal mixture on low speed and mix thoroughly.

4. Transfer the batter to the pans and top with remaining jalapeños. Bake for 35–45 minutes, or until golden. Cool in the pans for 15 minutes, then remove and slice.

Cake

1 cup cornmeal

⅔ cup all-purpose flour

1 teaspoon salt

¼ cup granulated sugar

1½ teaspoons baking powder

¼ teaspoon baking soda

1 container (8 ounces) sour cream

¼ cup whole milk

2 large eggs

1½ tablespoons unsalted butter, melted and cooled

3 tablespoons sliced jalapeño peppers

Molasses Sauce

Makes about 2 cups

¾ cup unsulfured molasses

1½ tablespoons unsalted butter

2 tablespoons freshly squeezed lemon juice

1 tablespoon cider vinegar

5. To make the molasses sauce, combine the molasses and butter in a small saucepan over medium heat. Bring to a boil and stir for 3–5 minutes. Remove from the heat and stir in the lemon juice and vinegar. Pour the sauce over the warm cake slices to serve.

Tomato Basil Cake

Makes about 6½ cups batter, enough for three 3 x 5½-inch loaves

2¼ cups all-purpose flour
¾ teaspoon baking powder
⅛ teaspoon salt
1 cup granulated sugar
Grated zest of 2 limes
3 tablespoons freshly squeezed lime juice
4 large eggs
¾ cup heavy cream
6 tablespoons (¾ stick) unsalted butter, melted and cooled
1½ cups cherry tomatoes, cut in half, or 2 medium beefsteak tomatoes, chopped
2 tablespoons chopped fresh basil
¼ cup grated Parmesan cheese

The abundance of tomatoes from my garden inspired me to develop this savory pound cake. The taste of store-bought tomatoes cannot compare with the taste of their fresh-from-the-garden counterparts—if you don't have the time or inclination to grow your own, visit a farmers market to buy local varieties.

1. Preheat the oven to 350°F. Butter and flour three 3 x 5½-inch loaf pans.

2. Combine the flour, baking powder, and salt in a mixing bowl.

3. Mix the sugar, lime zest, and lime juice in a large mixing bowl. Add the eggs one at a time, beating well after each addition, until foamy. Beat in the cream.

4. Gradually add the flour mixture, stirring with a wooden spoon until a thick batter forms. Fold in the butter.

5. Stir in the tomatoes, basil, and Parmesan cheese.

6. Pour the batter into the pans and bake for 45–55 minutes, or until a knife inserted in the center comes out clean. Cool in the pans for 10 minutes, then transfer to a rack to cool completely.

Variation

Tomato Chocolate Cake: Omit the basil and Parmesan and add ½ cup chopped bittersweet chocolate with the tomatoes.

Beet-Potato Pound Cake

Makes about 6 cups batter, enough for three 3 x 5½-inch loaves

1 cup potato flour

1 cup all-purpose flour

¼ teaspoon baking soda

¼ teaspoon salt

½ cup (1 stick) unsalted butter, at room temperature

1 cup granulated sugar

4 large eggs, separated

1 teaspoon vanilla extract

¾ cup buttermilk

1½ cups peeled and finely shredded fresh raw beets (about 3–4 medium)

1 cup clover honey

¼ cup confectioners' sugar

This honey-soaked pound cake is made with fresh beets and potato flour. It is a hearty everyday cake that transforms into something special when it's topped with Cream Cheese Frosting (page 352) or served with ice cream.

1. Preheat the oven to 350°F. Butter three 3 x 5½-inch loaf pans.

2. Combine both flours, the baking soda, and salt in a mixing bowl.

3. Cream the butter and sugar in a large mixing bowl with an electric mixer on medium speed until light and fluffy. Add the egg yolks and beat well. Beat in the vanilla and buttermilk.

4. Gradually add the flour mixture on low speed until blended. Stir in the beets; set aside.

5. In a clean bowl with clean beaters, beat the egg whites until soft peaks form. Gently fold the egg whites into the batter with a rubber spatula.

6. Transfer the batter to the pans and bake for 35–45 minutes, or until a knife inserted in the center comes out clean. Cool in the pan for 20 minutes, then remove from the pan.

7. Heat the honey in the microwave for 30 seconds to thin. Pour onto a serving plate and set the loaves on top of the honey. Dust the loaves with confectioners' sugar while warm.

Variations

Pineapple Potato Cake: Replace the beets with shredded potatoes. Add ¾ cup drained canned pineapple chunks to the cake. Slice the cake while slightly warm and pour Rum Honey Sauce (page 356) over the slices.

Spiced Beet Cake: Add ½ teaspoon each of ground cardamom, ginger, cinnamon, and nutmeg to the flour mixture.

Caraway Beet Potato Cake: Add 2 tablespoons caraway seeds to the flour mixture.

Chayote Cake

Makes about 10 cups batter, enough for one 8-inch two-layer cake

1 small chayote, peeled, seeded, and grated
2 cups all-purpose flour
2 teaspoons baking soda
1 teaspoon baking powder
1 teaspoon salt
1 teaspoon ground ginger
1 teaspoon ground cinnamon
1 teaspoon ground nutmeg
1¼ cups vegetable oil
1½ cups granulated sugar
3 large eggs
1 teaspoon vanilla extract
3½ cups Lemon Cream Cheese Frosting (page 352)

Chayote is a popular squash in many parts of the world. It can be baked whole, like an acorn squash, but I like to shred it first and then bake it in a cake. If you like zucchini cake or zucchini bread, you will like this cake, which is filled with an exotic-tasting medley of spices.

1. Preheat the oven to 350°F. Butter and flour two 8 x 8-inch square pans.

2. Combine the flour, baking soda, baking powder, salt, ginger, cinnamon, and nutmeg in a mixing bowl.

3. Combine the oil and sugar in a large bowl with an electric mixer on medium speed until creamy. Add the eggs one at a time, beating well after each addition. Beat in the vanilla.

4. Fold in the chayote.

5. Pour the batter into the pans and bake for 35–40 minutes, or until a knife inserted in the center comes out clean. Cool in the pans.

6. Place one cooled layer on a serving plate and top with one-fourth of the frosting. Top with the second layer and spread the remaining frosting on the sides and top of the cake.

Variations

Chayote Carrot Cake: Reduce the chayote to 1½ cups and add 1½ cups grated carrots. Add ¼ teaspoon ground allspice with the other spices.

Chayote Zucchini Rosemary Cake: Reduce the chayote to 1½ cups and add 1½ cups grated zucchini. Add 2 teaspoons chopped fresh rosemary to the dry ingredients.

Cassava Cake

Makes one 8-inch round cake

3 large eggs

2 large egg whites

1 pound grated cassava (about 3½ cups)

7 ounces sweetened condensed milk

7 ounces evaporated milk

14 ounces coconut milk

¼ cup granulated sugar

1 cup unsweetened flaked coconut

¼ cup toasted coconut curls for garnish (page 33)

Cassava, yucca, taro, and manioc are all names for the same root vegetable, which can be found in some supermarkets and most Asian and Latin American groceries. Choose small cassava, which are easier to peel and less woody than their larger counterparts. This sweet pudding cake is based on a traditional Filipino recipe.

1. Preheat the oven to 325°F. Butter and flour an 8-inch springform pan. Prepare a water bath large enough to fit the pan (see page 39) and set it in the oven on the middle rack.

2. Beat the eggs and egg whites in a medium mixing bowl with an electric mixer on medium speed for 2–3 minutes, or until thick.

3. Combine the cassava, all three milks, the sugar, and coconut in a large mixing bowl with the mixer on medium speed and mix well. Add the eggs and beat for 1 minute, or until the mixture is thick and creamy.

4. Pour the batter into the pan and set it into the water bath. Bake for 35–40 minutes, or until firm and the top is set and a knife inserted in the center comes out clean. Remove from the water bath and transfer to a rack to cool completely. Top with coconut curls.

SPICE, NUT, SEED, HERB, AND FLOWER CAKES

Nothing is more exciting to me than reinventing recipes we all know and love, giving them a healthful, modern spin. This section bridges the gap between wholesome cakes made with granola, sunflower seeds, and whole grains, which are almost a meal in themselves, and lighter cakes that get a boost from the sweetest of spices or even flowers. Here's a bonus: these cakes pack a lot of protein power—whenever you combine grains with nuts, or nuts with seeds, you create a complete protein.

Cinnamon Walnut Coffee Cake
Makes 9½ cups batter, enough for one 9-inch tube cake

Bake this simple, everyday cake in the morning to fill your home with the smell of cinnamon sugar.

1. Preheat the oven to 350°F. Butter and flour a 9-inch tube pan.

2. Combine the flour, baking powder, baking soda, and salt in a mixing bowl.

3. Beat the eggs and sugar in a large mixing bowl with an electric mixer on medium speed until pale in color. Beat in the vanilla and oil.

4. Gradually add the flour mixture on low speed, alternating with the yogurt, and mix until blended. Pour the batter into the pan to about one-third full.

5. To make the walnuts, combine the sugar, cinnamon, and walnuts in a mixing bowl. Sprinkle three-fourths of the walnuts over the batter in the pan and pour in the remaining batter. Sprinkle with the remaining walnut mixture. Bake for 50–60 minutes, or until a tester inserted in the center comes out clean. Cool in the pan for 20 minutes, then transfer to a rack to cool for 1 hour.

6. Set the cooled cake on a serving plate and top with the icing.

Cake
2¾ cups all-purpose flour
1 teaspoon baking powder
½ teaspoon baking soda
½ teaspoon salt
3 large eggs
2 cups granulated sugar
2 teaspoons vanilla extract
1 cup vegetable oil
1 cup plain yogurt

Cinnamon Walnuts
⅔ cup granulated sugar
1 teaspoon ground cinnamon
1¼ cups shelled walnuts, chopped

Topping
1½ cups Vanilla Icing (page 358)

Variations

Apple Raisin Coffee Cake: Replace the walnuts with 1¼ cups peeled shredded Red Delicious apples and 1 cup raisins.

Date Nut Spice Cake: Add 1 teaspoon ground cinnamon, ½ teaspoon ground ginger, and ¼ teaspoon ground nutmeg to the flour mixture. Add 1¼ cups chopped dried dates to the filling.

Blueberry Coffee Cake: Replace the yogurt with sour cream and the walnuts with 1½ cups fresh blueberries.

Almond Spice Cake

Makes about 8 cups batter, enough for one 8-inch cake

This spice cake makes a great snack when eaten plain, or when topped with cheese or butter and eaten with a side of fresh pears, as in the variation following.

3 cups sifted all-purpose flour
1½ teaspoons baking soda
1 teaspoon ground ginger
1 teaspoon ground cinnamon
¼ teaspoon ground white pepper
¼ teaspoon ground allspice
⅛ teaspoon salt
6 tablespoons (¾ stick) unsalted butter, at room temperature
¼ cup firmly packed dark brown sugar
2 large eggs
⅔ cup unsulfured molasses
⅓ cup orange juice
1 teaspoon vanilla extract
1 cup buttermilk
1 cup chopped almonds
2 cups sliced almonds

1. Preheat the oven to 350°F. Butter and flour an 8 x 8-inch square pan.

2. Combine the flour, baking soda, ginger, cinnamon, pepper, allspice, and salt in a mixing bowl.

3. Beat the butter and sugar in a large mixing bowl with an electric mixer on medium speed until fluffy. Beat in the eggs, molasses, orange juice, and vanilla.

4. Gradually add the flour mixture, alternating with the buttermilk, on low speed until blended. Stir in the chopped almonds.

5. Pour the batter into the pan and bake for 20 minutes. Scatter the sliced almonds on top and bake for an additional 10–15 minutes, covering loosely with foil if the almonds get too brown, and until a knife inserted in the center comes out clean. Cool in the pan for 10 minutes, then transfer to a rack to cool completely.

Variations

Spice Cake with Cheese and Pears: Omit the sliced almonds. After baking for 25 minutes, top the cake with 8 thin slices of Cheddar cheese. Bake for 2–3 minutes, until melted and golden. Serve warm, with sliced pears on the side.

Spice Cake with Butter and Pears: Combine 2 tablespoons melted butter and ¼ cup confectioners' sugar in a small bowl and brush on the cooled cake. To serve, top with an additional 1½ tablespoons melted butter, dust with confectioners' sugar, and arrange sliced pears on top or on the side.

Cream Cheese Spice Cake: Top the cooled cake with Cream Cheese Frosting (page 352) and sprinkle with almonds.

Sunflower Seed Cake

Makes about 5¾ cups batter, enough for one 7-inch cake

Sunflower seeds lend a delicious dimension to this coffee cake. It's an all-around good cake for snacking, alfresco breakfasts, and other informal occasions.

1¾ cups all-purpose flour
¼ teaspoon baking soda
¼ teaspoon salt
¼ teaspoon ground nutmeg
½ teaspoon ground cinnamon
¾ cup (1½ sticks) unsalted butter, at room temperature
½ cup granulated sugar
3 large eggs
¼ cup clover honey
1 teaspoon vanilla extract
1 teaspoon freshly squeezed lemon juice
½ cup sour cream
1 cup plus 3 tablespoons unsalted sunflower seeds

1. Preheat the oven to 350°F. Butter a 7-inch round decorative pan.

2. Combine the flour, baking soda, salt, nutmeg, and cinnamon in a mixing bowl.

3. Cream the butter and sugar in a large mixing bowl with an electric mixer on medium speed until light and fluffy. Add the eggs one at a time, beating well after each addition. Beat in the honey, vanilla, and lemon.

4. Gradually add the flour mixture, alternating with the sour cream, on low speed until blended. Stir in 1 cup of the sunflower seeds.

5. Pour the batter into the pan and bake for 45–50 minutes, or until a knife inserted in the center comes out clean. Cool in the pan.

6. Invert the cake onto a serving plate and sprinkle with the remaining 3 tablespoons sunflower seeds.

Variation

Sunflower Seed Cake with Crumb Topping: Make a crumb topping by mixing ¼ cup all-purpose flour, ¾ cup firmly packed light brown sugar, ¼ teaspoon salt, and ½ cup unsalted sunflower seeds in a medium bowl. Work in 4 tablespoons (½ stick) cold unsalted butter, cut into small pieces, with your hands until mixture is crumbly. Sprinkle over the cake batter and bake for 40–45 minutes, or until a tester inserted in the center comes out clean. Omit the 3 tablespoons sunflower seeds scattered over the cake before serving.

Opposite top left: Carob Nut Cupcakes; right: Granola Cakes; bottom left: Sunflower Seed Cake.

2¾ cups all-purpose flour
1½ cups granulated sugar
¾ cup carob powder
1½ teaspoons baking powder
¾ teaspoon baking soda
1 teaspoon salt
½ teaspoon ground cloves
1 teaspoon ground cinnamon
½ teaspoon ground nutmeg
½ pound (2 sticks) unsalted butter, at room temperature
¾ cup firmly packed light brown sugar
5 large eggs
¼ cup orange juice
1½ cups whole milk
½ cup chopped walnuts
½ cup chopped pecans
½ cup pine nuts
½ cup chopped hazelnuts

Carob Nut Cupcakes

Makes about 11 cups batter, enough for 15 large cupcakes

These cakes owe their smooth sweetness to their high carob content. Carob is naturally much sweeter than chocolate; therefore, I used less sugar in this recipe than I would have for chocolate cupcakes. I like to divide the batter into fourths and add a different type of nut to each portion.

1. Preheat the oven to 350°F. Butter and flour 15 large muffin cups.

2. Combine the flour, granulated sugar, carob powder, baking powder, baking soda, salt, cloves, cinnamon, and nutmeg in a medium bowl.

3. Beat the butter and brown sugar in a large mixing bowl with an electric mixer on medium speed until fluffy. Add the eggs one at a time, beating well after each addition. Beat in the orange juice.

4. Gradually add the flour mixture, alternating with the milk, on low speed until combined.

5. Divide the batter among four bowls. Stir the walnuts into one, the pecans into another, the pine nuts into another, and the hazelnuts into the last. Spoon the batters into the pans and bake for 30–35 minutes, or until a tester inserted into a cupcake comes out clean. Cool in the pan for 10 minutes, then transfer to a rack to cool completely.

Granola

Makes about 4 cups

2 tablespoons clover honey

2 tablespoons olive oil

2 tablespoons firmly packed light
   brown sugar

1 teaspoon vanilla extract

1½ cups rolled oats (not instant)

¼ cup raisins

¼ cup dried apricots, chopped

½ cup almonds, chopped

¼ cup wheat germ

¼ cup sweetened flaked coconut

Cake

4 cups all-purpose flour

1 tablespoon baking powder

1 tablespoon baking soda

½ teaspoon ground cinnamon

2 cups firmly packed light brown
   sugar

4 tablespoons (½ stick) unsalted
   butter, melted

4 large eggs

5 ripe large bananas

⅔ cup plain yogurt

1 tablespoon vanilla extract

Granola Cakes

Makes about 11 cups batter, enough for four 4-inch square cakes

Although it is intended to be mixed in with the batter, you can also prepare the granola in this recipe as a hearty breakfast in itself. These cakes are cooked in a decorative baking dish and serve with a spoon.

1. To make the granola, preheat the oven to 325°F. Butter a large rimmed baking sheet or jelly-roll pan.

2. Heat the honey, oil, sugar, and vanilla in a small saucepan over medium heat, stirring until the sugar dissolves. Put the oats in a medium bowl and coat with the honey mixture.

3. Transfer the oat mixture to the baking tray and bake for 30 minutes, or until crisp, stirring every 10 minutes. Cool on the baking tray, then stir in the raisins, apricots, almonds, wheat germ, and coconut.

4. To make the cakes, increase the oven heat to 350°F. Butter and flour four 4 x 4-inch square pans.

5. Combine the flour, baking powder, baking soda, and cinnamon in a mixing bowl.

6. Beat the sugar, butter, eggs, bananas, yogurt, and vanilla in a large mixing bowl with an electric mixer on medium speed until creamy.

7. Gradually add the flour mixture and three-fourths of the granola on low speed until blended.

8. Pour the batter into the pans and top with the remaining granola. Bake for 35–40 minutes, or until a knife inserted in the middle comes out clean. Cool in the pan. Once cooled, remove from pans or serve in the pans, and dig in with a spoon.

Oatmeal Cake

Makes about 6 cups batter, enough for one 7 x 11-inch cake

1 cup rolled oats (not instant)

1¼ cups hot whole milk

1½ cups all-purpose flour

1 teaspoon baking soda

¾ teaspoon ground cinnamon

½ teaspoon salt

½ cup (1 stick) unsalted butter, at room temperature

1 cup firmly packed light brown sugar

2 large eggs

1 teaspoon vanilla extract

2⅓ tablespoons Cinnamon Sugar (page 352)

If you love oatmeal and you love cake, you have to try this moist breakfast cake—like a bowl of hot, creamy oatmeal in cake form. Flavor this to suit your taste with raisins, dried cranberries, apples, or maple syrup, just as you would sweeten a bowl of oatmeal.

1. Preheat the oven to 350°F. Butter and flour a 7 x 11-inch pan.

2. Combine the oats and milk in a medium mixing bowl; let stand for 10 minutes.

3. Combine flour, baking soda, cinnamon, and salt in another mixing bowl.

4. Beat the butter and sugar in a large mixing bowl with an electric mixer on medium speed until creamy. Beat in the eggs and vanilla.

5. Gradually add the flour mixture on low speed until blended, and then stir in the oat mixture.

6. Pour the batter into the pan and bake for 45–50 minutes, or until a knife inserted in the center comes out clean. Sprinkle the cake with cinnamon sugar and let cool for 10 minutes. Serve warm.

Lavender Orange Cakes

Makes about 4 cups batter, enough for four 4-inch cakes

This delicately scented cake is flavored with flowers and a hint of orange. It is an ideal midafternoon snack on a sunny summer day. Enjoy it in a garden with a cup of tea.

But when adding fresh flowers to a cake, know your source: make sure they are one hundred percent organic. Don't use flowers that may have been treated with pesticides, chemicals, or fertilizers.

Orange Cream Topping

Makes about 1½ cups

½ cup confectioners' sugar

1 teaspoon finely grated orange zest

¼ cup freshly squeezed orange juice

7 ounces sweetened condensed milk

Cake

1½ cups all-purpose flour

2½ teaspoons baking powder

½ teaspoon salt

6 tablespoons (¾ stick) unsalted butter, at room temperature

½ cup granulated sugar

2 large eggs

1 teaspoon vanilla extract

½ teaspoon grated orange zest

½ cup freshly squeezed orange juice

2 tablespoons dried lavender flowers

Garnish

¼ cup sliced kumquats

2 teaspoons dried lavender flowers

Fresh lavender flowers

Fresh mint leaves

Front: Lavender Orange Cake; back: Lavender Chocolate Truffle Cake.

1. To make the topping, combine the sugar, orange zest, orange juice, and condensed milk in a small bowl, stirring until blended. Cover and chill for 3 hours.

2. To make the cake, preheat the oven to 350°F. Butter and flour 4 extra-large muffin cups.

3. Combine the flour, baking powder, and salt in a mixing bowl.

4. Beat the butter and sugar in a large mixing bowl with an electric mixer on medium speed until fluffy. Beat in the eggs one at a time, then add the vanilla and orange zest.

5. Gradually add the flour mixture, alternating with the orange juice, on low speed until blended. Stir in the lavender.

6. Divide the batter among the muffin cups and bake for 25–35 minutes, or until a knife inserted in the center comes out clean. Cool in the pan for 10 minutes, then transfer to a rack to cool completely.

7. Invert the cakes on plates. Spoon the orange topping over and garnish with the kumquats, dried and fresh lavender, and mint leaves.

Variations

Lavender Chocolate Truffle Cakes: Replace the orange juice in the cake with ½ cup whole milk. Add 4 ounces melted and cooled semisweet chocolate. Garnish with fresh blueberries.

Rose Petal Cakes: Replace the 2 tablespoons dried lavender in the cake with chopped petals from 2 roses. Top with sugared rose petals (page 295).

Dandelion Cakes: Replace the 2 tablespoons dried lavender in the cake with chopped dandelion flowers. Top with dandelions and make a wish while eating the cake.

Lemon Herb Pudding Cake

Makes about 4 cups batter, enough for one 7-inch cake

When I desire a savory snack instead of a sweet one, this moist pudding cake is one of my favorites. Like a cheesecake, it is made in a water bath, and it is flavored with herbs fresh from my garden. Dried herbs can be substituted, but in that case, use only ½ teaspoon of each. I am lucky enough to have a lemon tree, too, and I use its fruit to make fresh juice for this and other cakes.

1. Preheat the oven to 350°F. Butter and flour a 7-inch round pan. Prepare a water bath large enough to fit the pan (see page 41) and set it in the oven on the middle rack.

2. Beat the butter, sugar, and salt in a large mixing bowl with an electric mixer on medium speed until fluffy. Gradually add the flour, lemon zest, and juice on low speed.

3. Beat the egg yolks and milk in a small bowl, then beat into the butter mixture.

4. In a clean bowl with clean beaters, beat the egg whites until stiff peaks form. Gently fold the egg whites into the batter with a rubber spatula. Fold in the chives, dill, tarragon, and fennel.

5. Pour the batter into the pan and set it into the water bath. Bake for 35–40 minutes, or until lightly brown. Cool in the pan for 10 minutes, then top with the feta and serve warm.

---

3 tablespoons unsalted butter, at room temperature

¾ cup granulated sugar

⅛ teaspoon salt

¼ cup all-purpose flour

1 teaspoon grated lemon zest

¼ cup freshly squeezed lemon juice

3 large eggs, separated

1½ cups whole milk

1 teaspoon chopped fresh chives

1 teaspoon chopped fresh dill

1 teaspoon chopped fresh tarragon

1 teaspoon chopped fresh fennel fronds

½ cup crumbled feta cheese

CHEESECAKES

Do you have a craving for something creamy? Cheesecakes are sure to please. In this section, I highlight the variety of textures and flavors that cheesecakes deliver, from the subtle smoothness of mascarpone cheesecake to the marbled density of brownie cheesecakes. New York cheesecake takes a vacation to Florida and picks up southern flavors from Key lime and a coconut pecan crust. And for something totally different: cupcakes topped with macaroni and cheese!

Key Lime Cheesecake

Makes about 6½ cups batter, enough for one 8-inch cake

This creamy cake is inspired by the New York classic. Its texture is true to its roots, but the citrusy flavors are pure Florida snowbird. Beautifully crowned with pecans, thinly sliced Key limes, and toasted coconut, with coconut and pecans in the crust. The Cuban guava variation has the Nuevo Latino taste of the tropics.

Crust

1 cup graham cracker crumbs
¼ cup ground pecans
¼ cup desiccated coconut (available in Asian groceries)
3 tablespoons granulated sugar
½ teaspoon grated lime zest
4 tablespoons (½ stick) unsalted butter, melted

Filling

4 boxes (8 ounces each) cream cheese, at room temperature
1½ cups granulated sugar
2 teaspoons all-purpose flour
4 large eggs
½ cup bottled or freshly squeezed Key lime juice
½ cup heavy cream
2 teaspoons vanilla extract
2 teaspoons grated lime zest

Topping

1¼ cups Key Lime Curd (page 353), cooled

Garnish

4 Key limes, sliced
⅓ cup pecan halves
2 tablespoons toasted coconut curls (page 33)

1. Preheat the oven to 350°F. Butter and flour an 8-inch springform pan. Wrap the outside of the pan in foil. Prepare a water bath large enough to fit the pan (see page 41) and set it aside.

2. To make the crust, combine the crumbs, pecans, coconut, sugar, lime zest, and the butter in a medium bowl until well blended. Press the mixture into the bottom of the springform pan and ½ inch up the sides. Bake for 10 minutes, then transfer to a rack to cool for 10 minutes. Set the water bath in the oven on the middle rack.

3. Meanwhile, to make the filling, beat the cream cheese in a large mixing bowl with an electric mixer on medium speed until soft. Add the sugar and beat until fluffy. Add the flour and beat until combined. Add the eggs one at a time, beating well after each addition. Beat in the lime juice.

4. In another bowl, using clean beaters, combine the cream, vanilla, and lime zest until thick. Carefully fold the cream mixture into the batter with a rubber spatula.

5. Pour the batter over the crust and set the cheesecake into the water bath. Bake for 40–50 minutes, or until the cheesecake jiggles when tapped and a knife inserted in the center comes out clean. Turn off the oven, open the door slightly, and let the cheesecake cool in the oven for 1 hour. Transfer to a rack to cool completely, then cover and chill for 3 hours.

6. Just before serving, open the mold and place the cake on a serving plate. Spread the curd over the cake and top with lime slices, pecans, and coconut curls.

Variations

Cuban Guava Cheesecake: After pouring the batter over the crust, swirl in ¾ cup guava jam. Omit the lime curd and lime slices and top the cooled cake with sliced guavas.

Palm Beach Coconut Orange Cheesecake: Replace the lime zest and juice with orange zest and juice. Add ½ cup desiccated coconut to the batter. Top with 1 cup toasted coconut.

Marble Brownie Cheesecake

Makes one 10-inch cake

The blend of sour cream, cream cheese, and chocolate make this cake sweet, tangy, and chocolatey all at the same time. The chewy brownie crust and crunchy nuts make it even more delicious.

1. To make the crust, preheat the oven to 350°F. Butter a 10-inch springform pan and line it with parchment paper. Wrap the outside of the pan in foil.

2. Combine the flour, baking powder, salt, and cocoa powder in a mixing bowl.

3. Beat the butter and sugar in a large mixing bowl with an electric mixer on medium speed until fluffy. Add the vanilla and the eggs one at a time, beating well after each addition.

Brownie Crust

1 cup all-purpose flour

½ teaspoon baking powder

⅛ teaspoon salt

¾ cup unsweetened cocoa powder

½ pound (2 sticks) unsalted butter, at room temperature

2 cups granulated sugar

2 teaspoons vanilla extract

4 large eggs

1 cup chopped walnuts

1 cup chocolate chips

4. Gradually add the flour mixture on low speed, then blend in the walnuts and chocolate chips.

5. Pour the batter into the pan and bake for 15–20 minutes, until firm. Remove the pan from the oven, but leave the oven on.

6. Meanwhile, make the cheesecake. Beat the cream cheese and sugar in another large mixing bowl with clean beaters on medium speed until light and fluffy. Add the eggs and egg yolks one at a time, beating well after each addition. Beat in the sour cream, salt, and vanilla.

7. Carefully pour the batter over the brownie crust. Drop spoonfuls of the melted chocolate over the batter and use a knife to swirl. Bake for 30–35 minutes, or until golden. Turn off the oven, open the door slightly, and let the cheesecake cool in the oven for 1 hour. Transfer to a rack to cool completely, then cover and chill for 3 hours. Warm for 20 minutes to room temperature and serve.

Mascarpone Cheesecake

Makes one 8-inch cake

When I lived in Vienna—very close to northern Italy—American cream cheese was hard to find, and I quickly became a fan of mascarpone, an ultracreamy, highly flavorful Italian cheese. This recipe calls for making homemade ladyfingers, but if you can find high quality store-bought ladyfingers, you will have a completely no-bake cheesecake. It is inspired by one of my favorite Italian desserts, tiramisu.

1. Preheat the oven to 425°F. Fit a pastry bag with a ½-inch tip. Cut parchment paper to the size of a baking sheet and, using a pencil, draw 12 evenly spaced straight lines lengthwise (i.e., from the top of the long side to the bottom of the long side) on the paper. Repeat with another piece of parchment paper and another baking sheet. Flip the papers over and put them on the baking

Ladyfingers

5 large egg yolks

¾ cup granulated sugar

6 large egg whites

1 cup all-purpose flour

¼ cup confectioners' sugar

Filling

¼ cup sweet Marsala wine

2 cups mascarpone cheese

1 cup heavy cream

1 cup confectioners' sugar

½ teaspoon ground cinnamon

Zabaglione

4 large egg yolks

¼ cup granulated sugar

½ cup sweet Marsala wine

sheets. You should see the lines through the papers; if you don't, darken them.

2. To make the ladyfingers, beat the egg yolks and 2 tablespoons of the granulated sugar in a large mixing bowl with an electric mixer on medium speed for 2 minutes, or until well blended.

3. In a clean bowl with clean beaters, beat the egg whites until soft peaks form. Gradually add the remaining granulated sugar and beat until stiff peaks form. Gently fold the egg whites into the batter with a rubber spatula. Gradually fold in the flour.

4. Place half the batter into the pastry bag and pipe strips that are about 1 inch wide, 4 inches long, and ¾ inch high along the parchment-paper lines on one of the baking sheets. Repeat with the remaining batter and remaining baking sheet. Dust with confectioners' sugar.

5. Bake for 8–10 minutes. Slide the parchment paper onto racks and cool completely.

6. To make the cheesecake, line an 8-inch springform pan with parchment paper. Arrange 8 ladyfingers over the bottom and around the sides. Drizzle with one-third of the wine.

7. Combine the mascarpone, cream, confectioners' sugar, and cinnamon in a large mixing bowl with an electric mixer on medium speed, blending well.

8. Add half the mascarpone mixture to the pan. Place another 8 ladyfingers over the batter and drizzle with another one-third of the wine. Top with the remaining mascarpone mixture, ladyfingers, and wine. Cover and refrigerate for 4 hours, or until set. Open the mold and carefully invert on a serving plate. Remove the parchment.

9. To make the zabaglione, beat the egg yolks and sugar in a double boiler with an electric mixer on medium

speed until pale and thick. Add the wine and continue to beat over low heat for 7–10 minutes, or until very thick. Refrigerate at least 3 hours before serving. (The zabaglione will keep in the refrigerator for up to 2 days.)

10. Spoon zabaglione on serving plates and top with slices of cheesecake.

Variation

Chocolate Ladyfingers: Reduce the flour by 2 tablespoons and add ¼ cup Dutch-process cocoa powder with the flour. Dust the cooled cake with more cocoa powder.

Mac and Cheese Cupcakes

Makes 12 large cupcakes

Cake for lunch? How much more gratifying does eating get? These cheesy cupcakes are like no other cheesecake you have ever tasted—perfect for those who want to walk on the wild side. I really like adding corn flour to the all-purpose flour, as specified in this recipe, but if you can't find corn flour you can simply use 3 cups of all-purpose flour.

1. To make the cupcakes, preheat the oven to 350°F. Line 12 large muffin cups with paper or foil liners.

2. Combine the flours, baking powder, and salt in a mixing bowl.

3. Cream the butter and the sugar in a large mixing bowl with an electric mixer on medium speed until fluffy. Beat in the egg yolks and vanilla.

4. Gradually add the flour mixture, alternating with the buttermilk, on low speed until blended. Add the cheese and mix well.

5. In a clean bowl with clean beaters, beat the egg whites until stiff peaks form. Gently fold the egg whites into the batter with a rubber spatula.

Cupcakes

2 cups all-purpose flour

1 cup corn flour

1½ tablespoons baking powder

½ teaspoon salt

½ pound (2 sticks) unsalted butter, at room temperature

2 cups granulated sugar

4 large eggs, separated

2 teaspoons vanilla extract

1 cup buttermilk

1½ cups shredded sharp Cheddar cheese

Mac and Cheese

1¼ cups elbow macaroni

2 tablespoons unsalted butter

2 tablespoons all-purpose flour

1¾ cups whole milk

¼ teaspoon salt

⅛ teaspoon ground black pepper

1¾ cups shredded sharp Cheddar cheese, plus more for garnish

1 teaspoon chopped fresh parsley for garnish

6. Fill the liners about three-fourths full with batter. Bake for 20–25 minutes, or until a tester in the center comes out clean. Cool in the pan.

7. Meanwhile, make the mac and cheese. Cook the macaroni according to package directions and set aside. Melt the butter in a medium saucepan over low heat and add the flour to make a paste. Gradually add the milk, salt, and pepper, stirring constantly until blended. Stir in the cheese, a little at a time, until the sauce begins to thicken. Remove from the heat and stir in the macaroni. Spoon over the cupcakes and top with additional shredded Cheddar and parsley.

Left: Parsley-topped Mac and Cheese Cupcake; front right: Variation. For the variation: Prepare the cheese sauce in step 7 until thickened. Skip the macaroni and top with shredded cheese.

Queso Fresco Cheesecakes

Makes 24 cupcakes

Served at neighborhood *panaderías*, or bakeries, here in Los Angeles, this Salvadoran cheesecake is made with queso fresco, a fresh cheese that's similar to farmer cheese. Alternatively, mild feta cheese can be substituted for queso fresco. Crema agria is a smooth, tangy cheese dressing similar to sour cream. I prepare this recipe as individual cakes, but you can also bake the batter in an 8½ x 4½-inch loaf pan, increase the baking time to 35–40 minutes, and slice it to serve.

1. Preheat the oven to 350°F. Butter and flour 24 medium muffin cups.

1 cup all-purpose flour

1 cup whole wheat flour

2 teaspoons baking powder

¼ teaspoon ground cinnamon

½ pound unsalted queso fresco, grated

2 cups granulated sugar

4 large eggs, beaten

8 ounces crema agria or sour cream

1 teaspoon vanilla extract

½ pound (2 sticks) unsalted butter, melted and cooled

¼ cup sesame seeds

2. Combine both flours, the baking powder, and cinnamon in a mixing bowl.

3. Beat the queso fresco, sugar, eggs, crema agria, and vanilla in a large mixing bowl with an electric mixer on medium speed until smooth. Stir in the butter.

4. Gradually add the flour mixture on low speed until blended.

5. Pour the batter halfway into the cups and sprinkle with sesame seeds. Bake for 20–25 minutes, or until a knife inserted into the center comes out clean. Cool in the pans.

ICE CREAM CAKES

At what point does ice cream lose its identity and become a cake? What some people call ice cream cakes consist simply of softened ice cream packed into a mold or pan and frozen. But in my opinion, an ice cream cake isn't an ice cream cake until it's paired with an actual baked treat and layered and frozen into one dessert. The good news about ice cream cakes is that they are pretty simple to make, especially when using store-bought ice cream. Whether you make one large cake to slice, like the Mint Brownie Ice Cream Cake, or individual cakes such as the Cream Cakesicle Pops or the Playful Cream Puff Banana Split Sundaes, you'll want to try each one of these creamy, cooling treats. When you substitute your favorite ice cream flavors for those suggested in the recipes, the possibilities are endless.

Mint Brownie Ice Cream Cake

Makes one 5 x 10-inch cake

Fudgy brownies and mint ice cream combine to give this cake a meltingly fresh taste. Use your favorite ice cream or sorbet—coffee ice cream, raspberry sorbet, and chocolate sorbet are wonderful variations.

1. To make the crust, preheat the oven to 350°F. Butter and flour a 4 x 8-inch loaf pan.

Brownie Crust

2 ounces semisweet chocolate, chopped

½ cup (1 stick) unsalted butter, at room temperature

1 teaspoon vanilla extract

½ cup all-purpose flour

¾ teaspoon baking powder

½ cup granulated sugar

⅓ cup firmly packed dark brown sugar

2 large eggs

Ice Cream Layers

1 container (1½–1¾ quarts) mint chocolate chip ice cream

1½ cups semisweet chocolate chunks

1½ cups crushed chocolate wafer cookies

1 container (1 pint) vanilla ice cream, softened

3 cups Whipped Cream (page 359) for garnish

½ pint (6 ounces) fresh raspberries for garnish

2. Melt the chocolate and butter in a double boiler over simmering water, stirring until melted. Remove from the heat and stir in the vanilla. Set aside to cool.

3. Combine the flour and baking powder in a mixing bowl.

4. Beat both sugars and the eggs in a large mixing bowl with an electric mixer on medium speed until creamy.

5. Gradually add the flour mixture, alternating with the chocolate mixture, on low speed until well mixed.

6. Pour the batter into the pan and bake for 25–30 minutes, or until a tester inserted in the middle comes out clean. Cool in the pan, then transfer to a rack to cool completely.

7. To make the ice cream layers, line the bottom and sides of a 5 x 9-inch loaf pan with wax paper, leaving a 2-inch overhang on all sides.

8. Place the mint ice cream in a bowl and let it soften, but do not let it melt. Mix in the chocolate chunks. Make a rectangular well of ice cream in the pan, spreading it about ¾ inch thick on the bottom and ½ inch thick on the sides. Sprinkle the center of the well with crushed cookies.

9. Measure the thickness of the brownie crust. Spread the vanilla ice cream over the cookie crumbs, leaving enough room at the top of the loaf pan to fit the brownie crust. Press the brownie crust on top. Cover with foil and freeze for 3–4 hours, or until firm.

10. To serve, remove the cake from the freezer and let it sit for 5 minutes. Unmold the cake by lifting it by the wax paper and inverting it onto a serving plate. Cut with a sharp knife and serve with whipped cream and raspberries.

Cake

6 large egg whites

¼ teaspoon salt

1½ cups granulated sugar

½ cup almonds, ground

1 tablespoon cornstarch

1 container (1½–1¾ quarts)
  strawberry frozen yogurt,
  softened

2 cups sliced fresh strawberries

1 container (1½–1¾ quarts)
  vanilla frozen yogurt, softened

Chocolate-Covered Strawberries

8 ounces semisweet chocolate,
  chopped

6 ounces white chocolate, chopped

¾ pound strawberries with stems
  (about 12)

Garnish

1½ cups Whipped Cream (page
  359)

⅛ cup whole shelled almonds

Ice Cream Dacquoise with Chocolate-Covered Strawberries

Makes one 7-inch three-layer cake

A dacquoise is a nut-flavored meringue that's shaped into a disk. In this version, I flavor the meringue with almonds, layer the disks with strawberry and vanilla frozen yogurt and fresh berries, and garnish with chocolate-covered berries. It will definitely make the most ordinary day feel special.

1. Preheat the oven to 300°F. Place a sheet of parchment paper on each of three baking sheets and, using a pencil, draw three 7-inch circles on the paper. Flip the papers over and put them on the baking sheets. You should see the circles through the papers; if you don't, darken them.

2. Beat the egg whites and salt in a large mixing bowl with an electric mixer on medium speed until foamy. Gradually beat in the sugar until stiff glossy peaks form. Gently fold in the almonds and cornstarch. Spoon the batter into a pastry bag fitted with a ½-inch plain tip. Using the circles as a guide, pipe the batter in spirals onto the baking sheets, starting from the outside and working inward, filling in the rounds as you go. Bake for 70–80 minutes, or until crisp. Slide the parchment onto racks and cool the cakes for 30 minutes.

3. To assemble the cake, set one disk on a serving plate. Top with half the strawberry frozen yogurt, spreading it ½ inch from the edge. Top with about 1 cup of the sliced strawberries and then spread with about half the vanilla frozen yogurt. Add the next disk and press down. Repeat with the remaining strawberry yogurt, strawberries, and vanilla yogurt. Top with the third disk and press down. Cover and place in the freezer for 3 hours.

4. To make the chocolate-covered strawberries, line a baking sheet with wax paper. Melt the semisweet

chocolate in a double boiler. Holding each strawberry by the stem, dip it into the chocolate, twisting to let the chocolate drip back into the pan. Place each berry on the baking sheet to set. Use the remaining chocolate to pipe designs on the top of the cake.

5. Once the semisweet chocolate has set, melt the white chocolate in a double boiler. Spoon into a pastry bag fitted with a small round tip. Pipe designs over the strawberries in the pattern of your choice, and use the remaining chocolate to complete the designs on the cake.

6. When ready to serve, cut the dacquoise into slices and place on serving plates. Using a pastry bag fitted with a large star-shaped tip, pipe whipped cream onto the plates next to the cake. Top the whipped cream with chocolate-covered strawberries and almonds.

Variation

Vanilla Cream Dacquoise: Omit both frozen yogurts and the berries. Fill the dacquoise with Vanilla Pastry Cream (page 358). Top the cake with sliced almonds.

Cream Puff Banana Split Sundaes

Makes 4 sundaes

Dig into these ice cream sundae cakes with a long-handled spoon. In a twist on the traditional banana split, the vanilla, chocolate, and strawberry ice creams in this recipe are enclosed in choux pastry, but the sundaes are still covered with the usual molten flow of hot fudge, tangy strawberry sauce, and tart pineapple sauce. I usually use a spray bottle to mist water on the cream puffs before putting them in the oven: the moisture that evaporates during baking helps make the puffs puffier. Top the sundaes with maraschino cherries to make them truly authentic.

1. To make the pastry, preheat the oven to 375°F. Line a baking sheet with parchment paper.

Choux Pastry

¾ cup water

5⅓ tablespoons (⅔ stick) unsalted butter

¾ cup all-purpose flour

⅛ teaspoon salt

3 large eggs

2. Combine the water and butter in a medium saucepan and bring to a boil over medium heat, stirring to melt the butter. Remove from the heat and beat in the flour and salt.

3. Return the saucepan to low heat and cook, stirring constantly, until the mixture forms a ball and no longer sticks to the sides of the pan. Remove from the heat, add the eggs one at a time, and beat until the dough is smooth and satiny.

4. Spoon the dough by tablespoonfuls onto the baking sheet, making 4 groups of 3 mounds placed about 2

Hot Fudge

4 ounces unsweetened chocolate, coarsely chopped

4 tablespoons (½ stick) unsalted butter

½ teaspoon salt

1½ cups granulated sugar

¾ cup evaporated milk

Strawberry Sauce

½ cup water

½ teaspoon cornstarch

1½ cups diced fresh or drained frozen strawberries

½ cup granulated sugar

Pineapple Sauce

½ cup water

½ teaspoon cornstarch

1½ cups fresh or drained canned pineapple chunks

½ cup granulated sugar

Ice Cream

4 small or medium bananas, peeled and cut in half lengthwise

1 container (1 pint) vanilla ice cream

1 container (1 pint) chocolate ice cream

1 container (1 pint) strawberry ice cream

3 cups Whipped Cream (page 359)

½ cup maraschino cherries, with stems

inches apart. Lightly spray the mounds with water from a spray bottle. Bake for 18–22 minutes, without opening the oven door, until the cream puffs are golden. Transfer puffs to a rack to cool.

5. To make the hot fudge, melt the chocolate, butter, and salt in a double boiler. Add the sugar, ½ cup at a time, stirring after each addition until dissolved. Slowly add the milk, stirring until blended. Keep warm over low heat.

6. To make the strawberry sauce, put the water in a small saucepan. Add the cornstarch and stir over low heat until dissolved. Add the strawberries and sugar and cook, stirring, until the strawberries have softened and sauce thickens. Let cool to room temperature.

7. To make the pineapple sauce, boil the water in a small saucepan. Lower the heat to medium, add the cornstarch, and stir until dissolved. Add the pineapple and sugar and stir until the pineapple has softened and the sauce thickens. Let cool to room temperature.

8. To construct each sundae, put 2 banana slices in an ice cream dish. Cut three of the puffs in half and set the bottoms between the bananas. Add a scoop of each flavor ice cream onto each puff, then add the tops. Spoon strawberry sauce over the chocolate ice cream, hot fudge over the vanilla ice cream, and pineapple sauce over the strawberry ice cream. Put the whipped cream in a pastry bag fitted with a large star-shaped tip and pipe a dollop on each of the puffs. Top each puff with a maraschino cherry.

Variations

Choux Pastry Sundaes: Pipe the choux pastry into eight 3½-inch spiral disks and bake for 15–20 minutes. Once cooled, set on dessert plates. Top with the ice creams, sauces, whipped cream, and cherries.

Fudge Choux Pastry Sandwiches: Pipe the choux pastry into twelve 2½-inch disks. Bake for 15–20 minutes. When cool, add a scoop of softened ice cream and hot fudge to half the disks. Press the remaining disks gently onto the ice cream, taking care not to break them. Wrap in plastic and freeze for 2 hours before serving.

Sorbet Sponge Cake

Makes one 9-inch cake

7½ cups Sponge Cupcake batter (page 72)

1 container (1 pint) raspberry sorbet

1 container (1 pint) lime sorbet

1 container (1 pint) orange sorbet

Even though it's extremely simple to make, this cake still looks impressive—an array of brightly colored scoops of sorbet gleam like jewels. No one needs to know you simply piled the frozen scoops on top of the cake!

1. Bake the sponge cake batter in a 9-inch round pan for 30–35 minutes. Let the cake cool for 10 minutes in the pan, then transfer to a rack to cool completely.

2. Line a baking sheet with wax paper. Using an ice cream scoop, shape the sorbet into balls and place on the baking sheet. Cover with plastic wrap and freeze for 1 hour. Put the cake on a serving plate, pile the scoops on top of the cake, then cover again and freeze for 2 more hours. Remove from the freezer about 10 minutes before slicing.

Cream Cakesicle Pops

Makes about 4½ cups batter, enough for 18 cake pops

If you're familiar with my earlier books, you may already know of my fascination with ice pops and cream pops. I have been experimenting with these frozen treats for decades, and I am now proud to call myself the go-to person for everything "pops." Combine that with my passion for cakes and you end up with these delicious creations, which I like to call cakesicles. Making the preparation even more fun and easy is the fact that there is a variety of silicone popsicle molds now on the market, which can be used for both baking and freezing. If you don't have oven-safe ice pop molds, you can use oven-safe paper cups or a silicone muffin pan (see the variations).

1½ cups all-purpose flour

1 teaspoon salt

½ pound (2 sticks) unsalted butter, at room temperature

1½ cups granulated sugar

2 tablespoons freshly squeezed orange juice

4 large eggs

1 teaspoon grated orange zest

2 containers (1 pint each) orange sorbet

1 container (1 pint) vanilla ice cream

18 ice pop sticks

1. Preheat the oven to 350°F. Butter and flour three six-cavity oven-safe silicone ice pop molds.

2. Combine the flour and salt in a mixing bowl.

3. Beat the butter, sugar, and orange juice in a large mixing bowl with an electric mixer on medium speed until fluffy. Add the eggs one at a time, beating well after each addition. Stir in the orange zest.

4. Pour the batter into the molds until they are ⅓ full and bake for 15–20 minutes, or until a tester inserted in the center comes out clean. Let the cakes cool in the pan.

5. Unmold the cakes and clean the molds. Spread half the sorbet and half the vanilla ice cream into the molds, filling each cavity about one-fourth full and mixing the flavors together to marbleize. Insert an ice pop stick into each cake and set it over the ice cream; cover with the remaining sorbet and ice cream. Cover with foil and freeze for 8 hours, or until very firm.

Variations

To make Cream Cakesicle Pops in paper cups: Set eighteen 3-ounce paper cups on a baking sheet and fill about one-third full with batter. Bake according to directions and, once they are cooled, tear the cups off the cake. Spoon half the ice cream and sorbet into clean cups, filling about one-third full and swirling to marbleize. Top with cakes and fill the cups with the remaining ice cream and sorbet. Insert an ice pop stick into each cup, cover with foil, and freeze for 8 hours. Tear off the cups when ready to serve.

To make Cream Cakesicle Pops in silicone muffin pans: Fill eighteen muffin cups about one-third full with batter. Bake according to directions and, once they are cooled, remove the cakes and clean the pans. Fill the cups about one-third full with half the sorbet and ice cream, swirling to marbleize. Top with a cake and fill the cups with the remaining ice cream and sorbet. Press tightly, then remove from the mold and place on a baking sheet lined with wax

paper. Insert an ice pop stick into each cake, cover with foil, and freeze for 8 hours.

Lemon Cream Cakesicle Pops: Replace the orange juice, orange zest, and orange sorbet with lemon juice, lemon zest, and lemon sorbet.

Lime Cream Cakesicle Pops: Replace the orange juice, orange zest, and orange sorbet with lime juice, lime zest, and lime sorbet.

Cherry Gelato

Makes about ½ gallon

2¼ cups whole milk

1 cup granulated sugar

8 large egg yolks

1 cup heavy cream

1 teaspoon vanilla extract

3 cups fresh cherries, pitted and halved

Red food coloring

Cake

4 cups Golden Sponge Roll batter (page 83)

Amaretto Syrup (page 356)

Unsweetened cocoa powder for garnish

Zuccotto

Makes one 8-inch cake

This dome-shaped cake from Florence, Italy, is traditionally prepared with whipped cream and chocolate, nuts, or fruit, but I like to make it with fresh homemade gelato. If you don't have an ice cream maker or decide to use store-bought gelato or ice cream, I highly recommend taking advantage of the wide range of flavors available. Spumoni, which includes cherry, chocolate, and pistachio, is my favorite. Serve this dessert semifreddo, or partially frozen, for the best flavor.

1. Heat the milk and sugar in a medium saucepan over medium-low heat, stirring until the sugar dissolves. Turn off the heat.

2. Beat the egg yolks in a medium mixing bowl with an electric mixer on medium speed until thick.

3. Gradually add 1 cup of the warm milk mixture to the egg yolks, beating until blended. Add the egg yolk mixture to the milk in the saucepan. Cook over medium heat, stirring constantly, until thickened and the custard registers between 170°F and 180°F on an instant-read thermometer. Remove from heat and whisk in the heavy cream and vanilla. Cool slightly, then transfer the custard to a bowl, cover, and refrigerate for 3 hours.

4. Add the cherries and red food coloring as desired to the custard. Transfer to an ice-cream maker and freeze according to manufacturer's directions.

5. Line an 8 x 12-inch pan with parchment. Pour the cake batter into the pan. Bake and cool according to directions on page 83. Slice the cake into 2½-inch-wide strips.

6. Butter an 8-inch bowl, line with plastic wrap, and butter the plastic wrap. Arrange the cake strips around the interior of the bowl in a single layer. Brush the cake

with amaretto syrup. Add a second layer of cake, filling all the spaces between strips. Spoon the gelato in the middle of the cake. Cover and freeze for 4–6 hours, or until firm.

7. Remove the cake from the freezer and let it sit at room temperature for 10–20 minutes before serving. Then invert the cake onto a serving plate and dust with cocoa powder.

Birthday Cakes

BABY AND TODDLER BIRTHDAY CAKES

Should a baby's first few birthdays offer an opportunity to introduce him or her to traditionally sweet birthday cakes or to more nutritious alternatives? This is a topic for heated discussion among parents, so in this section I provide you with two birthday-party options. For those who prefer to serve healthful cakes to their young guests, the playfully shaped apple, banana, and zucchini cakes get their sweetness from fruits and vegetables, rather from than refined sugar. They are also made with whole grains to boost nutrients, and contain less fat than a typical birthday cake. If you're looking for more traditional fare, I offer bite-size selections such as miniature Swiss rolls, doughnuts, and cupcakes, scaled down to fit nicely in those tiny mouths and tummies.

Applesauce Cakes

Makes about 4½ cups batter, enough for fifty 1¾-inch cakes or six 4-inch cakes

Made with whole wheat flour, these baby birthday cakes are as healthful as cake can be. Low in fat and refined sugar, they are sweetened with agave nectar, applesauce, and apple juice.

1. Preheat the oven to 325°F. Butter and flour fifty 1¾ x ¾-inch heart-shaped pans or six 4-inch heart-shaped pans.

Hearts: Applesauce Cakes; Stars: Banana Agave Cakes; Flowers: Zucchini Cakes.

Cakes

1¾ cups whole wheat pastry flour

1 teaspoon baking soda

1 teaspoon ground cinnamon

½ teaspoon ground cloves

⅛ teaspoon ground allspice

½ teaspoon salt

5⅓ tablespoons (⅔ stick) unsalted
   butter, at room temperature

⅓ cup agave nectar

1 large egg

1 teaspoon vanilla extract

½ cup unsweetened apple juice

1¼ cups chunky unsweetened
   applesauce

Topping

1 Gala apple

3 tablespoons freshly squeezed
   lemon juice

¼ cup Lemon Icing (page 358)

2. Combine the flour, baking soda, cinnamon, cloves, allspice, and salt in a mixing bowl.

3. Beat the butter in a large mixing bowl with an electric mixer on medium speed until fluffy. Beat in the agave nectar, egg, and vanilla.

4. Gradually add the flour mixture on low speed until blended. Stir in the apple juice and applesauce.

5. Pour the batter into the pans. If making small cakes, bake for 12–15 minutes. If making larger cakes, bake for 20–25 minutes. Insert a tester into the center to test for doneness; cakes are ready when tester comes out clean. Cool in the pans for 5 minutes, then transfer to a rack to cool completely.

6. Peel, core, and slice the apple, then brush the slices with lemon juice. Top the cake with a small amount of lemon icing and apple slices.

Variations

Chocolate, Raisin, and Applesauce Bundt Cake: Replace 1 cup of the whole wheat flour with all-purpose flour and add ⅓ cup unsweetened cocoa powder. Stir in ½ cup golden raisins when you add the applesauce. Bake in a 7-inch Bundt pan for 40–50 minutes. Top with Chocolate Glaze (page 351).

Applesauce Ginger Spice Cake: Replace the whole wheat flour with all-purpose flour. Add 1 tablespoon grated fresh ginger with the applesauce. Bake in an 8 x 8-inch square pan for 30–35 minutes. Dust with confectioners' sugar. Cut into squares to serve.

Banana Agave Cakes

Makes about 4½ cups batter, enough for fifty 1¾-inch cakes or six 4-inch cakes

Extra-ripe bananas and tangy yogurt give this cake a flavor boost, plus it is low in fat and sugar. Bake these cakes in miniature or standard-size star-shaped molds, or spread the batter on a

Cakes

1¾ cups whole wheat flour

1 teaspoon baking soda

½ teaspoon salt

5⅓ tablespoons (⅔ stick) unsalted
butter, at room temperature

⅓ cup agave nectar

2 large eggs

1 teaspoon vanilla extract

2 very ripe medium bananas,
mashed (about 1 cup)

½ cup plain yogurt

Topping

1–2 perfectly ripe bananas, sliced
crosswise

3–6 tablespoons lemon juice

9 x 12-inch baking sheet and cut into star shapes with cookie cutters after the cake has cooled.

1. Preheat the oven to 325°F. Butter and flour fifty 1¾-inch or six 4 x 2-inch star-shaped pans.

2. Combine the flour, baking soda, and salt in a mixing bowl.

3. Beat the butter and agave nectar in a large mixing bowl with an electric mixer on medium speed until light and fluffy. Beat in the eggs, vanilla, and bananas.

4. Gradually add the flour mixture, alternating with the yogurt, on low speed until blended.

5. Pour the batter into the prepared pans. If making small cakes, bake for 15–20 minutes. If making larger cakes, bake for 25–30 minutes. Insert a tester into the center to test for doneness; cakes are ready when tester comes out clean. Cool in the pans for 5 minutes, then transfer to a rack to cool completely.

6. Toss banana slices with lemon juice, then garnish each cake with a single banana slice.

Variations

Grilled Banana Cake: Bake the cake in a 9 x 9-inch square pan for 25–30 minutes. Omit the lemon juice from the topping. Cut 3 bananas in half lengthwise and grill (see page 244) before topping the cake. Drizzle 3 tablespoons of honey over the banana.

Fried Banana Cake: Omit the lemon juice from the topping. Cut 1 banana crosswise into 3 equal pieces. Dip in a lightly beaten egg and then coat with plain bread crumbs. Deep-fry in 2 inches vegetable oil until golden. Arrange on top of the cake. Serve hot.

Vegan Banana Cake: Omit the eggs. Replace the yogurt with 1 cup unsweetened apple juice. Increase the mashed bananas to 4 (a total of 2 cups).

Cakes

1¼ cups whole wheat flour

1 teaspoon baking powder

1 teaspoon baking soda

1 teaspoon ground cinnamon

½ teaspoon salt

2 large eggs

⅓ cup firmly packed light brown
    sugar

¼ cup clover honey

½ cup vegetable oil

¾ cup unsweetened apple juice

1 medium zucchini, shredded
    (about 2 cups)

Topping

2 tablespoons Almond Icing (page
    358) or 1½ cups Cream Cheese
    Frosting (page 352)

1¼ cups shredded zucchini

Zucchini Cakes

Makes about 5½ cups batter, enough for six 4-inch cakes or fifty miniature cakes

Even adults will be so mesmerized by the playful shapes and sweet flavors in these nuggets of cake that they won't realize how healthful they are. If you're making the cakes as sandwiches, party guests of all ages will find the flower-shaped, cream cheese–filled treats to be a satisfying, fulfilling dessert.

1. Preheat the oven to 350°F. Butter and flour fifty 2 x ¾-inch or six 4½ x 2-inch flower-shaped cake pans.

2. Combine the flour, baking powder, baking soda, cinnamon, and salt in a mixing bowl.

3. Beat the eggs in a large mixing bowl with an electric mixer on medium speed until frothy. Beat in the sugar, honey, oil, and apple juice until blended.

4. Gradually add the flour mixture on low speed. Once combined, raise the speed to high and beat for 3 minutes until smooth. Stir in the zucchini.

5. Pour the batter into the pans. If making small cakes, bake for 15–20 minutes. If making larger cakes, bake for 25–30 minutes. Insert a tester into the center to test for doneness; cakes are ready when tester comes out clean. Cool on a rack for 5 minutes, then transfer to a rack to cool completely. Top the miniature flowers with the almond icing and zucchini shreds; cut the large flowers in half crosswise and fill with cream cheese frosting.

Variations

Cookie-Cutter Zucchini Flower Sandwiches: Bake the cake on a 9 x 12-inch rimmed baking sheet lined with parchment paper. Let cool. Cut the cake with a flower-shaped cookie cutter. Spread half the flowers with Cream Cheese Frosting (page 352) and top with the remaining flowers.

Lemon-Dill Zucchini Loaves: Add 2 teaspoons chopped fresh dill or 1 teaspoon dried dill to the flour mixture. Reduce the apple juice to ½ cup and add ¼ cup freshly squeezed lemon juice and ½ teaspoon lemon zest. Bake in 2½ x 4-inch loaf pans for 30–40 minutes.

Vegan Zucchini Nut Cakes: Replace the eggs with 2 very ripe mashed medium bananas. Add ½ cup chopped pecans with the zucchini.

Miniature Swiss Rolls

Makes 4 cakes

There is something about miniature sweets that is really appealing, especially for a toddler's birthday—perhaps because they fit so nicely in those little hands. Here, low-in-fat Swiss rolls are served up baby-style.

1. Preheat the oven to 350°F. Butter a 7½ x 11¾-inch jelly-roll pan, cover with parchment paper, and butter and flour the parchment.

3. Combine the flour and cornstarch in a mixing bowl.

4. Beat the egg yolks and vanilla in a large mixing bowl with an electric mixer on medium speed until thick; set aside.

5. In a clean bowl with clean beaters, beat the egg whites until foamy. Add the salt and beat until soft peaks form. Gradually add the sugar and continue beating until stiff peaks form. Gently fold the egg whites into the yolks with a rubber spatula. Sprinkle the flour mixture over the egg mixture and fold until blended.

6. Pour the batter into the pan, spreading ¼ inch thick. Bake for 12–15 minutes, or until springy to the touch.

7. Dust a clean towel with confectioners' sugar. Turn the cake onto the towel and remove the parchment paper. Tightly roll the cake from the long side and let sit for 1 minute, then unroll and let sit for 2 minutes. Roll again, remove the towel, and let cool completely on a rack.

Swiss Rolls

⅓ cup all-purpose flour

⅓ cup cornstarch

5 large eggs, separated

1 teaspoon vanilla extract

½ teaspoon salt

⅓ cup granulated sugar

Confectioners' sugar for dusting

Filling and Topping

3¼ cups Vanilla Buttercream (page 356)

Yellow food coloring

¼ cup yellow crystal sugar

8. Unroll the cake and spread with a thin coat of buttercream. Roll the cake again and cut into 1-inch pieces. Color the remaining buttercream yellow and spread on the outside of the cakes, then roll in crystal sugar.

Variation

Chocolate Swiss Rolls: Reduce the flour to ¼ cup and add ¼ cup unsweetened cocoa powder. Fill with Chocolate Buttercream (page 350). Cover the outside with chocolate sprinkles.

Chocolate-Covered Doughnuts

Makes 30 doughnuts

1 recipe Raised Doughnuts dough (page 225)
12 ounces dark (at least 60% cacao) chocolate
2 tablespoons unsalted butter
Vanilla Buttercream (page 356)
Green, blue, and yellow food coloring

Here, the doughnut's classic form is dressed up in its best birthday finery. Rich dark chocolate surrounds the tender rings of a classic raised doughnut recipe.

1. Roll out the doughnut dough to ½ inch thick and cut with a 2½-inch doughnut cutter (the centers should be 1 inch in diameter). Prepare the doughnuts as directed.

2. Set a cooling rack over a jelly-roll pan or a baking sheet. Melt the chocolate and butter in a double boiler. Dip the cooked doughnuts in the chocolate mixture so that one side is coated, and set on the rack to harden, coated side up.

3. Divide the buttercream among three bowls. Color one with green food coloring, one with blue food coloring, and another with yellow food coloring. Fit three pastry bags with small round tips. Fill each bag with its own color of buttercream and pipe designs on the tops and sides of the doughnuts.

Variation

White Chocolate Doughnuts: Replace the dark chocolate with white chocolate. Dip the doughnuts in the chocolate, and then in colored

Miniature Swiss Rolls, Chocolate Covered Doughnuts, Miniature Cupcakes.

sprinkles, chopped nuts, and chopped dried fruit such as cherries, apricots, or cranberries before the white chocolate hardens.

Miniature Cupcakes

Makes about 32 cupcakes

I baked these little luxuries in a very small muffin tin—each cavity is only about 2 inches in diameter and 1 inch high! One little squirt of buttercream through a pastry bag fitted with a star-shaped tip is all that is needed to create the decorations in the photo, but see page 143 for additional toppings to explore.

1. Bake the cake batter in 32 miniature muffin cups lined with paper or foil liners for 12–16 minutes, or until a tester comes out clean. Cool in the pan for 5 minutes, then transfer to a rack to cool completely.

2. Divide the buttercream among three bowls. Color one with green food coloring, one with blue food coloring, and another with yellow food coloring. Fit three pastry bags with large star-shaped tips. Fill each bag with its own color of buttercream and pipe a star in the center of each cupcake.

8 cups Golden Yellow Cake batter (page 69)
3¼ cups Vanilla Buttercream (page 356)
Green, blue, and yellow food coloring

Ten Minicupcake Toppings

- Pipe a small rose onto each cake (see page 319).
- Dip cupcakes in Lemon Icing (page 358)and sprinkle them with colored sugar.
- Create funny faces on each cupcake with candy.
- Pipe a letter onto each cupcake to spell "Happy Birthday" and the birthday child's name.
- Pipe a star onto each cake and then top with small berries or candy.
- Top with small fondant flowers (see page 156).
- Pipe with thin lines in detailed patterns, in the manner of petits fours.
- Cut a fondant circle the size of the cupcake, emboss it with a pattern, and press onto the cupcake.
- Attach an edible photo transfer based on a favorite character or book (see page 55).
- Top with crystallized flowers (see page 295).

KIDS' BIRTHDAY CAKES

Themes for kids' parties vary from bowling bashes to roller-rink roundabouts; from small and simple celebrations to over-the-top galas. There are even "snow play" parties here in Los Angeles for which snow is trucked in and dumped on front lawns in the middle of summer. No matter how grand the theme, the birthday cake remains the highlight of the celebration and is always chosen with care.

In this section, you will find such reinterpreted classics as whoopie pies, ice cream sandwiches, and lollipops. You will also find cute characters created on dome-shaped cakes and cakes inspired by bento box lunches. And what's a kid's birthday without cupcakes? If you're looking for new ways to decorate them, I show you twenty-four of my favorites. And there's no reason why adults who enjoy the pleasures of childhood can't enjoy one of these treats at a "grown-up" birthday party, too.

Lollipop Cakes

Makes about 4 cups batter, enough for 24 small cakes

What's better than a birthday cake? How about a birthday cake dressed up as candy? These bites of bliss are almost too good to be true, and they are easy and fun to make. Once the cakes are dipped in chocolate, they can be covered in almost any light-weight, flavorful topping. Serve them by setting their sticks upright in cups filled with candy or nuts.

1. Preheat the oven to 350°F. Butter and flour 48 small dome-shaped pans.

2. Combine the flour, baking powder, and salt in a mixing bowl.

3. Beat the butter and sugar in a large mixing bowl with an electric mixer on medium speed until fluffy. Add the eggs one at a time, beating well after each addition. Beat in the vanilla.

4. Gradually add the flour mixture on low speed until blended.

Opposite top left: Lollipop Cakes; bottom left: Woopie pies; right: Brownie Ice Cream Sandwiches.

Cakes

1½ cups all-purpose flour
½ teaspoon baking powder
¼ teaspoon salt
¾ cup (1½ sticks) unsalted butter, at room temperature
¾ cup granulated sugar
3 large eggs
1 teaspoon vanilla extract
2½ cups Chocolate Frosting (page 351)
24 lollipop sticks
16 ounces chocolate (white, milk, or dark), chopped

Toppings

Sweetened flaked coconut
Chocolate sprinkles
Chopped peanuts
Sliced almonds
Chopped walnuts
Colored sugar

5. Pour the batter into the molds and bake for 10–15 minutes, or until a tester inserted in the center comes out clean. Cool in the pans.

6. Unmold the cakes. Spread the flat side of each cake with frosting, then press two together, flat sides touching, to form balls. Press lollipop sticks three-quarters of the way into each ball.

7. Line a baking sheet with wax paper. Melt the chocolate in a double boiler. Hold a cake by the stick and dip it into the chocolate, covering it completely and twisting to let any excess chocolate fall back into the pan, then dip into your choice of toppings. Set on the baking sheet to dry.

Variation

Chocolate Lollipop Cakes: Reduce the flour to 1¼ cups and add ⅓ cup Dutch-process cocoa powder to the dry ingredients.

Whoopie Pies

Makes 10–12 sandwiches

Ready for a good time? These sandwich cakes are a quintessentially American treat. They supposedly got their name from the cries of joy uttered by Amish men whose wives would pack them in their lunch boxes. Creamy vanilla is the traditional filling, but I prefer the marshmallow filling called for here. Find your own favorite from the list on page 147. If you have a muffin-top pan, you can use it to bake the cakes instead of mounding the batter onto baking sheets.

1. Preheat the oven to 350°F. Line two baking sheets with parchment paper. Using a pencil, draw twelve three-inch circles onto each sheet of parchment. Flip the sheets over.

2. Combine the flour, cocoa powder, baking soda, and salt in a mixing bowl.

Whoopie Pies
2 cups all-purpose flour
½ cup unsweetened cocoa powder
1¼ teaspoons baking soda
1 teaspoon salt
5⅓ tablespoons (⅔ stick) unsalted butter, at room temperature
1 cup firmly packed light brown sugar
1 large egg
1 teaspoon vanilla extract
1 cup buttermilk

Filling
Marshmallow Frosting (page 345)

Topping
3 tablespoons unsweetened cocoa powder
3 tablespoons confectioners' sugar

3. Beat the butter and sugar in a large mixing bowl with an electric mixer on medium speed until fluffy. Beat in the egg and vanilla.

4. Gradually add the flour mixture, alternating with the buttermilk, on low speed until blended.

5. Using a ¼-cup measure and the circles as a guide, spoon the batter onto the baking sheets. Bake for 12–15 minutes, or until puffy. Cool on the baking sheets.

6. Spread half the cakes with filling on their flat sides; top with the remaining cakes. Dust with cocoa powder and confectioners' sugar, using stencils to create patterns if desired.

Tasty Fillings for Whoopie Pies

- Coffee Frosting (page 351)
- Cream Cheese Chocolate Chip Frosting (page 352)
- Vanilla Buttercream (page 356)
- White Chocolate Buttercream (page 350)
- Peanut Butter Frosting (page 180)
- Vanilla Ice Cream (page 357)—soften ice cream, then freeze pies for 1 hour after assembly
- Coconut Cream Cheese Frosting (page 352)
- Root Beer Frosting (page 355)

Brownie Ice Cream Sandwiches

Makes 20 sandwiches

Brownies offer the most intense chocolate satisfaction, and when made into sandwiches with vanilla ice cream they couldn't possibly be better. If you prefer a simpler treat, leave out the chocolate chips and walnuts, but if you really want to gild the lily, try one of the variations—they're amazing!

1. Preheat the oven to 350°F. Butter and flour two 8 x 8-inch square pans.

2. Combine the flour, baking powder, and salt in a mixing bowl.

2 cups all-purpose flour

1 teaspoon baking powder

⅛ teaspoon salt

½ pound (2 sticks) unsalted butter, at room temperature

1½ cups granulated sugar

6 large eggs

1½ pounds unsweetened chocolate, melted

¾ cup chopped walnuts (optional)

½ cup chocolate chips (optional)

1 container (1½–1¾ quarts) vanilla ice cream, softened

3. Beat the butter and sugar in a large mixing bowl with an electric mixer on medium speed until fluffy. Add the eggs one at a time, beating well after each addition. Beat in the chocolate.

4. Gradually add the flour mixture until well integrated. Stir in half the walnuts and half the chocolate chips, if desired.

5. Spread the batter into the pans, then top with the remaining walnuts and chocolate chips, if desired. Bake for 20–25 minutes, or until a knife inserted in the center comes out clean. Cool in the pans.

6. Remove the brownie cakes from the pans without cutting. Top one brownie cake with ice cream, then top with the remaining brownie cake. Cut into sandwiches about 1½ x 2 inches in size and set on a serving plate. Cover with plastic wrap and freeze for 2 hours before serving.

Variations

Peanut Butter–White Chocolate Ice Cream Sandwiches: Omit the walnuts and replace the chocolate chips with white chocolate chips. Combine ½ cup peanut butter with ½ cup confectioners' sugar and spread over the cooled brownies. Sprinkle with white chocolate chips. Melt 4 ounces of dark chocolate in a double boiler and spoon into a pastry bag fitted with a small tip. Pipe the chocolate over the peanut butter in a crosshatch pattern. Refrigerate for 1 hour to set, then assemble into sandwiches.

Brownie Ice Cream Sandwiches with White Chocolate Topping: Omit the walnuts and chocolate chips. Melt 4 ounces of white chocolate in a double boiler and spoon into a pastry bag fitted with a small tip. Pipe the chocolate over the brownies in a crosshatch pattern. Refrigerate for 1 hour to set, then assemble into sandwiches.

Character Cakes

Makes about 10 cups batter, enough for two 6-inch cakes

3½ cups cake flour

1 tablespoon baking powder

¾ teaspoon baking soda

1 teaspoon salt

½ pound (2 sticks) unsalted butter, at room temperature

2 cups granulated sugar

4 large eggs

¼ cup freshly squeezed orange juice

1 teaspoon grated orange zest

2 cups plain yogurt

6 cups Vanilla Frosting (page 357)

Red, green, and black food coloring

Marzipan (page 354)

Pink nonpareils

Kids will fall in love with these cute and buttery birthday cakes. If you like, make several small cakes instead of one large one. They will cook faster and leave you more time to play and decorate.

1. Preheat the oven to 350°F. Butter and flour two 6-inch dome-shaped cake pans.

2. Combine the flour, baking powder, baking soda, and salt in a mixing bowl.

3. Beat the butter and sugar in a large mixing bowl with an electric mixer on medium speed until fluffy. Add the eggs one at a time, beating well after each addition. Beat in the orange juice and zest.

4. Gradually add the flour mixture, alternating with the yogurt, on low speed until blended.

5. Transfer the batter to the pans and bake for 45–50 minutes, or until a tester inserted in the center comes out clean. Cool the pan for 10 minutes, and then transfer to a rack to cool completely.

For the porcupine: Add ¼ cup vanilla frosting to a pastry bag fitted with a small round tip. Color the remaining frosting medium pink and use half of it to frost the cake. Add the remaining pink frosting to a pastry bag fitted with a large round tip and make porcupine spikes around the cake, leaving one side of the cake "unspiked" for the face. Pipe the remaining vanilla frosting onto the tips of the spikes, then pipe outlines of an oval for the nose and smile for the mouth. Create two ¾-inch balls of marzipan, leaving one white and coloring the other black. Roll out the marzipan to ⅛ inch thick. Using ¾-inch circular cookie cutters, or a utility knife, cut out the whites of the eyes. Using ¼-inch circular cookie cutters, or the tip of a straw, cut out the black pupils. Attach the pupils to the whites with frosting. Using a utility knife, cut out an oval nose and smiley mouth. Press the eyes, nose, and mouth into the cake.

For the pig: Color the vanilla frosting light pink and use it to frost the cake. Add a ring of pink nonpareils around the base. Create two 1-inch balls of marzipan, leaving one white and coloring the other black. Roll out the marzipan to ⅛ inch thick. Using ¾-inch circular cookie cutters, or a utility knife, cut out the whites of the eyes. Using ¼ inch circular cookie cutters, or the tip of a straw, cut out the black pupils and black nostrils. Using a utility knife, cut out one white triangle for a nose and two white triangles for ears, and smaller black ear inserts. Cut out a black smiley mouth. With frosting, attach the pupils to the whites of the eyes, nostrils to the nose, and black triangles to the middle of the ears. Coil the remaining black marzipan into a spiral for the tail. Press the eyes, nose, mouth, ears, and tail into the cake.

For the ladybug: Color half the vanilla frosting red, one-fourth of it pink, and the remaining one-fourth of it green. Frost the body of the ladybug in red and the face in pink. Add the green frosting to a pastry bag fitted with a medium star-shaped tip and pipe "grass" around the base of the cake. Create two 1½-inch balls of marzipan, leaving one white and coloring the other black. Roll out the marzipan to ⅛ inch and, using 1½-inch circular cookie cutters or a utility knife, cut out the whites of the eyes. Using ½-inch circular cookie cutters, cut out the black pupils, black ladybug dots, and a black smiley mouth. Press the eyes, mouth, and dots into the cake. Roll and coil the remaining black marzipan into two spirals and attach them above the face as antennae.

Bento Birthday Bear

Makes one cake

Inspired by the bento box lunches so popular in Japan, this cake-in-a-box is yet another birthday surprise to unwrap. To feed a crowd, fill a larger box with more cakes.

4 cups Golden Yellow Cake batter (page 69)

2 tablespoons unsweetened cocoa powder

Green, blue, and pink food coloring

3 ounces milk chocolate

3 cups Vanilla Frosting (page 357)

Candy flowers (such as gummy flowers)

Candied cherries

Jelly beans in assorted colors

5 cups Chocolate Frosting (page 351)

Candy dots or buttons in assorted colors

4 cups Miniature Swiss Rolls batter (page 139)

Licorice sticks in assorted colors

One 7 x 5 x 2-inch box for display

One 8 x 10 sheet of acetate (see page 18) or parchment paper

Toothpicks

Permanent marker

1. To make the bear, preheat the oven to 350°F. Butter and flour a 5 x 3-inch loaf pan, a 4 x 2½-inch loaf pan, and two mini muffin tins.

2. Divide the Golden Yellow Cake batter equally among three bowls. Add the cocoa powder to one, and dark green food coloring to the second, and leave the remaining batter plain. Pour as much chocolate batter as will fill the 5 x 3-inch pan about ¾ inch deep, and pour the remaining chocolate batter into one mini muffin tin. Add the green batter to the 4 x 2½-inch loaf pan and the plain batter to the remaining mini muffin tin. Bake the mini cupcakes for 15–20 minutes and the loaf cakes for 25–30 minutes, or until a tester inserted into the cakes comes out clean. Let cool in the pans.

3. Once the cakes have cooled, cut out a bear shape from the 5 x 3-inch cake with a utility knife. Cut the green cake crosswise into ¼–½-inch thick strips, then make jagged cuts across the top of each strip to make grass.

4. Divide the vanilla frosting among one large and three small bowls. Color the large bowl green, one of the small bowls blue, and another pink, leaving one white. Put the white frosting into a pastry bag fitted with a large round tip and pipe the face and paws onto the bear. Put the pink frosting in another bag fitted with a medium star-shaped tip and pipe in the ears. Put the blue frosting into a pastry bag fitted with a medium tip and pipe stars and spirals onto the minicupcakes, topping them with candy flowers, cherries, and jelly beans.

5. Put the chocolate frosting in a pastry bag fitted with a small star-shaped tip. Pipe "fur" onto the bear. Check to make sure the white frosting for the face and paws has hardened, then use a toothpick dipped in chocolate frosting to draw the eyes, mouth, and claws. Add candy dots for the pupils and the nose.

6. Bake the Swiss roll cake batter in an 11¾ x 7½-inch pan according to the directions on page 139. Before rolling it into a log, cut two pieces of cake to fit the inside of the box. Place one piece in the box, spread with chocolate frosting, and then top with the second layer. Put the green frosting in a pastry bag fitted with a star-shaped tip; pipe it and chocolate frosting on the top of the cake. Roll the remaining cake as directed, then cut a 1½-inch slice for the snail shell. Draw the snail head with permanent marker on the acetate or parchment paper. Melt the milk chocolate in a double boiler and spread it in a circular motion on the drawing. Add candy to the tips of the ears and let set before attaching the chocolate to the Swiss roll.

7. To assemble, fill the box with the grass, bear, snail, and minicupcakes. Add licorice and candies to fill completely.

Chocolate Chocolate Chip Cupcakes, Decorated Twenty-Four Ways

Makes about 6½ cups batter, enough for 24 cupcakes

Cupcakes are friendly! Cupcakes are stylish! Cupcakes are nostalgic! This is why I love them—not to mention the fact that they provide infinite design opportunities. Nothing is more exciting to me than being confronted with a blank canvas, and every batch of cupcakes I bake offers the chance for a fresh new start. I don't understand why some people like to decorate each cupcake with the same design, when with a little creativity, inspiration, and very few ingredients you can create a multitude of unique expressions. Part of the fun—especially at a children's

2¼ cups all-purpose flour

1 cup granulated sugar

1 cup unsweetened cocoa powder

2 teaspoons baking powder

1 teaspoon baking soda

½ teaspoon salt

1 cup low-fat vanilla yogurt

2 large eggs

1 cup skim milk

1 teaspoon vanilla extract

1 cup chocolate chips

5 cups Chocolate Frosting (page 351)

2 cups Peanut Butter Frosting (page 180)

6 cups Vanilla Frosting (page 357)

2 cups Fondant (page 353)

Toppings

Candies

Berries

Cookies

Fruit slices

Nuts

Sprinkles

Colored sugar

birthday party—is choosing the cupcake you like best. For the cupcakes themselves, use this low-in-fat recipe, or make the birthday child's favorite flavor—then follow the techniques below to create your own designs.

1. Preheat the oven to 350°F. Line 24 medium muffin cups with paper or foil liners.

2. Combine the flour, sugar, cocoa powder, baking powder, baking soda, and salt in a large bowl. Add the yogurt, eggs, milk, and vanilla, blending until just combined. Fold in the chocolate chips.

3. Fill the liners three-fourths full with batter and bake for 18–22 minutes, or until a tester inserted in the center comes out clean. Transfer to a rack to cool completely.

4. To decorate, prepare the frostings and add food coloring and toppings to make the variations seen on page 156.

Variations

Fondant flower (front row, far left): Color the fondant pink and yellow. With flower-shaped cutters, make two different flower shapes and attach them to the top of the cupcake with vanilla frosting. Using a pastry bag fitted with a small round tip, pipe a dot of frosting in the center and pipe dots around the edge of the cupcake. Top with colored sugar and candy dots.

Chocolate raspberry (front row, second from left): Using a spoon, pool dark chocolate frosting in the center of the cupcake. Using a pastry bag fitted with a large round tip, pipe large dots of vanilla frosting around the chocolate and in the center. Place a raspberry on top. Change the tip to a small writing tip and pipe small chocolate dots over the white dots.

Flower garden (front row, second from right): Color the vanilla frosting green. Using a flat pastry tip, pipe "grass" over the cupcake. Color the a ½-inch ball of fondant yellow, another ½-inch ball pink, and leave a ¼-inch ball white. Cut out small flowers with flower-shaped

cutters and place them on the grass. Form the white fondant into smaller balls and attach them to the center of each flower with a tiny bit of water.

Tower of stars (front row, far right): Dollop a mound of vanilla frosting in the center of the cupcake. Using a medium star-shaped pastry tip, pipe vanilla-frosting stars in a circle around the outside edge of the cake, and create smaller concentric rings by piping over the mound. Using tweezers, place a small candy dot on the tip of each star.

Purple marshmallow sparkle (second row, far left): Add one part melted marshmallows to one part vanilla frosting, then color the mixture purple. Create a mound of frosting in the center of the cupcake. Using a large round pastry tip, pipe additional frosting in concentric circles on top of the cupcake. Top with purple sugar.

Blue star (second row, second from left): Color the vanilla frosting blue. Using a large star-shaped pastry tip, pipe one big star in the center. Top with blue sugar and a white chocolate chip.

Chocolate happy cupcake (second row, second from right): Using an icing spatula, lightly frost the cupcake with chocolate frosting. Using a small round pastry tip, pipe vanilla frosting on top of the cupcake to create eyes and curly hair. Color a small amount of vanilla frosting pink and, using a small writing tip, pipe the mouth below the eyes. Using a writing tip, pipe chocolate frosting for the pupils of the eyes.

Yellow rose (second row, far right): Color a large batch of vanilla frosting yellow and a small batch green. Using a large petal-shaped pastry tip, pipe yellow petals onto the cupcake, starting the center and working outward in concentric circles until they reach ¼ inch from the edge. Using a small flat tip, pipe green frosting "leaves" all the way around the flower.

White flowers (third row, far left): Using a small round pastry tip, pipe groups of five small dots of vanilla frosting on the cake to make ten flowers. Color a small amount of vanilla frosting pink, and, using a writing tip, pipe pink dots in the center of each white flower.

Peanut chocolate delight (third row, second from left): Using a large round pastry tip, pipe a lump of peanut butter frosting in the center of the cupcake. Top with a chocolate-covered peanut.

Vanilla happy cupcake (third row, second from right): Spoon a mound of vanilla frosting in the center of the cupcake. Using a large round pastry tip, pipe additional frosting in concentric circles on top of the mound. Pipe the face in chocolate and pink frosting. Top with a piece of pink candy.

Almond chocolate delight (third row, far right): Using an icing spatula, generously frost the cupcake with chocolate frosting. Add sliced almonds around the edge and top with chocolate-covered almonds in the center.

Pink flower (fourth row, far left): Color the vanilla frosting pink. Thicken it with a small amount of confectioners' sugar. Spoon a mound of pink frosting on the center of the cupcake. Using a large petal-shaped pastry tip, pipe pink petals over the mound. Top with a white chocolate chip.

Dark chocolate chunks (fourth row, second from left): Generously frost the cupcake with chocolate frosting. Using a small round pastry tip, pipe alternating dots of vanilla and pink frosting around the perimeter. Add dark chocolate chunks to the center.

Blueberry mountain (fourth row, second from right): Generously frost the cupcake with chocolate frosting. Cover with chocolate sprinkles and top with fresh blueberries.

Fondant bow and polka dots (fourth row, far right): Lightly frost the cupcake with vanilla frosting. Make a bow from yellow fondant and place it in the center of the cupcake. Cut pink fondant in small circles and place the dots over the vanilla frosting.

Chocolate yogurt (fifth row, far left): Using a large star-shaped pastry tip, starting from the outside and working toward the center, pipe chocolate frosting in a spiral over the center of the cupcake. Top with a yogurt-covered almond.

Yellow cupcake with bird (fifth row, second from left): Color three-fourths of the vanilla frosting yellow and, using an icing spatula, apply it to the top of the cupcake. Dip the edges of the cupcake in yellow sugar. Add a dot of white frosting to the center. Roll out some pink and white fondant and cut a bird shape out of the pink fondant with a utility knife. Cut out the white fondant in the shape of a wing. Wet the wing with a drop of water and press into the pink bird. Dip a toothpick into dark food coloring and draw an eye on the bird. Press the bird onto a toothpick and place it in the center of the cupcake.

Purple spiral (fifth row, second from right): Color the vanilla frosting purple. Using a small round pastry tip, pipe the purple frosting in a thin spiral over the cupcake. Top with purple sugar.

White chocolate with stars (fifth row, far right): Dollop a mound of vanilla frosting on the center of the cupcake. Using a medium star-shaped pastry tip, pipe yellow-frosting stars around the perimeter. Place white chocolate chips between the stars.

Sparkly yellow heart (back row, far left): Lightly frost the center of the cupcake with pink frosting. Roll out yellow fondant and cut it into a heart shape. Press the heart onto a toothpick and place it in the center of the cupcake. Wet the fondant with a few drops of water and sprinkle the entire cupcake with blue sugar.

Blue cupcake with coconut curls (back row, second from left): Generously frost the cupcake with blue frosting. Top with large coconut curls (see page 33).

Lime frosting with lime slice (back row, second from right): Add 1 teaspoon freshly squeezed lime juice and green food coloring to the vanilla frosting and thicken slightly with confectioners' sugar. Using a large star-shaped pastry tip, pipe a large lump on top. Top with a thin lime slice.

Vanilla with spiral cookie (back row, far right): Using a large star-shaped pastry tip, pipe vanilla frosting into a mound in the center of the cupcake. Top with a butter cookie spiraled with chocolate and a chocolate-covered almond.

BIRTHDAY CAKES FOR TEENAGERS

For teenagers, milestone birthdays—such as the two big birthdays for teenage girls, the Sweet Sixteen and the Quinceañera (the Latina fifteenth-birthday fete)—are usually celebrated in style, often with lavish parties and equally extravagant cakes. Birthdays also give aspiring teenage bakers a chance to show off their skills with a cake that suits their personalities and their palates. They'll find several options in this section, from easy yet awesome to more challenging cakes for those who want to learn new techniques. These cakes are equally at home at other teen celebrations, including a bar or bat mitzvah and a debutante ball. No matter which cake you choose, each one invites you to dig in for a good time.

Quinceañera Cake

Makes about 24 cups batter, enough for one four-tier cake

Say *hola* to this happy-fifteenth-birthday cake! Tiered Quinceañera cakes are usually frilly and glamorous—they often look exactly like wedding cakes—so this cake is a bit of a departure from tradition. Still, I think it fits the occasion perfectly and reflects the whimsical nature of teenage girls. For this cake, I recommend baking one set of graduated tiers at a time and storing the remaining batter in the refrigerator while the first set is baking. The buttercream can be colored any color you choose.

10 cups all-purpose flour

3 tablespoons baking powder

2 teaspoons salt

2¼ pounds (9 sticks) unsalted butter, at room temperature

4½ cups granulated sugar

18 large eggs

4½ tablespoons vanilla extract

3 cups whole milk

12 cups Vanilla Buttercream (page 356), colored with blue food coloring

5 cups Chocolate Frosting (page 351)

1¾ cups Marzipan (page 354)

1. Preheat the oven to 350°F. Butter and flour four round pans in graduated sizes (see the chart on page 163)—one 10-inch pan, one 8-inch pan, one 6-inch pan, and one 4-inch pan.

2. Combine the flour, baking powder, and salt in a large bowl.

3. Beat the butter and sugar in a very large mixing bowl with an electric mixer on medium speed until light and fluffy. In another large bowl, beat the eggs and vanilla. Add the egg mixture to the butter mixture, beating well. Gradually add the flour mixture, alternating with the milk, on low speed until blended.

4. Divide half the batter among the pans and bake according to the times listed on the chart on page 163. Cool in the pans for 20 minutes, then transfer to racks to cool completely. Repeat with remaining batter.

5. Level the cooled cakes with a serrated knife, so that the tops do not form a dome. Using the cake pans as templates, cut bases out of corrugated cardboard with a utility knife and cover them with foil, making one base for each tier. Place about 4 cups colored buttercream in a bowl (to use as a "crumb coat"). Set one cooled 10-inch cake layer on a base and add a thin layer of buttercream from the bowl. Top with the second 10-inch layer and thinly coat the top and sides of both layers with more buttercream. Now you have formed and crumb-coated the first tier. Measure the height of the tier and cut four ½-inch-diameter dowels to the same height. Set aside. Refrigerate the layers for at least 1 hour. Repeat with the 8-inch, 6-inch, and 4-inch layers—placing on bases and covering with a crumb coat—but omit the dowels for the 6-inch and 4-inch layers.

6. Place the 10-inch layers on a serving plate and frost the top and sides with about 3 cups of the buttercream. Insert the dowels evenly spaced about 2 inches from the edge. Frost the top and sides of the 8-inch layers with about 2½ cups of buttercream and insert the dowels about 2 inches from the edge. Frost and stack the 6-inch layers on top, then frost and stack the 4-inch layers.

7. Form the marzipan into one 3-inch ball and one 2-inch ball. Leave the large ball white and use food coloring to color the small ball dark brown. Dust a work surface with confectioners' sugar and roll out the marzipan balls to ⅛ inch thick. Using small circular cutters or a utility knife, cut four sets of the whites of the eyes and four sets of dark brown pupils in graduated sizes. Attach the pupils to the whites with frosting. Add to the cake.

8. Put three-fourths of the chocolate frosting in a pastry bag fitted with a large round tip. Pipe dots around the bottom of each cake layer and at the top of the top layer. Put the remaining chocolate frosting in a pastry bag fitted with a small round tip. Pipe the eyelashes and mouth onto each face.

9. To serve, cut the top layer in half down the middle. Remove the cardboard and cut the next layer into 6 equal wedges. Remove the cardboard and dowels and cut the 8-inch layer into 8 equal wedges. Remove the next layer of cardboard and dowels and cut the final layer into 10 equal wedges.

Quinceañera Cake Pans and Baking Times

To make this cake, you will need two pans in each size. Each should be 2 inches high.

DIAMETER	AMOUNT OF BATTER PER PAN	BAKING TIME
10 inches	5½ cups	35–40 minutes
8 inches	3 cups	30–35 minutes
6 inches	1¾–2 cups	25–30 minutes
4 inches	¾ cup	20–25 minutes

Cake Bars

6 tablespoons unsweetened cocoa powder

¾ cup boiling water

3 cups all-purpose flour

1½ teaspoons baking soda

½ teaspoon salt

¾ cup (1½ sticks) unsalted butter, at room temperature

1½ cups granulated sugar

3 large eggs

1½ teaspoons vanilla extract

¾ cup whole milk

Fudgy Cake Bars

Makes about 8½ cups batter, enough for one 9 x 13-inch cake

I don't know about you, but when I was a teenager, at least one of my daily meals consisted of a candy bar . . . and to tell you the truth, it often still does. Inspired by popular candy bar flavors, these fudgy cake bars are better than a birthday cake for a large crowd. Each is unique, tempting party guests to choose and eat their favorites.

1. Preheat the oven to 350°F. Line a 9 x 13-inch pan with parchment and butter the parchment.

2. Combine the cocoa and boiling water in a heatproof bowl; set aside to cool.

3. Combine the flour, baking soda, and salt in a mixing bowl.

Frostings

1⅛ cups Caramel Topping (page 350)

5 cups Dark Chocolate Frosting (page 351)

1½ cups Vanilla Frosting (page 357)

1½ cups Whipped Cream (page 359)

Toppings

Chocolate chips

Pecan halves

Sweetened flaked coconut

Unsweetened cocoa powder

Confectioners' sugar

Fresh raspberries

Fresh blackberries

Unsalted roasted peanuts

Dark chocolate malted milk balls

Yogurt- and chocolate-covered almonds

Miniature marshmallows

Salted almonds, ground

4. Beat the butter and sugar in a large mixing bowl with an electric mixer on medium speed until fluffy. Beat in the eggs and vanilla.

5. Gradually add the flour mixture, alternating with the milk, on low speed until blended. Stir in the cocoa mixture.

6. Spread the batter evenly in the pan and bake for 25–30 minutes, or until the top is firm and a tester inserted in the center comes out clean. Cool in the pan. Cut into individual portions (choose squares or rectangles and sizes based on your guests' ages and appetites).

7. Top each bar with frostings and assorted toppings.

3 cups all-purpose flour

1 teaspoon baking powder

½ teaspoon salt

¾ pound (3 sticks) unsalted butter,
   at room temperature

2 cups granulated sugar

4 large eggs

1 teaspoon vanilla extract

1 cup root beer

½ cup root beer–flavored candies,
   crushed

1 container (1¼ quarts) vanilla
   ice cream

Root Beer Ice Cream Trifles

Makes about 8 cups batter, enough for three trifles

Remember the days when teenagers hung out at soda fountains after school, sharing root beer floats? Neither do I, but I like the idea of it! This recipe lets you re-create that nostalgia in a cake-and-ice-cream trifle—all you need is two spoons and someone to share it with.

1. Preheat the oven to 350°F. Line a 10½ x 15-inch jelly-roll pan with parchment paper.

2. Combine the flour, baking powder, and salt in a mixing bowl.

3. Beat the butter and sugar in a large mixing bowl with an electric mixer on medium speed until fluffy. Add the eggs one at a time, beating well after each addition. Beat in the vanilla.

4. Gradually add the flour mixture, alternating with the root beer, on low speed until blended. Fold in ¼ cup of the candies.

5. Spread the batter into the pan and bake for 15–20 minutes, or until the cake is springy to the touch. Cool in the pan for 10 minutes, and then transfer to a rack. Remove the parchment paper and allow to cool completely.

6. To assemble the trifles, get out three tall beer mugs, tumblers, or glasses. Using a cookie cutter ¼-inch smaller than the base of the glasses, cut the cake into circles. Place a circle in the bottom of each glass, then add a scoop of ice cream. Repeat the layers until each glass is full, finishing with

a scoop of ice cream. Garnish with the remaining candies and serve with long-handled spoons.

Variations

Frosted Root Beer Trifles: Replace the ice cream with Root Beer Frosting (page 355).

Root Beer Layer Cake with Root Beer Frosting: Bake the cake in two 8-inch square cake pans for 35–40 minutes, or until a tester comes out clean. Frost the cake with Root Beer Frosting (page 355), leaving the sides exposed. Top with root beer candy.

Sarsaparilla Cake: Replace the root beer with sarsaparilla soda. Replace the root beer candies with hard licorice-flavored candy.

Cola Trifles: Replace the root beer with cola. Omit the root beer candies. Top the ice cream with Hot Fudge (page 127) and chopped peanuts.

Cola Cake with Malt Frosting

Makes about 8 cups batter, enough for one 8-inch tube cake

Teenagers like all kinds of soda pop, and this southern cola cake topped with malt-flavored frosting will be no exception. Scoop vanilla ice cream into the ring at the center of the cake if you want to re-create the flavors of an ice cream soda.

Cake

2½ cups sifted all-purpose flour

½ cup unsweetened cocoa powder

1½ teaspoons baking soda

1 teaspoon salt

½ cup (1 stick) unsalted butter, at room temperature

1⅓ cups granulated sugar

3 large eggs

⅔ cup buttermilk

1¼ cups cola

Malt Frosting

1 bag (12 ounces) semisweet chocolate chips

2 cups heavy cream

1¼ cups malt powder

⅓ cup confectioners' sugar

4 ounces cream cheese, at room temperature

1 teaspoon vanilla extract

Garnish

½ cup chopped pecans

1. Preheat the oven to 350°F. Butter and flour an 8-inch tube pan.

2. Combine the flour, cocoa powder, baking soda, and salt in a mixing bowl.

3. Beat the butter and sugar in a large mixing bowl with an electric mixer on medium speed until fluffy. Add the eggs, one at a time, and beat for 1 minute. Beat in the buttermilk and cola. Gradually add the flour mixture on low speed until blended.

4. Pour the batter into the pan and bake for 40–45 minutes, or until a tester inserted in the center comes out clean. Cool in the pan for 5 minutes, then transfer to a rack to cool completely.

5. To make frosting, melt chocolate chips in a double boiler, stirring until smooth. Set aside and let cool.

6. Beat the cream and malt powder in a medium mixing bowl with an electric mixer on medium speed until stiff. Cover and refrigerate for 30 minutes.

7. Beat the sugar, cream cheese, and vanilla in a large bowl with the mixer on medium speed until creamy. Beat in the chocolate, then beat in the malt mixture. Cover and refrigerate for 1–2 hours.

8. Place the cake on a serving plate. Frost the cake and top with pecans.

Rainbow Sweet Sixteen Cake

Makes about 30 cups batter, enough for one 9 x 12¼-inch six-layer cake

This cake is inspired by the cake I made for my own Sweet Sixteen party. I was an aspiring baker and, because the party had a rainbow theme, I wanted to make a rainbow-colored cake but I didn't quite know how. Instead, I made a huge cake that was shaped like the number "16" and decorated it with rows of frosting to look like a rainbow.

Now I know how to make rainbow-colored cakes, and in this recipe I show you how—the secret is to bake each color individually. You can frost the entire cake, leaving the colors of the inside as a surprise, or frost only the top and leave the sides of the cake exposed to show off your masterpiece. If you frost the entire cake, you don't need to trim the sides.

1. Preheat the oven to 325°F. Line two 9 x 12¼ x 1-inch pans with parchment paper.

2. Combine the flour, baking powder, and salt in a mixing bowl.

3. Beat the butter and sugar in a very large mixing bowl with an electric mixer on medium speed until fluffy. Beat in the vanilla.

10½ cups all-purpose flour
¼ cup baking powder
1½ teaspoons salt
2 pounds (8 sticks) unsalted butter, at room temperature
6 cups granulated sugar
2½ tablespoons vanilla extract
4¾ cups whole milk
24 large egg whites
¾ teaspoon cream of tartar
Red, orange, yellow, green, blue, and purple food coloring
6 cups Vanilla Frosting (page 357; use 12 cups if you plan to frost the sides of the cake)
¼ cup light blue crystal sugar

4. Gradually add the flour mixture, alternating with the milk, on low speed until blended.

5. In a clean bowl with clean beaters, beat the egg whites and cream of tartar until soft peaks form. Gently fold the egg whites into the batter with a rubber spatula.

6. Divide the batter among six bowls, coloring each with a different food coloring. Spread one bowl of batter into one of the baking pans and another bowl of batter into the other baking pan. Cover the remaining bowls and refrigerate until ready to use. Bake for 18–22 minutes, or until a tester inserted in the center comes out clean. Transfer to a rack to cool. Repeat with the remaining batter.

7. Place the red layer on a serving plate and top with a thin layer of frosting. Place the orange layer on top and spread with a thin layer of frosting. Repeat with the yellow, green, blue, and purple layers, frosting the purple layer more thickly than the others. Trim about ¼ inch from each side before frosting to give the cake a clean edge. Frost the top of the cake and dust with crystal sugar, using a stencil in a pattern of your choice.

Variation

Marbleized Rainbow Cake: Once the batters are colored, pour half the red, orange, and yellow batters together in a 9 x 13-inch pan and the second half in another 9 x 13-inch pan. Use a spatula to swirl the colors, and bake for 30–35 minutes. Let cool in the pan for 10 minutes, then transfer to a rack to cool completely. Repeat with 2 more cakes and the blue, purple, and green marbleized batters. Once cooled, stack the layers in alternating colors.

ADULT BIRTHDAY CAKES

Of all the ways to say happy birthday, a homemade cake is the absolute best. No matter how messy or lopsided the result may be, the gesture is especially welcome and always appreciated. With the cakes in this section, however, you won't have to make excuses for how your cake looks or console yourself with the fact that it's the thought that counts. These step-by-step instructions will help you create cakes that are as beautiful as they are flavorful.

When deciding which cake to make, I consider the recipient's favorite type of cake first: mousse cake for a chocolate lover, carrot cake for a spice-cake aficionado, perhaps chocolate-dipped cheesecake for the creamy-cake devotee—or maybe a princess cake, which I actually developed for my friend Allan, who is far from a princess but who loves the cakes all the same. Next, I think about the plating and the birthday message, and I create a design that focuses on the dramatic moment when the singing, wishing, and blowing out of candles take place. When the birthday genie rises from the smoke . . . we adults believe, too.

Wish Cakes

People have been singing "Happy Birthday" for more than one hundred years, and although the song doesn't change, the cakes we ask for or make for loved ones do. I prefer to prepare several smaller cakes rather than one large cake, because then I have more opportunities for flavor combinations and decorating, and it gives guests more opportunities for enjoying their favorites. If you're concerned about fitting birthday candles on smaller cakes, I suggest one for each decade, plus one for good luck.

For the Happy Birthday Cake: Prepare 14 cups of the devil's food cake batter according to the directions on page 76, but use three 8-inch round pans instead of three 9-inch pans. Bake for 35–45 minutes, or until a tester comes out clean. When cool, level the top layer with a serrated knife so that it is not domed. Fill a pastry bag fitted with a star-shaped tip with 1 cup chocolate frosting and set aside; frost

Devil's Food Cake batter (page 76)
Golden Yellow Cake batter (page 69)
Chocolate Frosting (page 351)
Vanilla Frosting (page 357)
Chocolate Fondant (page 353)
Fondant (page 353)
Royal Icing (page 355)
Blue and green food coloring
White candy dots
Blue candy dots

the cake with the remaining frosting. Color 1½ cups fondant green and roll it out to ¹⁄₁₆ inch thick. Cut out flower shapes with cookie cutters. Color 1½ cups royal icing blue and place it in a pastry bag fitted with a small writing tip. Pipe spirals of icing in the center of the flowers. Let harden before adding the flowers to the cake. With blue royal icing, write "Happy Birthday." Add white candy dots to the top of the cake, around the inside circumference. Pipe chocolate frosting stars around the dots and around the bottom circumference of the cake.

For the Oh Happy Day Cake: Prepare 12 cups of the devil's food cake batter according to the instructions on page 76, except use a 10 x 10-inch square pan instead of three 9-inch pans. Bake for 35–45 minutes, or until a tester comes out clean. When cool, level the top with a serrated knife so that it is not domed. Frost with chocolate frosting. Color 1½ cups fondant green and roll it out to ¹⁄₁₆ inch thick. Cut out the letters to spell "Oh Happy Day" with alphabet cookie cutters and place the letters on the cake. Color 1 cup royal icing blue and place it in a pastry bag fitted with a small writing tip. Use it to pipe icing stripes on the cake and to make the exclamation point.

For the Happiness Cake: Prepare 8 cups of the golden yellow cake batter according to the instructions on page 69, except use an 8 x 8-inch square pan instead of round pans. Bake for 20–25 minutes, or until a knife inserted in the center comes out clean. When cool, level the top of the cake with a serrated knife so that it is not domed. Frost with vanilla frosting. Measure the height and top of the cake. Roll out green fondant to ⅛ inch thick by 3 inches wide by a length that will allow it to go up the side of the cake, across the top, and down the other side. Then cut the fondant into a long narrow strip of that size. Emboss a raised flower pattern into the fondant. Wrap the strip around the cake. Put ½ cup white royal icing in a pastry bag fitted with a small writing tip. Use the icing to attach candy dots to the center of each flower. Roll out the chocolate fondant to ¹⁄₁₆ inch thick and cut out several large chocolate flowers and a long oval. Place the oval and flowers on the cake. Attach a blue candy dot to the center of each chocolate flower with royal icing. Color ½ cup royal icing blue and place it in a pastry bag fitted with a small writing tip. Use it to write "Happiness" in the oval and to pipe a blue border around the oval. Pipe blue dots on the strip, between the flowers, and pipe a blue border around the bottom of the cake.

For the Happy Everything Cake: Bake 10 cups of the golden yellow cake batter according to the instructions on page 69, except use two 7-inch round pans instead of the 9-inch pans. Bake for 35–45 minutes, or until a tester comes out clean. When cool, level the tops with a serrated knife so that they are not domed. Prepare 4½ cups vanilla frosting and use it to frost the top, sides, and between the layers. Roll out 1 cup chocolate fondant to 1/16 inch thick and cut out letters to spell "Happy Everything" with alphabet cookie cutters. Place the letters on top of the cake. Roll out ¼ cup green fondant to 1/16 inch thick and cut out two hearts, one smaller than the other, and stack them on the cake. Color ¼ cup royal icing blue and place it in a pastry bag fitted with a small writing tip. Use it to pipe a blue border around the heart and blue dots around the top border. Add blue candy dots to the piped dots. Put 1½ cups chocolate frosting into a pastry bag fitted with a medium star-shaped tip and pipe the frosting around the bottom of the cake. Add blue candy dots to the borders.

Chocolate Lover's Mousse Cakes

Makes 6 cakes

Earn your stripes by making these four-tier cakes in pyramid molds. Three layers of mousse made from three kinds of chocolate—white, milk, and bittersweet—on a base of chocolate cake look oh-so-impressive! I like to serve this semifreddo on a plate next to an arrangement of chocolate sheets.

1. To make the cakes, preheat the oven to 350°F. Line a 9 x 12-inch pan with parchment.

2. Combine the flour, cocoa powder, baking powder, and salt in a mixing bowl.

3. Beat the egg yolks and sugar in a large mixing bowl with an electric mixer on medium speed until thick. On low speed, gradually add the water and vanilla. Gradually add the flour mixture to the egg yolk mixture.

Chocolate Cake

1 cup all-purpose flour

¼ cup unsweetened cocoa powder

2½ teaspoons baking powder

⅛ teaspoon salt

5 large eggs, separated

½ cup granulated sugar

⅓ cup hot water

1 teaspoon vanilla extract

Mousse

1 packet (¼ ounce) unflavored
  gelatin

¼ cup granulated sugar

2 tablespoons water

1 teaspoon vanilla extract

1½ cups whole milk

5 large egg yolks

⅛ teaspoon salt

1 cup whipped cream

7½ ounces white chocolate, melted

3 ounces milk chocolate, melted

3 ounces bittersweet chocolate,
  melted

Chocolate Sheets

14 ounces bittersweet chocolate

One 8½ x 11 sheet of acetate (see
  page 18) or parchment paper

4. In a clean bowl with clean beaters, beat the egg whites
    until soft peaks form. Gently fold the egg whites into
    the batter with a rubber spatula.

5. Spread the batter onto the pan and bake for 18–22
    minutes, or until the cake springs back when touched.
    Transfer to a rack to cool completely. Once cooled, peel
    off the parchment and cut into 3 x 3-inch squares.

6. To make the mousse, combine the gelatin, sugar, and
    water in a small saucepan over low heat, stirring until
    the gelatin and sugar are dissolved. Remove from the
    heat and add the vanilla. Set aside to cool completely.

7. Heat the milk in a saucepan over low heat to warm.

8. Working off the heat, beat the egg yolks and salt in a double boiler with an electric mixer on medium speed. Set the egg yolk mixture over low heat and gradually add the milk. Remove from the heat and let cool. Once cooled, add the gelatin mixture.

9. Divide the mousse among three bowls. Fold one kind of melted chocolate into each, then fold ⅓ cup of the whipped cream into each.

10. Spoon the white chocolate mousse into six 3 x 3-inch pyramid molds, filling each about one-fourth full. Cover with plastic wrap and freeze for 30 minutes, or until the surface has hardened. Add the milk chocolate layer to the molds, filling so they are about half full, then cover and freeze for an additional 30 minutes, or until the milk chocolate surface has hardened. Add a layer of bittersweet chocolate mousse to the molds and top with the cake squares. Cover with plastic and freeze for an additional 3 hours.

11. To make the chocolate sheets, melt the bittersweet chocolate in a double boiler. Spread half the chocolate to ¹⁄₁₆ inch thick on an 8½ x 11-inch sheet of acetate or parchment paper, leaving ½-inch border all around, and let set. Put a small amount of the remaining chocolate in a pastry bag fitted with a large round tip and pipe 6 dots of chocolate on the border of the acetate. Set aside. Reserve the remaining chocolate for assembly.

12. Using square cookie cutters or a knife, cut the hardened chocolate into squares of graduated sizes. Reheat the reserved chocolate in the double boiler and spoon a little bit onto one side of each of six serving plates, allowing enough room to place the pyramids alongside the chocolate pool. Stand the chocolate squares on their sides in the pools, then place the plates in the refrigerator to allow the chocolate to harden.

13. About 20–30 minutes before serving, remove the pyramids from the freezer. Unmold and place them on the plates; top with reserved chocolate dots. Let stand to defrost, then serve semifreddo.

Variation

Square Chocolate Mousse Cake: Bake the cake in an 8 x 8-inch square pan. Once cooled, remove the cake and line the pan with plastic wrap, allowing 2 inches overhang on each side. Return the cake to the pan and top with mousse layers. Freeze for 4 hours. Lift the cake by the plastic wrap and transfer to a plate to serve. Let defrost for 30 minutes and slice.

Carrot Cake

Makes about 6½ cups batter, enough for one 8-inch cake

When I buy carrot cakes in bakeries, I wonder why the marzipan carrots used to garnish the cakes are always so tiny. In one bite, they are totally gone, and I want more! When I make carrot cake at home, I take control of the size of the carrot, and bigger is definitely better. For special birthdays, I like to garnish individual slices with white chocolate flowers. The secret to the rich moist cake? Crushed pineapple and pineapple juice.

1¾ cups all-purpose flour
¾ teaspoon baking soda
1 teaspoon ground cinnamon
½ teaspoon salt
¼ teaspoon ground cloves
½ teaspoon ground ginger
2 large eggs
½ cup firmly packed light brown sugar
¼ cup vegetable oil
2 teaspoons vanilla extract
4 ounces drained canned crushed pineapple (with juice reserved)
¼ cup pineapple juice from the can of crushed pineapple
2 medium carrots, grated (about 1 cup)
½ cup golden raisins
⅓ cup chopped walnuts
4¾ cups Cream Cheese Frosting (page 352)

1. Preheat the oven to 350°F. Butter and flour an 8 x 8-inch square pan.

2. Combine the flour, baking soda, cinnamon, salt, cloves, and ginger in a mixing bowl.

3. Beat the eggs, sugar, oil, and vanilla in a large mixing bowl with an electric mixer on medium speed until creamy. Stir in the pineapple, reserved juice, carrots, raisins, and walnuts.

4. Gradually add the flour mixture on low speed until blended.

5. Transfer the batter to the pan and bake for 30–35 minutes, or until a tester inserted in the center comes

out clean. Let cool in the pan, then transfer to a rack to cool completely.

6. To serve, cut the cake into rectangular slices and set on dessert plates. Spread the top of each slice with frosting. You should have about 1¼ cups frosting left over. Put the remaining frosting in a pastry bag fitted with a small round tip and pipe a border of frosting around the top of each slice of cake. If desired, attach marzipan carrots (see below) to the plates with frosting, and add white chocolate flowers (see below) to the top of each slice. Attach the flowers by mounding a bit of frosting on the slices to support them.

Marzipan Carrots and White Chocolate Flowers

3³/₄ cups Marzipan (page 354)
Orange and green food coloring
8 ounces white chocolate
One 8½ x 11 sheet of acetate (see page 18)
    or parchment paper
Colored sugar

MARZIPAN CARROTS: Color 3¼ cups marzipan orange and form it into rounded cones, each about 3½ inches long. Emboss lines into the cones by pressing the side of a toothpick gently into the surface. Color ½ cup marzipan green, and roll it out to ⅛ inch thick. Cut into stem shapes and attach to the top of the carrots with frosting.

WHITE CHOCOLATE FLOWERS: Melt the white chocolate in a double boiler. Spread it ¼ inch thick on the sheet of acetate or parchment paper. Let cool until set. Using a 1½-inch flower-shaped cookie cutter, cut out the flowers. Add a dot of frosting to the center of each and sprinkle with colored sugar. Make the leaves by rolling out green marzipan to ¹/₁₆ inch thick and cutting out leaf shapes with a utility knife. Emboss veins with a toothpick. Gently press onto a rounded surface and let harden into curls.

Custard Filling

1½ cups whole milk

¾ cup granulated sugar

1 tablespoon cornstarch

¼ teaspoon salt

3 large egg yolks

1 tablespoon vanilla extract

Almond Yellow Cake

1½ cups all-purpose flour

2 teaspoons baking powder

¼ teaspoon salt

½ cup (1 stick) unsalted butter, at room temperature

1 cup granulated sugar

2 large eggs, separated

1 teaspoon almond extract

½ cup whole milk

Seven-Minute Frosting

Makes about 3 cups

1½ cups granulated sugar

¼ teaspoon cream of tartar

⅛ teaspoon salt

2 large egg whites

¼ cup water

2 teaspoons vanilla extract

Filling

¾ cup Strawberry Sauce (page 127)

Garnish

4 cups Fondant (page 353)

Red, green, and black food coloring

Princess Cake

Makes about 4 cups batter, enough for one 4¼ x 8½-inch cake

I've made a lot of different cakes over the last few years, but princess cake—a traditional Swedish dessert—is my favorite platform for experimentation. It may have a lot of parts, but that's what makes it so much fun. I've come up with several variations on the theme, and this one, which uses almond-flavored yellow cake, custard filling, and seven-minute frosting covered in fondant, is baked in a loaf pan, unlike traditional Swedish versions made in a dome pan. Don't level the top layer of this cake—you want the domed loaf to give you a rounded, log-shaped cake.

1. To make the custard, heat the milk in a saucepan, but do not boil. Add the sugar, cornstarch, and salt. Continue to cook over low heat, stirring until dissolved.

2. Add the egg yolks and cook for 1–2 minutes, or until creamy. Remove from the heat and stir in the vanilla. Cover and refrigerate until ready to assemble cake.

3. To make the cake, preheat the oven to 350°F. Butter and flour a 4¼ x 8½-inch loaf pan.

4. Combine the flour, baking powder, and salt in a mixing bowl.

5. Cream the butter and sugar in a large mixing bowl with an electric mixer on medium speed until fluffy. Beat in the egg yolks and then the almond extract.

6. Gradually add the flour mixture, alternating with the milk, on low speed until blended.

7. In a clean bowl with clean beaters, beat the egg whites until stiff peaks form. Gently fold the egg whites into the batter with a rubber spatula.

8. Pour the batter into the pan and bake for 35–45 minutes, or until a tester inserted in the center comes out clean. Cool in the pan for 20 minutes, then transfer to a rack to cool completely.

9. To make the frosting, beat the sugar, cream of tartar, salt, egg whites, and water in a double boiler until peaks form, about 5–7 minutes. Remove from the heat and continue to beat until the frosting reaches spreading consistency. Stir in the vanilla.

10. To assemble the cake, cut the loaf horizontally into three layers. Place the bottom layer on a serving plate and top with strawberry sauce. Add the second layer and top with custard and about half the frosting. Add the top layer and frost the top and sides of the cake with the remaining frosting, shaping it into a round top.

11. Make four small balls from about ½ cup fondant. Leave one white and color one red, one dark green, and one black. Roll out the balls and cut out a flower from the white and roll a marble-size ball from the red for the center of the flower. Cut out leaves from the green fondant and make veins by drawing on the leaves with a toothpick. Cut out black loops to place on top of the cake. Let sit until dry.

12. Color the remaining fondant bright green. Measure the height and top of the cake and add 2 inches to determine the size of the fondant sheet needed to cover the cake (see page 54). Roll out the fondant to ⅛ inch thick and wrap it around the cake, pressing it flat against the frosting. Trim any excess fondant at the base. Decorate the top of the cake with the loops, leaves, and flowers.

Sesame-Coated Peanuts

⅓ cup unsalted roasted peanuts

2 tablespoons clover honey

2 tablespoons sesame seeds

Peanut Roll Cake

⅓ cup all-purpose flour

⅓ cup cornstarch

5 large eggs, separated

1 teaspoon vanilla extract

½ teaspoon salt

⅓ cup granulated sugar

½ cup chopped unsalted roasted
    peanuts

Peanut Butter Frosting

¾ cup (1½ sticks) unsalted butter,
    at room temperature

1½ cups firmly packed light brown
    sugar

¼ cup water

1⅓ cups smooth or crunchy peanut
    butter

2 tablespoons vanilla extract

Filling and Topping

1½ cups raspberry jam

1½ cups fresh raspberries

¼ cup Hot Fudge (page 126)

¼ cup chopped unsalted roasted
    peanuts

1 teaspoon sesame seeds

Peanut Sesame Raspberry Roll

Makes one 7½-inch rolled cake

Most adults I know to like to stay as youthful as possible, and it is for them that the term "kidult"—an adult who's really a kid at heart—was coined. Kidults also inspired me to create this sophisticated but playful birthday cake, based on the classic peanut butter and jelly combo that kids of all ages enjoy. An added bonus is that the sesame seeds, which cover the peanuts and cake, combine with the other ingredients to make a complete protein.

1. To make the sesame-coated peanuts, mix the peanuts and honey in a small bowl. Spread the sesame seeds on a plate and roll the peanuts in the seeds, coating thoroughly. Set aside.

2. To make the cake, preheat the oven to 350°F. Cover a 7½ x 11¾-inch jelly-roll pan with parchment paper and butter the parchment.

3. Combine the flour and cornstarch in a mixing bowl.

4. Beat the egg yolks and vanilla in a large mixing bowl with an electric mixer on medium speed until creamy.

5. In a clean bowl with clean beaters, beat the egg whites until foamy. Add the salt and beat until soft peaks form. Gradually add the sugar and continue beating until stiff peaks form. Gently fold the egg whites into the yolks with a rubber spatula. Sprinkle with the flour mixture and ⅓ cup of the (uncoated) peanuts, folding until blended.

6. Sprinkle the remaining (uncoated) peanuts on the jelly-roll pan and spread the batter on top. Bake for 12–15 minutes, or until springy to the touch.

7. Dust a clean towel with confectioners' sugar. Turn the cake onto the towel and remove the parchment. Roll the cake from the short side and let sit for 1 minute, then unroll and let sit for 2 minutes. Roll again and let cool completely.

8. To make the frosting, bring the butter, brown sugar, and water to a boil in a saucepan over high heat. Boil for 2 minutes. Remove from the heat. Add the peanut butter and vanilla and beat until smooth. Let cool.

9. To assemble, unroll the cake and spread with jam, then frosting, and then some of the raspberries. Roll the cake again and place on a serving plate, seam side down. Drizzle with hot fudge and top with the remaining raspberries, the sesame-coated peanuts, the ¼ cup chopped peanuts, and the sesame seeds.

Variation

Fluffernutter Cake: Replace the jam with Marshmallow Frosting (page 345).

Chocolate-Covered Cheesecake

Makes one 8-inch cake

An over-the-top decadent dessert deserves an over-the-top extravagant presentation, so in this recipe I show you how to go all out. This cheesecake is denser than most, to keep the slices from crumbling when you dip them into the chocolate, but if you like a creamy cheesecake, reduce the flour to 3 tablespoons and pour the chocolate over the cake.

1. Preheat the oven to 325°F. Butter and flour an 8-inch springform pan. Prepare a water bath large enough to fit the pan (see page 41).

2. To make the crust, combine the gingersnap crumbs, butter, and sugar in a mixing bowl until the crumbs are moistened. Press the crumbs into the bottom of the pan and about one-fourth of the way up the sides. Bake for 10 minutes, or until slightly darkened. Remove from the oven and let cool slightly.

3. To make the cake, beat the cream cheese, sugar, and vanilla in a large mixing bowl with an electric mixer on

Crust

1½ cups gingersnap crumbs

5⅓ tablespoons (⅔ stick) unsalted
butter, melted

1 tablespoon granulated sugar

Cake

4 boxes (8 ounces each) cream
cheese, at room temperature

1⅓ cups granulated sugar

2 teaspoons vanilla extract

4 large eggs, beaten

¼ cup all-purpose flour

¼ cup heavy cream

¼ cup sour cream

Garnish

8 ounces unsweetened dark (at least
70% cacao) chocolate

24 maraschino cherries, with stems

4 ounces milk chocolate, melted

4 ounces white chocolate, melted

3 cups Whipped Cream (page
359)

2 cups Strawberry Sauce (page
127)

medium speed until fluffy. Beat in the eggs, then the
flour. Add the heavy cream and sour cream and continue
to beat until fully incorporated.

4. Wrap the bottom and sides of the cooled pan with foil
and place in the water bath. Pour the batter into the pan
and bake for 50–60 minutes. To test for doneness, look
for tiny cracks around the edge of the cake, then gently
shake the pan. If the filling does not wobble, the cake
is set. Turn off the oven, open the door slightly, and
let the cheesecake cool in the oven for 1 hour. Transfer
to a rack to cool completely, then cover and chill for
3 hours. Cut the cake into 8 slices, wrap each slice
individually in plastic wrap, and freeze for 1 hour.

5. To make the garnish, hold the cherries by the stems
and dip them into the melted white and milk chocolate.
Place on parchment, then, using a spoon, drizzle the
cherries with the contrasting chocolate and let set.

6. Melt the dark chocolate in a double boiler. Dip
the cheesecake slices into the chocolate and set on
individual dessert plates. Allow the cheesecake to
defrost for 1 hour.

7. Put the remaining dark chocolate in a pastry bag fitted
with a small writing tip and pipe "Happy Birthday" onto
the rim of one plate. Pipe chocolate patterns (dots,
stripes) on the other plates.

8. Pool the strawberry sauce on the plates, set the
cheesecake slices on top, then top the cheesecake with
the cherries. Using a pastry bag fitted with a star-shaped
tip, pipe the whipped cream onto each slice. Add a
candle to the "Happy Birthday" slice to serve to the
guest of honor.

Cake

⅔ cup golden rum

3½ cups all-purpose flour

1 tablespoon baking powder

½ pound (2 sticks) unsalted butter,
  at room temperature

1½ cups granulated sugar

6 large eggs, separated

2 teaspoons grated lemon zest

3 tablespoons freshly squeezed
  lemon juice

Pecan Brittle

½ cup light corn syrup

1 cup granulated sugar

1 cup chopped pecan halves

1 tablespoon unsalted butter

1 teaspoon golden rum

1½ teaspoons baking soda

Filling and Topping

3 cups Rum Buttercream (page
  355)

3½ cups Apricot Filling (page
  349)

Garnish

12 maraschino cherries

Frankfurt Crown Cake

Makes one 8-inch cake

You don't find many adults wearing paper crowns at their parties, so here is another way to honor the birthday man or woman. Named after the town of its origin, Frankfurt, Germany, this crown-shaped rum cake is baked in a tube pan, then cut into layers and filled with sweetened apricots and rum-flavored buttercream. This recipe is unique in that it is topped with a chopped caramel-coated nut brittle called krokant. I have given you recipes for apricot filling and pecan brittle, but feel free to substitute high-quality store-bought apricot jam and your favorite nut brittle.

1. To make the cake, preheat the oven to 325°F. Butter and flour an 8-inch tube pan.

2. Reserve 4 tablespoons of rum for assembly. Combine the flour and baking powder in a mixing bowl.

3. Cream the butter and sugar in a large mixing bowl with an electric mixer on medium speed until light and fluffy. Add the egg yolks one at a time, beating well after each addition. Beat in the lemon zest, lemon juice, and remaining rum.

4. Gradually add the flour mixture on low speed until blended.

5. In a clean bowl with clean beaters, beat the egg whites until stiff peaks form. Gently fold the egg whites into the batter with a rubber spatula.

6. Pour the batter into the pan and bake for 40–45 minutes, or until a tester inserted in the center comes out clean. Cool in the pan for 20 minutes, then transfer to a rack to cool completely.

7. To make the pecan brittle, butter a large baking sheet.

8. Combine the corn syrup, sugar, and pecans in a microwave-safe bowl. Cover with a ventilated lid and microwave on high until the syrup is golden, about 5

minutes. Stir in the butter and rum, then microwave for 1½ minutes longer. Stir in the baking soda, then quickly pour the mixture onto the baking sheet, spreading it into a thin, even layer. Cool and let harden for 30 minutes. Crush it into small pieces in a food processor or blender. The size of the pieces is up to you. They can be as small as crumbles or as large as dimes, if you prefer a crunchier texture.

9. Slice the cake horizontally into three layers and place the bottom layer on a serving plate. Sprinkle with 2 tablespoons of the reserved rum, then top with one-fourth of the buttercream and then one-fourth of the apricot filling. Place the second layer on top and repeat with more rum, buttercream, and apricot filling. Top with the third layer and cover the outside of the cake with apricot filling. Frost the cake with the remaining butter cream, press in the brittle and garnish with maraschino cherries.

Variations

Frankfurt Crown Cake with Pine Nuts and Sour Cherries: Replace the rum with Kirsch. When you make the filling, replace the apricots with whole pitted sour cherries. In the brittle, replace the pecans with pine nuts.

Frankfurt Crown Cake with Almonds and Peaches: Replace the rum with amaretto. When you make the filling, replace the apricots with fresh sliced peaches. In the brittle, replace the pecans with almonds.

Miniature Frankfurt Crown Cakes: Bake the cakes in mini Bundt pans for 30–35 minutes.

PET BIRTHDAY CAKES

Because my husband and I do a lot of traveling, the only pet we can own and leave for weeks at a time is our turtle, George. He really isn't a cake lover, so on his birthday I make him a little salad with carrots and lettuce, which he loves. But when I was growing up, I had a dog named Fluffy, whose birthday we celebrated with as much enthusiasm as we did our own birthdays. So if, like me, you think that having a homemade cake for a dog's or cat's birthday is a must, here are some healthy recipes to choose from.

Carob Peanut Cake

Makes one 6-inch cake

Dogs can spot a good birthday cake when they see one, and even if they remain unaware of their birthdays (I guess we can't be sure of that), they will know something special must be going on when you serve them this cake. Chocolate makes dogs sick, but carob and peanuts are acceptable, so this is the ideal cake for them. If you like carob and peanuts, you may dig in, too.

1. To make the cake, stir the peanuts into the carob cake batter, then pour into a 6-inch dome-shaped pan. Bake for 45–50 minutes, or until a tester inserted in the center comes out clean.

2. To make the frosting, beat the confectioners' sugar, butter, and vanilla in a medium mixing bowl with an electric mixer on medium speed until smooth. Reserve one-fourth of the frosting for piping. Add the carob powder to the remaining frosting.

3. Place the cake on a serving plate and spread with the carob frosting. Add the halved peanuts to the bottom rim of the cake.

4. Divide the reserved frosting among three bowls and color each with a different food coloring. Transfer to pastry bags fitted with small round tips. Pipe a crown and birthday message onto the cake.

Cake
½ cup unsalted roasted peanuts, chopped
5½ cups Carob Nut Cupcake batter (page 109)

Carob Frosting
2 cups confectioners' sugar
1 tablespoon unsalted butter, melted
1 teaspoon vanilla extract
¼ cup carob powder

Garnish
¾ cup unsalted roasted peanut halves
Yellow, pink, and blue food coloring

Beef Cake

This sugar-free birthday treat made with meat can be served as a meal to dogs and cats. Substitute liver-, tuna-, or chicken-flavored baby food for the beef and you can customize this recipe to accommodate your pet's favorite flavors.

¾ cup whole wheat flour

¾ teaspoon baking powder

¼ cup (½ stick) unsalted butter, at room temperature

¼ cup corn oil

2 large eggs

1 jar (4 ounces) strained beef baby food

2 strips beef jerky for dogs, chopped

¼ teaspoon finely chopped fresh rosemary

1 clove garlic, minced

½ cup cottage cheese

1. Preheat the oven to 350°F. Butter and flour a 4 x 4-inch square pan.

2. Combine the flour and baking powder in a mixing bowl.

3. Beat the butter, oil, and eggs in a large mixing bowl with an electric mixer on medium speed until fluffy. Beat in the baby food.

4. Gradually add the flour mixture on low speed until blended. Stir in the jerky, rosemary, and garlic.

5. Pour into the prepared pan and bake for 25–30 minutes, or until a tester inserted in the center comes out clean. Let cool in the pan.

6. Using an ice cream scoop, place the cottage cheese on top of the cake. Cut into 2-inch slices to serve.

Grassy Carrot Cupcakes for Cats

⅛ cup whole wheat flour

3 tablespoons powdered milk

½ teaspoon baking soda

¼ teaspoon baking powder

¼ cup light brown sugar, firmly
  packed

¼ cup vegetable oil

1 large egg

2 medium carrots, finely grated
  (about 1 cup)

2 teaspoons chopped fresh parsley

¼ cup Lemon Icing (page 358)

½ cup alfalfa sprouts

Crazy about both cakes and cats? If you're trying to get your cat into healthy eating, these energy-rich carrot cupcakes are just right—the grassy sprouts are simply the "icing" on the cake.

1. Preheat the oven to 350°F. Butter and flour 12 mini muffin cups.

2. To make the cupcakes, combine the flour, powdered milk, baking soda, and baking powder in a bowl and set aside.

3. Mix the sugar, oil, and egg with a wooden spoon until blended. Stir in the carrots and parsley. Gradually add the flour mixture until combined.

4. Pour the batter into the prepared pan and bake for 15–20 minutes, or until a tester inserted in the center comes out clean. Let cool in the pan for 5 minutes, then transfer to a rack to cool completely.

5. Spoon the lemon icing on the tops of the cakes and top with alfalfa sprouts.

Special-Occasion Cakes

WEDDING CAKES

When planning what might turn out to be the biggest party of their lives—their wedding—couples put tremendous thought into the type of cake to serve at the celebration. In this section, I have included recipes to fit every couple's style. Traditionalists might choose the classic tiered wedding cake decorated with a 1960s-style lovebird theme; couples looking for a more modern alternative might choose cupcakes; and those looking for the best of both worlds might opt for miniature tiered cakes. For a favor that fits the theme, consider giving individual portions of cake packaged in a decorative box.

Miniature Tiered Wedding Cakes

Makes about 15 cups batter, enough for 6 miniature cakes

If you believe that everything is cuter, better, and easier in miniature, you'll want to take this approach to wedding cakes, too. Although these tiny tiers can be made with any type of cake, I chose a simple recipe in wedding-gown white. The batter can be baked in small pans of graduated sizes, in muffin tins in a variety of cup sizes, or in a large sheet pan from which the tiers can be cut, as I suggest in this recipe.

5¼ cups cake flour

2½ tablespoons baking powder

1 teaspoon salt

1 pound (4 sticks) unsalted butter, at room temperature

3¼ cups granulated sugar

1 tablespoon vanilla extract

2¼ cups whole milk

14 large egg whites

⅓ teaspoon cream of tartar

2 cups Chocolate Frosting (page 351)

8 cups Vanilla Frosting (page 357)

Blue, orange, pink, yellow, and green food coloring

1. Preheat the oven to 350°F. Butter and flour two 9 x 13-inch pans.

2. Combine the flour, baking powder, and salt in a mixing bowl.

3. Beat the butter and sugar in a large mixing bowl with an electric mixer on medium speed until fluffy. Beat in the vanilla. Gradually add the flour mixture, alternating with the milk, on low speed until blended.

4. In a clean bowl with clean beaters, beat the egg whites and cream of tartar until soft peaks form. Gently fold the egg whites into the batter with a rubber spatula.

5. Spread the batter in the pans and bake for 25–30 minutes, or until a tester inserted in the center comes out clean. Cool in the pans for 10 minutes, then transfer to a rack to cool completely.

6. Cut the cakes into the desired shapes and sizes, using a serrated knife to cut squares or rectangles and cookie cutters or biscuit cutters to make circles. Apply a very thin layer (a "crumb coat") of vanilla or chocolate frosting as desired. Transfer to serving plates and refrigerate for 1 hour.

7. Divide the remaining vanilla frosting into two batches. Leave one batch white and divide the other batch among five bowls. Color each with a different food coloring. Once the thin coating of frosting has hardened, frost, assemble, and decorate the cakes per the instructions below.

To make the orange flower cake: Cut the cake into 4-inch and 2¾-inch circles; level the tops so that the layers are 2 inches high. Frost with vanilla frosting. Using orange frosting and a pastry bag fitted with a petal-shaped tip, pipe roses on the top of the cake. Using the same bag fitted with a small flower-shaped tip, pipe small orange flowers around the sides of the cake. Using white frosting and a small round tip, pipe dots around the bottom layer of cake, and use yellow frosting to pipe small dots in the centers of the flowers. Using green frosting and a small round tip, pipe leaves around the roses and vines connecting the flowers on the sides of the cake.

To make the striped cake: Cut the cake into squares. Make the bottom tier 3¼ inches x 2 inches high, the center tier 2¼ inches x 1 inch high, and the top tier a 1-inch cube. Cover with vanilla frosting. Using orange frosting and a pastry bag fitted with a small round tip, pipe stripes on the large and small tiers, overlapping each other to create a checkerboard. Using blue frosting and a small round tip, pipe stripes in the same pattern on the middle tier. Assemble the cake and, using a small round tip, pipe orange dots on the base of the large tier and a blue star on the top.

To make the chocolate and white tiered cake: Cut the cake into rectangles. Make the bottom layer 4 x 3 x 2 inches, the middle layer 2½ x 2 x 2 inches, and the top layer a 1-inch cube. Frost the top and bottom tiers with chocolate frosting and the middle tier with vanilla frosting. Assemble the cake. Using pink frosting and a pastry bag fitted with a small round tip, pipe dots around the top border of the bottom layer and on top of the cake. Change to a small flower-shaped tip and pipe a pink flower in the center. Using green frosting and a petal-shaped tip, add leaves to the flower. Using yellow frosting and a small round tip, pipe dots around the bottom and top edges of the middle tier.

To make the white and blue cake: Cut the cake into three circles, all 1 inch high. Make the bottom tier 4 inches in diameter, the middle layer 2¾ inches in diameter, and the top layer 2 inches in diameter. Frost the sides of each layer with vanilla frosting, using an icing spatula to create a wavy texture. Assemble the cake. Using blue frosting and a pastry bag fitted with a small star-shaped tip, pipe shells around the borders for each layer. Using a petal-shaped tip, pipe a blue rose on top. Using green frosting and a petal-shaped tip, add green leaves to the rose.

To make the white, blue, and chocolate cake: Cut the cake into squares. Make the bottom tier 3½ inches x 1 inch high, the center tier 2 inches x 1 inch high, and the top tier 1 inch x ¾ inch high. Frost the bottom layer with white frosting, the middle layer with blue frosting, and the top layer with chocolate frosting. Assemble the cake. Using pink frosting and a pastry bag fitted with a star-shaped tip, pipe shells on the top and bottom edges of the bottom layer and on the top edge of the top layer. Using yellow frosting and a round tip, pipe dots on the top edge of the middle layer. Using white frosting and a petal-shaped tip, pipe a rose on top. Using green frosting and a petal-shaped tip, add leaves to the base of the rose.

Wedding Cupcakes

Makes 36 medium cupcakes, 1 large cupcake, and 16 mini cupcakes

We all know by now that weddings are one of the best times to show off your cupcake-making skills. These cupcakes are much easier to make than a tiered wedding cake covered with fondant. These include one extra-large cupcake for the bride and groom (including the topper), medium cupcakes for most guests, and the miniature cupcakes for the flower girls and ring bearers.

1. Preheat the oven to 350°F. Line 16 medium muffin cups, 6 mini muffin cups, and 1 large muffin cup (or a 4-inch round pan) with paper or foil liners. Divide the batter among the liners and bake the mini cupcakes for 13–16 minutes, the medium for 20–25 minutes, and the large for 30–35 minutes, or until a tester inserted in the center comes out clean. Transfer to a rack to cool completely.

2. Divide the fondant into two large batches and one small batch. Color the small batch peach, and one large batch green, and leave the other large batch white.

To make rock candy cupcakes: Dust a work surface with confectioners' sugar. Roll out the white fondant to 1/16 inch thick. Cut circles large enough to top the cupcakes you wish to decorate. Attach the fondant to the cupcakes with royal icing. Pipe additional royal icing around the edges. Attach the rock candy to the center with royal icing.

To make embossed cupcakes: Dust a work surface with confectioners' sugar. Roll out the white fondant to 1/8 inch thick. Dust rubber stamps (such as dots, flowers, and other patterns) with confectioners' sugar and gently press them into the fondant, taking care not to press all the way through. Cut the fondant into circles large enough to top the cupcakes you wish to decorate. Attach the fondant to the cupcakes with royal icing. Pipe additional royal icing around the edges.

---

15 cups Miniature Tiered Wedding Cake batter (page 192)

4 cups Fondant (page 353)

Green and peach or orange food coloring

3½ cups Royal Icing (page 355)

Rock candy

To make rose cupcakes: Dust a work surface with confectioners' sugar. Roll out the white fondant to ¹⁄₁₆ inch thick. Cut the fondant into circles large enough to top the cupcakes you wish to decorate. Attach the fondant to the cupcakes with royal icing. Pipe additional royal icing around the edges. If necessary, dust the work surface with more confectioners' sugar. To make the roses, form a ¼-inch ball of the peach fondant into a cone shape—one cone for each of the cupcakes you want to decorate. You will use this core to support the rose petals. Roll the remaining peach fondant into tiny balls, one for each petal of the rose. Flatten the balls into petal shapes, slightly thicker at one end. Starting at the wide end of the cone, wrap a petal around the cone, with the thicker end on the bottom, and press it in. Use your fingers to curl the ends of the petal outward. Overlap a second petal onto the first petal. Repeat with 3–4 additional petals. Then roll out the green fondant to ¹⁄₁₆ inch thick. Use a utility knife to cut out leaf shapes, then use a toothpick to draw veins on the leaves. With royal icing, attach two leaves to each rose and then attach the roses to cupcakes. Pipe around the edges with royal icing.

To make the flower cupcakes: Dust a work surface with confectioners' sugar. Roll out the white fondant to ¹⁄₁₆ inch thick. Emboss lines in the fondant with an embossing tool or the back of a knife. Cut the fondant into circles large enough to top the cupcakes you wish to decorate. Attach the fondant to the cupcakes with royal icing. Using a pastry bag fitted with a shell tip, pipe additional royal icing around the edges. Cut flower petals out of the peach fondant and the centers out of the white fondant, using flower-shaped cutters in graduated sizes. Attach with royal icing.

To make basketweave cupcakes: Dust your work surface with confectioners' sugar. For each cupcake you wish to decorate, roll out the two colors of fondant to ⅛ inch thick. Cut each color into eight strips about the same length as the diameter of the cupcake you are decorating. Lay out one color of strips parallel to each other, with ⅛ inch between each strip, then weave the second color of strips perpendicular to, and in and out of, the first set of strips. Trim the basketweave into a circle with a cookie cutter the size of the cupcake. Attach the fondant to the cupcake with royal icing. Pipe additional royal icing around the edges.

To make the polka-dot cupcakes: Dust a work surface with confectioners' sugar. Roll out green and white fondant to ⅛ inch thick. Cut the fondant with circular cutters of varying sizes and place the white circles in the green fondant voids and the green circles in the white fondant voids. Roll the polka-dot fondant again to press the colors together without distorting the circles. Cut the fondant with a circular cutter large enough to top the cupcake. Attach to the cupcake with royal icing. Pipe additional royal icing around the edges.

To make the striped cupcakes: Dust a work surface with confectioners' sugar. Roll out green and white fondant to ⅛ inch thick. Cut the fondant into vertical stripes with a utility knife; the stripes can be straight or curvy. Place the white stripes in between the green stripes and the green stripes in between the white stripes. Roll the striped fondant again to press the colors together without distorting them. Cut the fondant with a circular cutter large enough to top the cupcake. Attach to the cupcake with royal icing.

Tiered Wedding Cake

Makes one seven-tiered cake

58½ cups cake batter (choose from among the varieties listed on page 198)

12 cups Vanilla Buttercream (page 356)

Blue, green, and pink food coloring

Edible silver-plated leaves or green fondant leaves (page 353)

Inspired by a vintage lovebird cake topper and the pastel colors of Jordan almonds, this retro-style cake was designed in honor of everybody who loves the pop culture of the 1960s. I couldn't decide whether to make this cake round or square, so I chose a rounded square. Whichever shape you choose, remember that a cake this tall needs the support of the wooden dowels embedded inside.

Rather than transporting this finished tiered cake to a wedding, I strongly recommend that you do as many professionals do: assemble the cake at the reception location instead. Insert the dowels, crumb-coat the cake, and prepare your labor-intensive decorations at home. (See page 62 for tips on traveling.) Then, when your crumb coat has hardened, take your cake to the wedding venue and add the remaining frosting and decorative details on-site.

Whether you choose to make all seven layers the same flavor or each layer different, be sure to use batter from one of the very dense cakes in this book (see page 198 for recommendations). I chose buttercream frosting for simplicity, although you may use

Great Cakes for Tiering

- Chocolate Cherry Fruitcake (page 342)
- Carrot Cake (page 176)
- Chocolate Chip Sour Cream Cake (page 80)
- Quinceañera Cake (page 160)
- Honey Almond Cake (page 313)
- Pine Nut–Basil Cake (page 230)
- Espresso Cake (page 264)
- Pumpkin Rum Cake (page 322)

fondant and marzipan if you're looking for an additional challenge.

This cake serves between 50 and 65 people, depending on the size of the slices.

1. Bake the cake batter in square pans, using the amounts and times on page 199. Cool the cakes completely, according to the directions in whatever recipe you use.

2. Level the cooled cakes with a serrated knife to 2-inch (or identical) heights, so that the tops do not form a dome. Using the cake pans as templates, cut bases out of corrugated cardboard with a utility knife, making one rounded-square base for each tier. Place each cake on its corresponding board. Cut 1-inch-diameter dowels into 2-inch lengths (or the length of the height of the cakes) and insert the dowels 1½ inches from the corners of each cake.

3. Divide the vanilla buttercream between two bowls, one containing ⅔ of the frosting and the second containing ⅓ of the frosting. Cover the smaller batch until ready to use. Using a total amount equivalent to about ⅓ of the frosting from the larger batch, thinly coat each cake with a layer of frosting. Cover the remaining frosting until ready to use. Chill the cakes for 1 hour.

4. Once chilled, frost the cakes with the remaining frosting from the larger batch and stack them, centering the layers on top of one another and pressing each layer down so that the dowels support the tier above them. Smooth out the frosting once the tiers are completely assembled.

5. Using small and large flower-shaped and circular cookie cutters, press the outlines of flower shapes into the sides of the second, fourth, and sixth tiers and circle shapes into the sides of the first, third, fifth, and seventh tiers.

6. Divide the small batch of frosting into 4 bowls. Leave one batch white and color the others pink, blue, and green. Add the white frosting to a pastry bag fitted with a medium round tip, the pink frosting to a pastry bag fitted with a medium petal-shaped tip, and the green frosting to a pastry bag fitted with a small round tip. Divide the blue frosting into two pastry bags, one fitted with a small petal-shaped tip and one fitted with a small writing tip.

7. Using a skewer, draw lines in the frosting next to the circles in the first, third, fifth, and seventh tiers. Add silver leaves to some of the flowers and pipe pink frosting inside the outline of the petals, working from the center outward. Using the bag fitted with the small petal-shaped tip, pipe blue flowers from the center outward. Pipe green spirals to form the centers of all the flowers. Using the pastry bag with the small round tip, pipe vertical blue stripes and blue rings into their respective outlines. Then pipe the green rings. Pipe the white dot borders on the top and bottom of the tiers that have stripes and circles. Add a topper.

8. After the cake-cutting ritual, take the cake out of sight. Remove each layer by lifting its cardboard tier, and remove the dowels. Cut the cake in squares and serve.

Pan Sizes and Baking Times for Tiered Wedding Cake

You will need one square pan in each size, and they should each be two inches high.

PAN SIZE	AMOUNT OF BATTER PER PAN	BAKING TIME
12 inches	14 cups	40–45 minutes
10 inches	12 cups	35–40 minutes
9 inches	10 cups	35–40 minutes
8 inches	8 cups	35–40 minutes
6 inches	6 cups	25–30 minutes
5 inches	5 cups	25–30 minutes
4 inches	3½ cups	20–25 minutes

Wedding Cake Favors

Makes eight 3½–4-inch cakes

Many couples save the top tier of their wedding cake to eat on their first anniversary. These small cakes, packaged in boxes and given as favors for guests to take home and eat or freeze, allow the couple's family and friends to share in this tradition. The cakes are made from fruitcake batter because it's sturdy enough to withstand the journey home from the reception, and with fondant and royal icing because those substances won't smudge or smear when the cakes are placed into and removed from their boxes. A tip: purchase the boxes first, then make the cakes slightly smaller than their dimensions.

10 cups Chocolate Cherry Fruitcake batter (page 342)
Food coloring (in the colors of the
wedding)
6 cups Fondant (page 353)
3½ cups Royal Icing (page 355)
Jordan almonds for garnish

1. Bake the fruitcake batter in 3½–4-inch round, square, or rectangular pans. Cool for 10 minutes in pans, then transfer to a rack to cool completely. If necessary, level the cakes so they are slightly shorter than the height of the boxes, and trim the sides to fit.

2. Color the fondant and royal icing in the wedding colors. Frost the top and sides of each cake with royal icing.

3. Measure the height and top of the cakes, then roll out the fondant to ¹⁄₁₆ inch thick. Cut fondant sheets in a size big enough to drape over each cake (see page 54). Smooth the fondant over each cake and cut off any excess at the bottom of the cakes.

4. Pipe patterns or flowers and borders onto each cake with royal icing. Secure the Jordan almonds to the cakes with icing. Let harden, then place each cake in a box.

Groom's Cake

Makes about 11 cups batter, enough for one 10 x 10-inch square cake

A Southern tradition, the groom's cake is made by the bride for her intended on or right before the big day. Groom's cakes are typically chocolate with chocolate frosting, although that's usually the only thing that remains constant. Each bride covers her groom's cake with personalized images, representing his favorite hobbies, sports teams, or alma mater. Whether your wedding day is coming soon or it's years in the past, make this cake to show your creativity to—and your love for—your main man.

1. Preheat the oven to 350°F. Butter and flour a 10 x 10-inch square pan.

2. Melt the chocolate in a double boiler and set aside to cool.

Cake Toppers

Cake toppers have a place on all kinds of cakes, not just wedding cakes. Sculptural ornaments like Kewpie dolls, jeweled monograms, Buddha figures, and Sexy Sue dolls adorn cakes for every occasion. There are fairy-tale enchanted castles for new-home celebrations and macho men for bachelorette parties. There are leprechaun toppers for Saint Patrick's Day and Stars of David for bar mitzvahs. The double happiness symbol adorns Chinese wedding cakes, and in Mexico, a skull-and-crossbones topper decorates a cake made in honor of long-gone ancestors.

Cake toppers are nonedible keepsakes that last much longer than the cake itself. They function as three-dimensional narrative elements that personalize the cake and reflect the theme of the party or event. Frosting, fondant, and marzipan are sometimes sculpted to add to the scene. Cake toppers can be serious—like the miniature bride and groom standing proudly on a buttercream staircase—or humorous, like a group of plastic firemen putting out the lit candles at a seventieth birthday party.

Queen Victoria's marriage to Prince Albert in 1840 began the evolution of the wedding cake topper as one of the most recognizable symbols of matrimony. The royal couple's three-hundred-pound, nine-foot-wide wedding cake was topped with an ice sculpture of Britannia surrounded by cupids staring down at the couple, along with two turtledoves and a dog. At this time, pastry chefs were in major competition with each other to produce the most elaborate special-occasion desserts, so you can imagine the thought that went into the queen's wedding cake. Fruitcake was the cake of choice for weddings, and this dense cake was perfect for supporting ornaments. Anything Queen Victoria did caught on fast, and over the next eighty years, ornamental sculptures of cupids, doves, hearts, gold rings, horseshoes, and lovebirds began to appear on the tops of wedding cakes as harbingers of good luck.

In the 1920s, Sears devoted an entire section of its catalog to bride-and-groom cake toppers, which created a mass-market trend. During the following decade, it was rare to see a cake anywhere in America that wasn't adorned with a topper, and other cultures were soon to follow. The cutesy Kewpie doll was a well-loved character that commonly topped cakes during this time. Brides and grooms in 1930s toppers wore contemporary art deco fashions; in 1940s toppers, wartime grooms wore their uniforms, and in 1950s toppers—my personal favorites—brides sported bouffant hairdos and puffy skirts.

Throughout the twentieth century, the craze for cake toppers expanded to embrace other occasions: clowns, balloons, animals, sports teams, astronauts, and favorite characters like Minnie Mouse and Spider-Man for kids' birthdays; hobbies and career icons (like the scales of Justice and the caduceus) for adults. Some toppers depict shoppers with a bag full of gifts; you can also buy toppers in the likenesses of fishermen, golfers, skiers, police badges, computers, and cell phones. There are crosses for christenings; planes, trains, and cars for bon voyage cakes; and, yes, Viking warriors just for fun.

Today, Indian and Korean cake toppers feature couples in full traditional dress, even though their real-life counterparts wear contemporary fashions. Brides and grooms can be purchased separately to reflect differences in race, weight, height, and hair color. Gay and lesbian wedding cake toppers are also available, along with pregnant brides, geeky grooms, and couples with babies and kids. A couple can even send their photos to artists who will create custom cake toppers in their own likeness—

whether realistic or in caricature—or they can opt to have a cake topper that depicts their pets or their favorite celebrities. The wedding cake topper is a matter of choice: some people love them, and some people don't. For those who do, there is a huge selection available.

Some of my favorites include:

- Sugared fresh roses
- A small bowl of candy
- Miniature stacked cakes tied with a bow to look like presents
- A marzipan horseshoe
- A candy wreath
- A large bow
- Doves
- Wedding bells

3 ounces semisweet chocolate

2 cups all-purpose flour

1 cup Dutch-process cocoa powder

½ teaspoon baking powder

½ teaspoon salt

¾ pound (3 sticks) unsalted butter, at room temperature

2½ cups granulated sugar

½ cup firmly packed light brown sugar

5 large eggs

2 teaspoons vanilla extract

1¼ cups buttermilk

5 cups Chocolate Frosting (page 351)

3 cups Vanilla Frosting (page 357)

Food coloring

3. Combine the flour, cocoa powder, baking powder, and salt in a mixing bowl.

4. Beat the butter and both sugars in a large mixing bowl with an electric mixer on medium speed until blended. Add the eggs one at a time, beating well after each addition. Beat in the vanilla.

5. Gradually add the flour, alternating with the buttermilk, on low speed until blended.

6. Pour the batter into the pan and bake for 35–40 minutes, or until a tester inserted in the center comes out clean. Let cool in the pan for 10 minutes, then transfer to a rack to cool completely.

7. Place the cake on a serving plate and frost with chocolate frosting. Color the vanilla frosting with the groom's favorite colors and decorate the cake with images of his favorite hobbies.

CAKES FOR BABY CELEBRATIONS

The foods we eat as children have tremendous power over the psyche, and cakes are no exception. As we grow, these treats become touchstones for nostalgic good feelings, which is why we want to create good memories with beautiful cakes whenever we have the chance—especially for the youngest among us—and why retro-style cakes are especially suitable for celebrations involving new babies. From an amusing take on a Twinkie to angel food cakes that welcome a little angel; from cream-filled cupcakes to candy cakes for the sweetest of the sweet, each cake in this collection is an indulgence worthy of your next baby shower, christening, or party for a new arrival.

Chocolate Fried Twinkies

Makes 6 cakes

6 Twinkies
3 cups plus 1 teaspoon vegetable oil
1 cup all-purpose flour
½ cup unsweetened cocoa powder
1 teaspoon baking powder
½ teaspoon salt
1 cup whole milk
1 teaspoon vanilla extract
2 tablespoons cider vinegar
Confectioners' sugar for dusting

I think of Twinkies as being designed and scientifically engineered with a sense of humor—an American snack staple with a reputation for kitsch. But whether they are eaten straight from the package as an everyday treat, deep-fried and served on a stick at a state fair, or lavishly frosted—even with edible gold leaf!—and stacked to form a wedding cake, Twinkies are sure to make guests smile.

1. Freeze the Twinkies for 3 hours.

2. Heat 3 cups of vegetable oil in a large, deep saucepan over low heat until it reaches 325°F. Test the oil by throwing in a small cube of bread; the oil is ready when the bread sizzles and browns. Remove the bread cube.

3. Combine ¾ cup of the flour, the cocoa powder, baking powder, and salt in a large mixing bowl.

4. Beat the milk, vanilla, vinegar, and 1 teaspoon oil in a medium mixing bowl with an electric mixer on medium speed. Add to the flour mixture and beat on low speed until smooth.

5. Roll the Twinkies in the remaining flour and coat with batter, letting the excess drip back into the bowl.

Opposite top left: Mini "Popcorn" Cakes; bottom left: Fried Twinkies; right: Cream-Filled Cupcakes.

Carefully slide the Twinkies into the oil and fry on all sides until golden. Transfer to a plate lined with paper towels. Cool for 5 minutes, then dust with confectioners' sugar. Serve within 2 hours.

Variations

Original Fried Twinkies: Omit the cocoa powder and increase the flour to 1½ cups.

Chocolate Chili Fried Twinkies: Add ⅛ teaspoon chili powder to the flour mixture.

Golden Twinkie Tower: Omit everything but the Twinkies. After freezing, frost them with vanilla frosting and top with gold luster dust and small tiny pieces of edible gold leaf. Stack into a tower.

Mini "Popcorn" Cakes

Makes about 6 cups batter, enough for 24 miniature cupcakes

For a retro-inspired presentation, bake these bite-size corn cakes in white or yellow paper liners and pile them in a popcorn box to serve. They're so tasty, you can't stop (and why would you want to?) at just one.

1 cup cornmeal
⅔ cup all-purpose flour
1 teaspoon salt
¼ cup granulated sugar
1½ teaspoons baking powder
¼ teaspoon baking soda
1½ cups whole milk
2 large eggs
1½ tablespoons unsalted butter, melted and cooled

1. Preheat the oven to 375°F. Line 24 mini muffin cups with yellow or white paper liners.

2. Combine the cornmeal, flour, salt, sugar, baking powder, and baking soda in a mixing bowl.

3. Combine the milk, eggs, and butter in a large mixing bowl with an electric mixer on medium speed. Gradually add the cornmeal mixture and blend on low speed.

4. Pour the batter into the liners and bake for 12–16 minutes, or until golden and a tester in the center comes out clean. Transfer to a rack to cool.

4 cups all-purpose flour

2 teaspoons baking powder

1 teaspoon salt

2 cups firmly packed light brown
sugar

2 cups whole milk

6 large egg yolks

10 ounces unsweetened chocolate,
chopped

1 cup (2 sticks) unsalted butter, at
room temperature

2 cups granulated sugar

½ cup heavy cream

2 teaspoons vanilla extract

6 large eggs, seperated

3½ cups Pastry Cream (page 358)

3 cups Vanilla Frosting (page
357)

Blue food coloring

3 ounces semisweet chocolate,
melted

Cream-Filled Cupcakes

Makes 16 cups batter, enough for 20–24 large cupcakes

Cupcakes are amazing enough by themselves, but cupcakes with a hidden surprise filling are the best! These were inspired by my favorite store-bought cream-filled cupcakes. Enjoy them with a tall glass of milk.

1. Preheat the oven to 350°F. Line 20–24 large muffin cups with paper or foil liners.

2. Combine the flour, baking powder, and salt in a mixing bowl.

3. Combine the brown sugar, ½ cup of the milk, and 3 egg yolks in another mixing bowl.

4. Melt the unsweetened chocolate in a double boiler. Add the brown sugar mixture, stirring constantly, until shiny and thick. Set aside to cool.

5. Beat the butter and granulated sugar in a large mixing bowl with an electric mixer on medium speed until creamy. Add the 3 remaining egg yolks, beating until combined. Pour in the cooled chocolate mixture and beat until smooth. Add the heavy cream, remaining ½ cup milk, and vanilla and beat until combined. Gradually add the flour mixture on low speed until blended.

6. In a clean bowl with clean beaters, beat the egg whites until soft peaks form. Gently fold the egg whites into the batter with a rubber spatula.

7. Fill the liners three-fourths full with batter and bake for 25–30 minutes, or until a tester inserted in the center comes out clean. Cool in the pans.

8. When the cupcakes have cooled, cut a circle about 1½ inches around and about 1 inch deep out of the center of each cake. Cut ¼ inch off the top of the removed piece and reserve. Discard the remainder of the removed piece. Pipe the pastry cream into the hole and

replace the ¼-inch top. Color the vanilla frosting light blue, and use it to frost the tops of the cupcakes. Using a pastry bag fitted with a large round tip, pipe a line of melted chocolate down the center of each cake.

Angel Food Cake

Makes 7 cups, enough for one 9-inch cake

Celebrating a "little angel" with angel food cake at a baby shower, christening, or baby event is symbolic of the infant's future good fortune. You can make angel food cakes in both the plain and chocolate varieties. Or welcome a baby who has a mischievous personality with Devil's Food Cake (page 76). Here, I made two cakes, one plain and one chocolate, and baked them in pans of slightly different sizes so that I could create a unique construction. To serve, I alternated the slices.

1 cup cake flour
1½ cups granulated sugar
12 large egg whites
1½ teaspoons cream of tartar
¼ teaspoon salt
1½ teaspoons vanilla extract
Unsweetened cocoa powder for dusting

1. Preheat the oven to 375°F. Butter and flour a 9-inch angel food tube pan.

2. Combine the flour and ¾ cup of the sugar in a mixing bowl.

3. Beat the egg whites, cream of tartar, salt, and vanilla in a large mixing bowl with an electric mixer on medium speed until soft peaks form. Gradually add the remaining ¾ cup sugar, continuing to beat until stiff peaks form.

4. Dust the flour mixture over the egg whites and fold it in using a rubber spatula, being careful not to deflate the batter.

5. Pour the batter into the pan, filling it three-fourths full. Bake for 45–55 minutes, or until the cake springs back when touched. Invert the cake over a cooling rack and cool completely. If it has not dropped from the pan by the time it is cool, gently run a knife around the inside of the pan to loosen.

6. Slice the cake and sift cocoa powder over the top, using a stencil to create your design.

Variations

Chocolate Angel Food Cake: Add ¼ cup unsweetened cocoa powder to the dry ingredients. Sift confectioners' sugar over the top of the cooled cake, using a stencil to create your design.

Marble Angel Food Cake: Before pouring the batter into the pan, divide it between two bowls. Add ¼ cup unsweetened cocoa powder to one bowl. Pour one of the batters into the pan and then the other batter on top of it, swirling with a knife to marbleize.

Candy Cakes

Makes about 8 cups batter, enough for nine 3-inch cakes

Candy and cake bring out nostalgic thoughts of childhood, plus they taste and look great together. The bright colors and playful shapes of candy are a fun way to decorate cake cubes. This cake is flavored with licorice, which is intensified by the apricot jam between the layers. If you are feeding those with simple palates, you can substitute Golden Yellow Cake batter (page 69) or the Devil's Food Cake batter (page 76). For a real attention-getter, present the cake cubes on a tiered cake stand.

3 cups all-purpose flour

2 teaspoons baking powder

½ teaspoon salt

½ pound (2 sticks) unsalted butter, at room temperature

2 cups granulated sugar

4 large eggs, separated

2 teaspoons licorice extract or anise extract

1 cup whole milk

1 cup apricot jam

5 cups Chocolate Frosting (page 351)

3 cups Vanilla Frosting (page 352)

Candy dots, candy hearts, jellied fruits, gummy candies, and licorice candies for garnish

1. Preheat the oven to 350°F. Butter and flour two 9 x 9-inch square pans.

2. Combine the flour, baking powder, and salt.

3. Cream the butter and sugar in a large mixing bowl with an electric mixer on medium speed until fluffy. Add the egg yolks one at a time, beating well until blended. Beat in the licorice or anise extract.

4. Gradually add the flour mixture, alternating with the milk, on low speed until blended.

5. In a clean bowl with clean beaters, beat the egg whites until stiff peaks form. Gently fold the egg whites into the batter with a rubber spatula.

6. Pour the batter into the pans and bake for 30–35 minutes, or until a tester inserted in the center comes

out clean. Cool in the pans for 10 minutes, then transfer to a rack to cool completely.

7. Place one cooled layer on a serving plate. Spread with the jam, then place the second layer on top. Cut into 3-inch cubes. Frost the cakes with an icing spatula and decorate with candy.

MOTHER'S DAY AND FATHER'S DAY CAKES

Mother's Day and Father's Day are occasions that give us the opportunity to show our appreciation for our parents, and what better way to do this than baking a cake? And, for simplicity, or for making a letter-shaped cake, isn't it lucky that "Mom" and "Dad" are only three letters each? For a simple but garden-fresh Mother's Day treat, try the chocolate rose roulade recipe. Mud cake is perfect for little bakers (under supervision), and the fried beer cakes use Dad's favorite drink as a leavener and flavoring.

Mom Cake

Makes three 10-inch cakes

36 cups Golden Yellow Cake batter (page 69)
2 cups Fondant (page 353)
9 cups Vanilla Buttercream (page 356)
Yellow, purple, pink, brown, blue, and green food coloring
3 cups sweetened flaked coconut

Cutting cakes into letters or numbers is one of my favorite ways to serve a large crowd. That way, instead of baking one large sheet cake, I can make several smaller and more manageable cakes and then cut them into shapes before decorating. The shapes can then be arranged so that they form a large, festive design—like this one, for example. Any mom would agree that this cake is a gift in itself—and it can also be cut so that it spells "Dad" for Father's Day. To shorten the prep time, leave the cakes whole, place them next to each other, pipe the letters in the center with frosting, and then add borders around the edges.

1. Preheat the oven to 350°F. Bake the cake batter in three 10 x 10-inch square pans. Cool in the pans for 10 minutes, then transfer to racks to cool completely.

2. Level the cakes with a sharp serrated knife, so that the tops do not form domes. Create letter templates out of paper and place them on top of the cakes. Cut out the letters around the template with the knife and place on individual serving plates.

3. Divide the buttercream into one large batch and two smaller batches. Color the large batch yellow and the smaller ones green and purple. Coat the cakes with a

very thin layer of yellow frosting, and place them in the refrigerator to harden for 1 hour.

4. Divide the fondant into 3 large balls and 3 small balls. Color the large balls with purple, pink, and green food coloring and 2 of the small balls with brown and blue food coloring. Leave one small ball white. Roll out the fondant one color at a time, starting with the purple and pink, to ⅛ inch thick. Using fondant cutters or a utility knife, cut out various sizes of flowers and dots. Wet the pieces and press them together. Press the flowers into the sides of a shallow bowl to form curves. Let set to harden. Roll out the green fondant to ¹⁄₁₆ inch and cut out leaf shapes with small fondant cutters or a utility knife. Press veins into the leaves with the back of a knife. Press the leaves into the sides of a shallow bowl to form curves. Roll out the brown fondant to ⅛ inch and cut out the branch, and the bird's beak and eyes. Texture the bark with a knife. Roll out the blue and white fondant balls to ⅛ inch. Cut out the body and breast of the bird. Wet the beak, eyes, and breast and press them into the bird. Let set to dry.

5. Frost the top and sides of each cake with yellow frosting. Cover the sides with coconut. Using green frosting and a pastry bag fitted with a medium round tip, pipe vines onto the cakes. Arrange the branch, bird, and some of the flowers and leaves on the cakes. Using purple frosting and a shell tip, pipe a scalloped border around the letters, then add the remaining leaves and flowers so they overlap the border.

Chocolate Rose Roulade

Makes one 15-inch rolled cake

Roses are a favorite treat for the deer who visit my garden, and, to tell you the truth, I eat roses, too. I especially love them paired with chocolate—just be sure to use roses that have not been treated with any pesticides or fertilizers. This is a really simple yet impressively pretty cake to make for Mom on Mother's Day.

Cake

8 cups Chocolate Sponge Roll
    batter (page 62)
1 teaspoon rose water

Chocolate Rosewater
Cream

2 cups heavy cream
½ teaspoon rose water
2½ tablespoons granulated sugar
2 tablespoons unsweetened cocoa
    powder

Garnish

2 tablespoons unsweetened cocoa
    powder
Petals from 1 small rose
5 small rosebuds
½ teaspoon pink crystal sugar

1. Make the cake batter according to the directions on page 82, replacing the vanilla with 1 teaspoon rose water and omitting the dark chocolate stripes on top. Bake in a 10½ x 15-inch jelly-roll pan for 15–18 minutes. Transfer to a rack to cool.

2. To make the rosewater cream, beat the cream, rose water, sugar, and cocoa powder in a large mixing bowl until stiff.

3. Once the cake has cooled, lay it on a clean kitchen towel and spread with a thin layer of the cream, leaving a ¼-inch border around the edges. Working from the long side, tightly roll the cake away from you. Place it on a plate, seam side down. Dust with cocoa powder, then garnish with rose petals, rosebuds, and pink crystal sugar.

Mississippi Mud Cake

Makes about 7 cups batter, enough for one 8 x 12-inch two-layer cake

Named after the muddy banks of the Mississippi River, this crumbly sheet cake is ideal for kids to make for parents on Mother's or Father's Day. You'll find dozens of recipes for mud cake, but the one thing they all have in common is that the finished cake is messy—in fact, the messier the better! This cake boasts two layers—chocolate and vanilla—as well as walnuts, vanilla buttercream, and marshmallow filling. For an extra kick, dip marshmallows in milk chocolate to serve on the side. The fillings and frostings can be customized with Mom's or Dad's favorites.

1. Preheat the oven to 350°F. Butter and flour two 8 x 12-inch pans.

2. Combine the flour, baking powder, and salt in a mixing bowl.

3. Combine the butter, sugar, milk, and corn syrup in a saucepan over low heat. Cook, stirring, until the butter melts and the sugar dissolves. Remove from heat, stir in the vanilla, and set aside to cool.

Cake

3 cups all-purpose flour

1 tablespoon baking powder

⅛ teaspoon salt

¾ cup (1½ sticks) unsalted butter

1½ cups firmly packed light brown
  sugar

½ cup whole milk

⅓ cup light corn syrup

1 teaspoon vanilla extract

3 large eggs

⅓ cup unsweetened cocoa powder

3 ounces semisweet chocolate,
  melted

½ cup marshmallow cream

2¼ cups Vanilla Buttercream
  (page 356)

1½ cups walnut halves

Chocolate Icing

3 ounces semisweet chocolate

1 tablespoon unsalted butter

¼ cup hot water

1 cup confectioners' sugar

4. Gradually add the flour to the cooled butter mixture. Beat in the eggs.

5. Pour one-third of the batter into one of the pans. Stir the cocoa powder into the remaining batter and pour into the second pan. Bake the vanilla cake for 20–25 minutes and the cocoa cake for 30–35 minutes, or until a tester inserted into the center of each comes out clean. Cool in the pans for 10 minutes, then transfer to a rack to cool completely.

6. Cut the chocolate cake in half horizontally with a serrated knife. Place the bottom layer on a piece of parchment paper or over a rack. Spread with the marshmallow cream, then with about three-fourths of the vanilla buttercream. Place the vanilla cake on top and spread with the remaining buttercream. Place the second chocolate layer on top of the buttercream. Arrange the walnut halves on the top.

7. To make the icing, combine the chocolate, butter, and hot water in the top of a double boiler over low heat, stirring until melted and smooth. Stir in the confectioners' sugar until the icing reaches a pouring consistency. Pour the icing over the cake, allowing it to drip over the sides. Cut into squares to serve.

Variation

Crunchy Mud Cake: Add 2 cups crushed chocolate wafers in between the layers of the cake.

Fried Beer Cakes

Makes 12–16 cakes

Fried dough is what I call a fundamental foodstuff. These puffy bites of fried dough use beer—another fundamental foodstuff—as a leavener, which also adds to the tangy taste. Dads will love them for Father's Day. They're also ideal for Saint Patrick's Day or Super Bowl Sunday. Serve them in paper cones.

½ cup (1 stick) unsalted butter

1 cup amber beer

⅔ cup granulated sugar

1 teaspoon vanilla extract

4 large eggs

2¼ cups all-purpose flour

1 teaspoon baking powder

1 teaspoon ground cinnamon

¼ teaspoon salt

3 cups vegetable oil

2⅓ tablespoons Cinnamon Sugar
  (page 352)

1. Combine the butter, beer, and 3 tablespoons of the sugar in a saucepan over low heat. Bring to a boil and stir until the sugar is dissolved. Remove from the heat, stir in the vanilla, and set aside to cool in the pan. Once cool, add the eggs one at a time, beating well after each addition.

2. Combine the remaining sugar, flour, baking powder, cinnamon, and salt in a mixing bowl. Gradually add the flour mixture to the butter mixture, stirring until it forms a ball.

3. Heat the vegetable oil to 365°F in a wok or a large, deep saucepan; the oil is ready when ½ teaspoon of batter dropped in it browns and sizzles. Using a small ice cream scoop or two teaspoons, drop 4–6 scoops of batter into the oil. Fry for about 2–2½ minutes on each side, turning with tongs, until puffy and golden. Remove one cake from the pan and cut it open to see if the center has cooked. Adjust frying time accordingly. Use a slotted spoon to transfer to paper towels to drain.

4. Roll the cakes in cinnamon sugar while still warm and serve immediately.

Variations

Saint Paddy's Day Beer Cakes: Add 6 drops of green food coloring to the batter with the vanilla.

Fried Honey-Beer Cakes: Prepare with honey beer instead of amber beer, reduce the sugar to ½ cup, and add 2 tablespoons honey to the batter with the vanilla. Drizzle the cakes with additional honey instead of cinnamon sugar before serving.

GRADUATION CAKES

Graduation cakes are typically decorated with a mortarboard cake topper or a rolled diploma, or they may be cut into the shape of the honoree's year of graduation. School colors, team mascots, and decorations related to the graduate's chosen profession or field of study are also popular. My favorite graduation cakes are custom-made to reflect individual achievements—and the three cakes in this section make ideal "blank canvases" for personalization.

Diploma Cake

9 cups *White Cake batter (page 75)*

1¼ cups *Royal Icing (page 355)*

5 cups *Dark Chocolate Frosting (page 351)*

If you have some time to plan, try topping this cake with an edible icing photo transfer (see page 55) of the graduate or of the diploma—it's as classy as they come. For a class reunion, make several small cakes and decorate each with the diplomas of the attendees. Be sure to bake the cake in a pan that is 1½–2 inches larger on all sides than the dimensions of the photo transfer.

1. Scan the diploma, or take a photo of it, and scale the digital image to roughly 7 x 9 inches. Alternatively, take the original to a cake-decorating shop and have them do this for you.

2. Bake the cake batter in an 8 x 12-inch pan for 35–40 minutes, according to the instructions on page 75. Let cool in the pan for 15 minutes, then transfer to a rack to cool completely. Place the icing transfer in the freezer for 30 minutes to stiffen.

3. Place the cake on a serving plate and cover the top with royal icing. Before it hardens, peel the backing sheet from the icing transfer and place the diploma on top of the icing, pressing carefully to smooth. Allow the royal icing to set for 1–2 hours.

4. Frost around the diploma and the sides of the cake with half the chocolate frosting. Put the remaining frosting in a pastry bag with a shell-shaped tip and pipe a border around the diploma and the bottom of the cake.

Book Cakes

Makes 8 cups, enough for 24 small cakes

These cakes are ideal for a graduation party and easy to customize.

3 cups all-purpose flour

2 teaspoons baking powder

½ teaspoon salt

½ pound (2 sticks) unsalted butter, at room temperature

2 cups granulated sugar

4 large eggs, separated

2 teaspoons vanilla extract

1 cup whole milk

6 cups Vanilla Frosting (page 357)

Food coloring in school colors

1. Preheat the oven to 350°F. Butter and flour two 9 x 9-inch square pans.

2. Combine the flour, baking powder, and salt in a mixing bowl.

3. Cream the butter and sugar in a large mixing bowl with an electric mixer on medium speed until fluffy. Add the egg yolks one at a time, beating well until blended. Beat in the vanilla extract.

4. Gradually add the flour mixture, alternating with the milk, on low speed until blended.

5. In a clean bowl with clean beaters, beat the egg whites until stiff peaks form. Gently fold the egg whites into the batter with a rubber spatula.

6. Pour the batter into the pans and bake for 30–35 minutes, or until a tester inserted in the center comes out clean. Cool in the pans for 10 minutes, then transfer to a rack to cool completely.

7. Level the cakes with a knife and transfer to a work surface. Cut into assorted-size "books"—around 2 x 3 inches, 1 x 2 inches, and 2½ x 3 inches.

8. Divide the vanilla frosting into two batches. Use an icing spatula to apply one of the batches of frosting to three of the four sides of each cake. Create a grooved pattern in the frosting to represent the pages of the books. Color the second batch of vanilla frosting with the school colors. Reserve one-fourth of each color for piping. Frost the "spines" (i.e., the fourth side of each cake) and "covers" (i.e., the cake tops) with the remaining colored frosting. Place the reserved frosting into pastry bags fitted with small writing tips and use it to pipe borders onto the spines and covers, and to pipe messages or "titles" on the covers.

36 cups *Golden Yellow Cake batter (page 69)*

12 cups *Vanilla Buttercream (page 356)*

Food coloring in school colors

Sprinkles in one of the school colors

Class of Cake

Makes 36 cups, enough for four 8-inch cakes

This cake is especially striking when cut into the shape of your class year and decorated in school colors. It then becomes a blank slate for guests to decorate: just place a pastry bag filled with frosting next to it. To keep things simple, you can prepare this cake as one large sheet cake (in a 13 x 9-inch pan, using 14 cups of batter) and have people sign it in frosting.

1. Preheat the oven to 350°F. Pour the cake batter into four 8-inch square pans. Bake the cakes for 30–35 minutes. Cool in the pans for 10 minutes, then transfer to racks to cool completely.

2. Level the cakes with a sharp serrated knife, so that the tops do not form domes. Create number templates out of paper and place them on top of the cakes. Cut out the numbers around the template with the knife and place on individual serving plates.

3. Divide the buttercream into one large batch and two smaller batches. Color the large batch with one school color and the smaller batches with the other school color and another color of your choice. Place the frosting from the batch in the color of your choice in a pastry bag fitted with a small writing tip and save it for the party. Coat the cakes with a very thin layer of frosting from the larger batch, then place them in the refrigerator to harden for 1 hour.

4. To decorate, frost the top and sides of each cake with the remaining frosting from the larger batch. Cover the sides with sprinkles. Using the remaining smaller batch of frosting and a pastry bag fitted with a medium shell-shaped tip, pipe a scalloped border around the numbers.

5. At the party, place the pastry bag fitted with the writing tip next to the cake. Have all your guests "sign" the cake with messages.

Chapter 5

Party Cakes

BRUNCH CAKES

I often host brunch parties, because deer visit our hillside home in the mornings and our urban L.A. friends get a kick out of watching them. Besides, cake for breakfast can't be beat. It's a mainstay in many cultures, and in our house, too. Whether your taste runs to classic yeast-risen doughnuts or to loaves made with fresh flavors like blackberry, caramel walnut, or lemon and poppy seed, you'll find plenty of options in this chapter. But first, you're up for an early-morning walk on the wild side with a cake-and-eggs combination.

Cake and Eggs

Makes about 8 cups batter, enough for twelve 3½-inch cakes

Once you try cake and eggs, you might forget all about steak. Still, purists might find the cake-and-egg combination a little crazy, but that's the title of this book. These lemon-sesame corn cupcakes, topped with eggs and served with a couple of strips of bacon and some coffee, are a great way to start the day.

1. Preheat the oven to 350°F. Butter and flour 12 large muffin cups.

2. Combine the flour, cornmeal, baking soda, and salt in a mixing bowl.

Cake

2½ cups all-purpose flour

½ cup cornmeal

½ teaspoon baking soda

½ teaspoon salt

½ pound (2 sticks) unsalted butter,
    at room temperature

2 cups granulated sugar

4 large eggs

1 teaspoon grated lemon zest

1 tablespoon freshly squeezed
    lemon juice

2 tablespoons sesame seeds

1 cup whole milk

Topping

12 large eggs

3 tablespoons sesame seeds

⅛ teaspoon salt

⅛ teaspoon pepper

3. Cream the butter and sugar in a large mixing bowl with an electric mixer on medium speed until fluffy. Add the eggs one at a time, beating well after each addition. Beat in the lemon zest, lemon juice, and sesame seeds.

4. Gradually add the flour mixture, alternating with the milk, on low speed until blended.

5. Fill the muffin cups about one-third full with batter. Bake for 18–22 minutes, or until a tester inserted in the center comes out clean. Transfer to a rack to cool.

6. Cut each cake horizontally into two layers. Using a 3-inch round cutter, punch a hole out of the top layers. Reassemble the cakes and set on serving plates.

7. To make the topping, poach the eggs until done to taste. Using the same round cutter, cut each egg so that the whites are neatly trimmed, then place them in the holes cut out of the cakes. Top with sesame seeds, salt, and pepper.

Classic Raised Doughnuts

Makes about 18 doughnuts

Doughnuts are hot—literally! They are the latest culinary trend in America, and bakers everywhere are experimenting with new flavor combinations. This is my favorite doughnut recipe—it's easy to memorize, because it includes a half cup of almost everything—and it's a perfect starting place for bakers looking to play with mix-ins and decorations (see page 227). Instead of decorating the tops only, I like to give the sides of doughnuts the appreciation they deserve. Use square, round, and flower-shaped cookie cutters to customize the shapes. The playful abacus-inspired display will be a great hit at brunch.

1. Combine the yeast, water, and 1 teaspoon of the sugar in a small bowl. Let sit for 10 minutes, or until foamy.

3½ teaspoons active dry yeast

½ cup warm water

½ cup granulated sugar

½ cup (1 stick) unsalted butter, at room temperature

½ cup whole milk

2 large eggs

4½–6 cups all-purpose flour

3 cups vegetable oil for frying

3 cups Vanilla Frosting (page 357)

2½ cups Chocolate Frosting (page 351)

Crystal sugars, nonpareils, nuts, and sprinkles

2. Heat the butter, milk, and remaining sugar in a medium saucepan until the butter is melted and the sugar is dissolved. Cool for 3 minutes.

3. Transfer to a large bowl and beat in the eggs with an electric mixer on medium speed. Beat in the yeast mixture.

4. Add 4½ cups of flour and mix well on low speed. If the dough is sticky, continue to add flour, ½ cup at a time, stirring until smooth. Transfer to a floured work surface and knead until the dough is smooth and satiny, about 10 minutes. Place in a buttered bowl, cover loosely, and let sit for 75 minutes. Punch down the dough, cover again, and let rise for an additional hour, or until doubled in volume.

5. Roll out the dough in batches on a floured work surface to ¼ inch thick. Using doughnut cutters fitted with a 1-inch center, or using 4-inch, 3½-inch, and 2½-inch cookie cutters and a 1-inch cutter to cut the insides, cut out circles, squares, or flowers, making about 18 doughnuts. Reroll the scraps after cutting until all the dough is used. Cover lightly with plastic and let rise for an additional 30 minutes.

6. Heat the oil in a large, deep saucepan until it reaches 400°F. Test the heat by frying one doughnut until lightly browned on both sides. It will take about 60–90 seconds per side in the beginning and a little less time in later batches. Smaller doughnuts will also take less time to fry than larger doughnuts. Cut open the first doughnut to see if the center is cooked. Adjust the frying time accordingly and fry the doughnuts in batches. Drain on paper towels. Cool for 10 minutes before frosting.

7. Spread the doughnuts with frosting using an icing spatula, or pipe it on with a pastry bag, and then dust with sugars, nonpareils, nuts, and sprinkles, or choose your favorites from the list of mix-ins on page 227.

Doughnut Mix-Ins

Here are some suggestions for customizing your doughnuts with mix-ins or toppings. Choose up to ½ cup total and stir them into the dough after it reaches the desired consistency (chop large items into bite-size pieces)—or just sprinkle on top of the cooked doughnut. Experiment with combinations—the sky's the limit. My favorites all begin with *C*: cherries, cashews, coconut, and chocolate.

DRIED AND CANDIED FRUIT

Apple rings
Apricots
Banana chips
Candied cherries (red and green)
Candied ginger
Candied orange peel
Candied mixed fruit peel
Cranberries
Currants
Dates
Figs
Ginger slices
Guava
Mango
Papaya
Peaches
Pineapple
Prunes
Raisins (golden or dark)
Shredded or flaked sweetened
    coconut
Sour cherries
Toasted coconut (page 33)

FRESH FRUIT AND VEGETABLES

Apples
Apricots
Bananas
Bing cherries
Blueberries
Cranberries
Figs
Fruit cocktail
Kiwifruit
Mandarin oranges
Mangoes
Maraschino cherries
Papayas
Peaches
Pears
Pineapple
Sun-dried tomatoes
Black or green pitted olives

CANDY

Caramels
Carob-covered raisins
Chocolate chips or chunks
Chocolate-covered espresso beans
Chocolate-covered raisins
Chocolate sprinkles
Chopped candy bars
Colored sprinkles
Fruity cereal
Ground butterscotch candies
Ground citrus-flavored candies
Ground peppermint candies
Ground root beer candies
Marshmallows
Peanut brittle
Turkish delight
Yogurt-covered raisins

NUTS AND SEEDS

Almonds
Brazil nuts
Caraway seeds
Cashew butter
Cashews
Fennel seeds
Hazelnuts
Honey-roasted peanuts
Macadamia nuts
Peanut butter
Peanuts
Pecans
Pine nuts
Poppy seeds
Pumpkin seeds
Roasted chestnuts
Sesame seeds
Sunflower seeds
Walnuts

Lemon Poppy Loaves

Makes 8 cups, enough for seven 2½ x 4-inch loaves

2¾ cups all-purpose flour

½ teaspoon baking powder

½ teaspoon baking soda

½ teaspoon salt

½ pound (2 sticks) unsalted butter, at room temperature

2 cups granulated sugar

4 large eggs

1½ teaspoons vanilla extract

3 tablespoons freshly squeezed lemon juice

1 cup whole milk

¼ cup poppy seeds

1 drop yellow food coloring

¾ cup Lemon Icing (page 358)

Fill your brunch table with individual loaves baked fresh that morning, or prepare them the night before if you're on the go.

1. Preheat the oven to 350°F. Place 7 stiff paper liners (found online or at cake-decorating stores or restaurant supply stores), each about 2½ x 4 inches—or 7 mini loaf pans—on a baking sheet.

2. Combine the flour, baking powder, baking soda, and salt in a mixing bowl.

3. Beat the butter and sugar in a large mixing bowl with an electric mixer on medium speed until light and fluffy. Add the eggs one at a time, beating well after each addition. Beat in the vanilla and lemon juice.

4. Gradually add the flour mixture, alternating with the milk, on low speed until blended. Stir in the poppy seeds.

5. Divide the batter among the liners and bake for 30–35 minutes, or until a tester inserted in the center comes out clean. Cool in the liners on the baking sheet.

6. Stir the food coloring into the icing and place it in a pastry bag fitted with a small round tip. Pipe the icing over the cakes.

Variations

Caramel Walnut Loaves: Replace the lemon juice with 3 tablespoons pure maple syrup. Replace the poppy seeds with 1 cup chopped walnuts. Drizzle Caramel Glaze (page 350) on top of the cakes instead of the lemon icing.

Blackberry Loaves: Replace the poppy seeds with 1½ cups sliced fresh blackberries. Drizzle Vanilla Icing (page 358) on top of the cakes instead of the lemon icing.

Cream Cheese Filling

1 box (8 ounces) cream cheese, at
  room temperature
⅔ cup granulated sugar
2 large eggs

Cake

1 cup all-purpose flour
1½ teaspoons baking powder
½ teaspoon salt
½ cup (1 stick) unsalted butter, at
  room temperature
½ cup granulated sugar
3 large eggs
2 teaspoons vanilla extract
½ teaspoon almond extract
1 cup fresh or frozen thawed
  raspberries
1 cup sliced almonds

Topping

2 tablespoons confectioners' sugar
2½ cups Raspberry Sauce (page
  274)

Raspberry Cream Coffee Cake

Makes 7 cups, enough for one 10-inch cake

I often bake this coffee cake for brunch guests, and if there is any left,
I thoroughly enjoy it for breakfast the following day. Coffee cakes
can be prepared plain, but they often feature fruits or other goodies
mixed into the batter as well as fillings layered between the batter or
toppings added after baking. This recipe includes all three.

1. Preheat the oven to 375°F. Butter and flour a 10-inch
   springform pan.

2. To make the filling, combine the cream cheese, sugar,
   and eggs in a large mixing bowl with an electric mixer
   on medium speed. Set aside.

3. To make the cake, combine the flour, baking powder,
   and salt in a mixing bowl.

4. Beat the butter and sugar in a large mixing bowl with
   an electric mixer on medium speed until fluffy. Add the
   eggs one at a time, beating well after each addition. Beat
   in the vanilla and almond extracts.

5. Gradually add the flour mixture on low speed until just
   blended. Stir ¾ cup raspberries and ½ cup almonds into
   the batter.

6. Pour half the batter into the pan. Drop spoonfuls of
   the filling over the batter and swirl it in with a knife.
   Add the remaining batter, then top with the remaining
   raspberries and almonds.

7. Bake for 35–40 minutes, or until a knife inserted in the
   center comes out clean. Cool in the pan. Dust with
   confectioner's sugar before slicing. Spoon raspberry
   sauce on the serving plates or over the top of the slices.

Variations

Pear Coffee Cake: Replace the raspberries with chopped fresh pears
and the cream cheese filling with almond paste.

Apple Coffee Cake: Replace the raspberries with chopped apples. Add 1 teaspoon ground cinnamon, ½ teaspoon ground ginger, and ¼ teaspoon ground nutmeg to the flour mixture. Replace the cream cheese filling with Vanilla Custard (page 356).

Currant Coffee Cake: Replace the raspberries with fresh currants or ¾ cup dried currants. Add 1 teaspoon ground cardamom and ¼ teaspoon caraway seeds to the flour mixture. Replace the almonds with hazelnuts.

TEA PARTY CAKES

Afternoon tea, the late-afternoon meal enjoyed in much the world, features dainty delights and highbrow conversation. What I appreciate most about tea parties are the simple flavors and the pretty styling of the sweet or savory cakes. Don't miss indulging in the delicate sandwiches made with tea leaves, the savory pine nut–basil financiers, and the tropical flavors of the coconut banana cream cake. And you can always count on a cake from Wonderland to add some character to a tea party!

Pine Nut–Basil Financiers

Makes 6½ cups, enough for 18 small cakes

> Financiers are small French tea cakes that are commonly made with almond flour and baked in rectangular molds, resembling a block of gold. I play a bit of dress-up with the financier—my recipe is made with pine nuts and basil and baked in small oval tart pans. Invert the cakes when you serve them to show off the pine-nut studs.

1½ cups pine nuts
1½ cups all-purpose flour
1½ teaspoons baking powder
¼ teaspoon salt
¾ cup (1½ sticks) unsalted butter,
  at room temperature
¾ cup granulated sugar
2 teaspoons vanilla extract
3 large eggs
18 fresh basil leaves

1. Preheat the oven to 350°F. Butter and flour eighteen 2½–3-inch tart pans.

2. Grind ¾ cup of the pine nuts in a food processor or blender. Add the flour, baking powder, and salt.

3. Beat the butter and sugar in a large mixing bowl with an electric mixer on medium speed until fluffy. Beat in the vanilla and the eggs, one at a time.

4. Gradually add the flour mixture on low speed until blended. Stir in the remaining pine nuts and half the basil, chopped.

Opposite top left: Mousse Cakes; bottom left: Pine Nut-Basil Financiers; right: Teacake Sandwiches.

5. Pour the batter into the pans and bake for 18–22 minutes, or until a knife inserted in the centers comes out clean. Cool in the pans for 10 minutes, then transfer to a rack to cool completely. To serve, invert the financiers onto plates and garnish with the remaining basil.

Pistachio Mousse Cakes

Makes two 8-inch cakes

Pistachio mousse makes for an extravagantly rich cake, so serve this in small portions. If you are as passionate about mousse cakes as I am, you'll also want to try the three variations that follow—a perfect spread for your next elegant tea party.

1. Bake the batter in two 8-inch square pans lined with parchment paper, according to the directions on page 72. Cool in the pans.

2. To make the mousse, combine the gelatin, sugar, and water in a small saucepan, stirring over low heat until dissolved. Remove from the heat and add the rose water. Set aside to cool completely.

3. Heat the milk in a medium saucepan over low heat until warm.

4. Beat the egg yolks and salt in the top of a double boiler over low heat. Gradually add the milk. Remove from the heat and let cool, then stir in the gelatin mixture.

5. Grind ½ cup of the pistachios in a food processor or blender and stir into the batter.

6. Beat the heavy cream in a medium mixing bowl with an electric mixer on medium speed until soft peaks form. Gently fold into the batter with a rubber spatula. Add 2–3 drops of food coloring to turn the batter the desired shade of pistachio.

7. Place the cooled cakes on serving plates and spread the mousse over the cakes. Chop some of the remaining

Cake

8 cups Sponge Cupcake batter (page 72)

Pistachio Mousse

Makes 3 cups

1 packet (¼ ounce) unflavored gelatin
¼ cup granulated sugar
2 tablespoons water
1 teaspoon rose water
1½ cups milk
5 large egg yolks
⅛ teaspoon salt
¾ cup whole shelled pistachios
½ cup heavy cream
Green food coloring

pistachios and leave some whole, then sprinkle them over the cakes. Cover with plastic and freeze for 3 hours. Let sit for 5 minutes, then slice into 2-inch squares. Serve at room temperature.

Variations

Lemon Mousse Cakes: Omit the pistachios and green food coloring. Replace the rose water with 1 tablespoon freshly squeezed lemon juice. Add 1 teaspoon lemon zest along with the lemon juice. While the cakes are frozen, cut out individual servings with 2-inch round cutters. Top with candied fruit and fondant leaves (page 322).

Strawberry Mousse Cakes: Omit the pistachios and green food coloring. Place about 1 cup fresh strawberries in a blender and pulse until you have ⅔ cup strawberry purée. While the cakes are frozen, cut out individual servings with 2-inch round cutters. Top with candied fruit and fondant leaves (page 322).

Raspberry Mousse Cakes: Omit the pistachios and green food coloring. Place about ¾ cup fresh raspberries in a blender and pulse until you have ½ cup raspberry purée. While the cakes are frozen, cut out individual servings with 2-inch hexagonal cutters. Top with candied fruit. Pipe a border with icing.

Chai Tea Cake Sandwiches

Makes 18 sandwiches

I can seldom resist preparing these cakes as elegant tea sandwiches, and I love that they are flavored with tea. Change the flavor by substituting another type of tea and filling. Here, a lemony cream cheese frosting highlights the flavor of the tea. Orange flavors taste great with Earl Grey tea, jasmine works well with raspberry, hibiscus with peach, and orange spice tea with honey. For a different presentation, bake these cakes in teacups.

1. Preheat the oven to 350°F. Butter and flour two 9 x 9-inch square pans.

2. Combine the flour, baking powder, salt, and tea leaves in a mixing bowl.

2½ cups all-purpose flour

1 tablespoon baking powder

½ teaspoon salt

1½ teaspoons finely ground chai tea leaves

½ pound (2 sticks) unsalted butter, at room temperature

1¾ cups granulated sugar

6 large eggs

1 teaspoon vanilla extract

2 tablespoons freshly squeezed lemon juice

1¼ cups double-strength brewed chai tea, cooled

3½ cups Lemon Cream Cheese Frosting (page 352)

3. Beat the butter and sugar in a large mixing bowl with an electric mixer on medium speed until light and fluffy. Add the eggs one at a time, beating well after each addition. Beat in the vanilla and lemon juice.

4. Gradually add the flour mixture, alternating with the brewed tea, on low speed until blended.

5. Pour the batter into the pans and bake for 25–30 minutes, or until a tester inserted in the center comes out clean. Cool in the pan.

6. Place one cooled layer on a serving plate and top with the frosting. Place the second layer on top. Cut into 3 x 3-inch squares, then cut each square on the diagonal to form triangles.

Variations

Earl Grey Nut Cakes: Replace the chai tea and leaves with Earl Grey tea and leaves. Add ½ cup chopped walnuts. Replace the lemon juice in the cake and frosting with orange juice. Cut into 3 x 3-inch square sandwiches.

Tea Cakes in Cups: Butter and flour twelve 6-ounce ovenproof teacups and place the cups on a rimmed baking sheet. Pour batter into the cups three-fourths full. Bake for 18–22 minutes. Top with the frosting and serve in the cups, with a spoon alongside.

Almond Marzipan Cake

Makes about 7 cups batter, enough for one 9-inch cake

To my mind, there is no such thing as almond overload, and this cake features the nut in all three of its parts—the cake, the icing, and the topping. The dense texture of this amaretto-infused treat makes it plenty sturdy, capable of holding the cornucopia of marzipan fruits on top.

1. Preheat the oven to 350°F. Butter and flour a 9 x 9-inch square pan.

2. Combine the flour, baking soda, and salt in a mixing bowl.

How to Make Marzipan Fruits

Marzipan (page 354) is an almond-flavored edible paste that can be colored any color of the rainbow and molded into a variety of playful shapes. Marzipan fruits are common in dozens of countries, from Italy to Thailand, although the style of sculpting them varies from region to region.

Banana

Roll yellow marzipan into a ball, then roll it into a banana shape, pressing to taper one edge and curving it slightly. Square off the thick end by pinching it with your fingers. Let it dry for 1 hour. With a food-safe brush, paint the banana with green and brown food coloring diluted with a little bit of water, depending on how ripe you would like it to look.

Strawberry

Roll red marzipan into a ball and green marzipan into a smaller ball. Taper one side of the red ball to make it look like a strawberry. Use a toothpick to poke dots into the surface for texture. Shape the green ball into a pointed star, so that it looks like a hull with a stem. Flatten the leaves and use icing to attach it to the top of the strawberry.

Orange

Roll orange marzipan into a ball and green marzipan into a smaller ball. Use a toothpick to poke dots into the surface for texture. Press the back of a knife into the orange to make an indented groove. Roll out the green marzipan and use a utility knife to cut out a leaf shape, then draw the veins with a skewer. Curve the leaf on a rounded surface and let it harden. Attach the leaf to the orange with icing.

Pear

Roll brown or greenish yellow marzipan into a ball and green marzipan into a smaller ball. Taper one end of the brown marzipan into a pear shape. Roll out the green marzipan and use a utility knife to cut out a leaf shape, then draw the veins with a toothpick. Curve the leaf on a rounded surface and let it harden. Attach the leaf to the pear with icing.

Cherry

Roll purple marzipan into a tiny ball and green marzipan into a smaller ball. Make an indentation in the top of the cherry. Roll the green marzipan into a stem and attach it to the cherry with icing.

2 cups all-purpose flour

1 teaspoon baking soda

½ teaspoon salt

½ cup (1 stick) unsalted butter, at room temperature

2 cups granulated sugar

4 large eggs

¼ cup amaretto liqueur

½ teaspoon almond extract

1 cup plain yogurt

1 cup ground almonds

2 tablespoons sliced almonds

¾ cup Almond Icing (page 358)

½ cup confectioners' sugar

3¾ cups Marzipan (page 354), shaped into fruits (see page 236)

3. Beat the butter and sugar in a large mixing bowl with an electric mixer on medium speed until light and fluffy. Beat in the eggs, amaretto, and almond extract, and continue to beat for 2 minutes.

4. Gradually add the flour mixture, alternating with the yogurt, on low speed until blended. Stir in the ground almonds.

5. Pour the batter into the pan and bake for 25–30 minutes, or until a knife inserted in the center comes out clean. Cool in the pans for 5 minutes, then transfer to a rack to cool completely.

6. Reserve 4 sliced almonds and chop the rest. If necessary, add water to the almond icing so it is thin enough to spoon.

7. Place the cake on a serving plate and spoon a circle of almond icing in the center, surrounded by chopped almonds. Set a sliced almond in each corner of the cake. Add about ½ cup confectioners' sugar to the icing to thicken it, and, using a pastry bag fitted with a small round tip, pipe a detailed design around the sliced almonds. Set the marzipan fruits on top.

Variation

Hazelnut Cake: Replace the almonds with hazelnuts in the cake and in the icing.

Coconut Cake

2 cups all-purpose flour

2 teaspoons baking powder

½ teaspoon salt

1 teaspoon ground cinnamon

½ pound (2 sticks) unsalted butter,
at room temperature

1½ cups granulated sugar

1 tablespoon vanilla extract

5 large eggs, separated

1 cup coconut milk

1½ cups fresh or packaged unsweetened shredded coconut

Banana Cream

½ pound (2 sticks) unsalted butter,
at room temperature

4 cups confectioners' sugar

1 teaspoon vanilla extract

¼ cup coconut milk

2 very ripe medium bananas,
mashed (about ¾ cup)

Topping

2 cups fresh or packaged unsweetened shredded coconut

Garnish

Fresh orchids (not edible)

Coconut Banana Cream Cakes

Makes about 6½ cups batter, enough for six 4-inch cakes

One of the many culinary thrills of teatime in the American South is the availability of fresh coconut, a popular ingredient in cakes from Georgia to Texas. I spend several weeks every year in Palm Beach, Florida, at my parents' home, where I can walk outside and pick fresh coconuts and also find them in local markets. Made with coconut milk and banana, and spiced with a touch of cinnamon, this cake is simplicity itself and sweetness at its best.

1. To make the cake, preheat the oven to 350°F. Butter and flour six 4-inch round pans or large muffin cups.

2. Combine the flour, baking powder, salt, and cinnamon in a mixing bowl.

3. Beat the butter, sugar, and vanilla in a large mixing bowl with an electric mixer on medium speed until blended. Add the egg yolks one at a time, beating well after each addition.

4. Gradually add the flour mixture, alternating with the coconut milk, on low speed until blended. Stir in the coconut.

5. In a clean bowl with clean beaters, beat the egg whites until stiff peaks form. Gently fold the egg whites into the batter with a rubber spatula.

6. Divide the batter among the pans and bake for 20–25 minutes, or until golden and a knife inserted in the center comes out clean. Cool in the pans for 10 minutes, then transfer to a rack to cool completely.

7. To make the banana cream, beat the butter, 1 cup of the sugar, and the vanilla in a large mixing bowl with an electric mixer on medium speed until blended. Add the remaining sugar, alternating with the coconut milk, to reach the desired spreading consistency. Divide the cream between two bowls, adding the banana to one.

8. Cut each cake in half horizontally. Place the bottoms onto a work surface, spread with the banana cream, and add the top layer. Frost each cake with plain coconut cream. Cover with shredded coconut. Transfer to individual plates and top with orchids.

Variations

Coconut Cake with Rum Syrup and Coconut Cream: Bake the cake in an 8-inch springform pan for 40–45 minutes. Brush with Rum Syrup (page 355) before frosting the cake.

Coconut Cake with Pineapple Filling: Replace the mashed bananas with pineapple jam.

14 cups Devil's Food Cake batter (page 76)

2½ cups Chocolate Frosting (page 351)

4 cups Chocolate Fondant (page 353)

2 cups Fondant (page 353)

Blue, yellow, red, green, and brown food coloring

3½ cups Royal Icing (page 355)

Candy heart

Silver dragées

Tea with Alice

Makes one 9 x 13-inch cake

The best in all of Wonderland, this cake is a tribute to my all-time favorite storybook friends: Alice, the Cheshire Cat, and the White Rabbit.

1. Bake the cake in a 9 x 13-inch pan, as directed on page TK. Once the cake has cooled, level the top with a serrated knife so that it does not form a dome. Frost the cake with a thin coat of chocolate frosting.

2. Dust a work surface with confectioners' sugar and roll out the chocolate fondant to a rectangle approximately 13 inches wide, 17 inches long, and ⅛ inch thick. Center the fondant on top of the cake, allowing the extra to drape over the sides. Press down, smoothing to flatten the fondant onto the cake. Cut off the excess fondant with a utility knife.

3. Divide the plain fondant into one large ball and four small balls. Color the small balls blue, yellow, pink, and purple, leaving the large ball white.

4. Dust the work surface with more confectioners' sugar, if necessary. Roll out the white fondant to 1/16 inch thick. Cut out pieces for Alice's face, dress, and legs. Cut out the White Rabbit's head with ears, and his arms and legs.

5. Roll out the blue fondant and cut out Alice's shirt, shoes, and bows.

6. Roll out the yellow fondant and cut out Alice's hair.

7. Roll out the purple fondant and cut out the Cheshire Cat.

8. Roll out the pink fondant and cut out the Rabbit's shirt, the inside of his ears, and the Cheshire Cat's face. Allow all the fondant pieces to dry and harden.

9. Using a small amount of the royal icing, attach the fondant pieces to the top of the cake, then place the

candy heart in between Alice's hands and the silver
dragées in the center of her bows.

10. Divide the icing into bowls and color them pink, blue,
green, and brown, leaving one bowl white. Place about
⅓ of each of the colored icings in pastry bags fitted
with small round tips and cover the remaining royal
icing with plastic wrap to keep it from drying out.
Pipe outlines around the fondant pieces, then pipe the
outlines of the patterns that will go in the corner of the
cake, and finally pipe the dots. Let dry.

11. Fill in the outlines of the corner patterns with the
remaining colored icings, using a toothpick to push the
icing against the borders. Let harden before serving.

Canelés de Bordeaux

Makes 8 small cakes

These French cakes are creamy and custardy on the inside and
caramelized on the outside. You can prepare them in traditional
canelé molds if you have them; if not, use muffin tins.

> 2 tablespoons unsalted butter,
> chilled
> ¾ cup cake flour
> ¼ teaspoon salt
> 1 cup granulated sugar
> 2 cups whole milk
> 4 extra-large egg yolks
> 1 tablespoon dark rum
> 1 teaspoon vanilla extract

1. Combine the butter, flour, and salt in a food processor
or blender, and pulse until the mixture resembles coarse
meal. Add the sugar and pulse until mixed.

2. Heat the milk in a saucepan almost to a boil. Add to the
flour mixture and pulse until blended.

3. Add the egg yolks, rum, and vanilla, process for about
30 seconds, or until a sticky dough forms. Refrigerate
the dough for 12 hours.

4. Preheat the oven to 375°F. Butter and flour 8 canelé
molds or medium muffin cups. Fill the molds about
three-fourths full with the batter and bake for 60–75
minutes, or until a tester inserted in the center comes
out clean. Cool in the molds for 15 minutes, then
transfer to a rack to cool completely.

SUMMER PARTY CAKES

Ready for a good time? Whether you fire up the barbecue to grill fruit and slices of pound cake, whip up a cake to cook over a campfire, or make a s'mores-inspired cake entirely in your kitchen, you'll find plenty of ideas here for outdoor parties.

Barbecued Pound Cake with Grilled Fruit

Barbecued cake is like no other cake you have tasted—its slightly charred flavor is one you will get hooked on right away. To barbecue, you can use a gas, charcoal, or stove-top grill. To feed a crowd or for a buffet, arrange the cake on a bed of fresh grilled fruit. Another option is to plate the cake slices individually and serve with the fruit alongside, garnishing each with whipped cream and chocolate sauce. Use whatever fruits are in season, and cook them according to the chart on page 244.

2 pounds sliced fresh fruit

7 tablespoons unsalted butter, melted

2 tablespoons firmly packed light brown sugar

¼ cup orange juice

2 tablespoons freshly squeezed lemon juice

2 tablespoons freshly squeezed lime juice

Olive oil

1 Pound Cake (page 67), cut into ½–¾-inch slices

1. Thread the small fruit onto skewers. Combine 3 tablespoons of the butter, the sugar, and the orange, lemon, and lime juices in a small mixing bowl. Brush the fruits lightly with the sauce.

2. Set the grill up for direct grilling and preheat to high. Brush olive oil on the grates. Grill the fruit, turning several times, until softened; see page 244 for specific times. Place the fruit on a serving plate.

3. Brush the pound cake slices on both sides lightly with the remaining 4 tablespoons butter. Grill for 1½–3 minutes on each side, or until toasted. Arrange the slices with the fruit and serve.

Variations

Plated Barbecued Pound Cake: Place the grilled cake slices on dessert plates. Remove the fruit from the skewers after grilling and spoon over the cake, then top with Whipped Cream (page 359) and Chocolate Sauce (page 352).

Grilling Fruit

For best results and even cooking, cut the fruit into pieces of approximately equal size. When you thread the fruit onto skewers, put fruits that are similar in size and texture or density on the same skewer. When you grill rings or larger fruits, you may want to thread them onto two skewers to keep them from spinning, put them in a grill basket, or grill them directly on the grate and turn them with tongs.

FRUIT	HOW TO PREPARE	GRILLING TIME
Apples	Core and cut into 3/4-inch rings	6–8 minutes
Apricots	Cut in half	4–6 minutes
Bananas	Leave whole and unpeeled	4–6 minutes
Blueberries	Leave whole	3–4 minutes
Cherries	Leave whole	3–4 minutes
Citrus fruits	Leave unpeeled; cut into 3/4-inch slices	4–5 minutes
Figs	Cut in half lengthwise	4–6 minutes
Grapes	Leave whole	3–4 minutes
Melons	Cut into 1-inch wedges	3–4 minutes
Nectarines	Cut in half	6–8 minutes
Papayas	Cut into 3/4-inch slices	5–8 minutes
Peaches	Cut in half	6–8 minutes
Pears	Cut into 3/4-inch wedges	6–7 minutes
Pineapple	Cut into 3/4-inch rings	6–8 minutes

Manly Cakes

There is an odd question being tossed around the baking world these days—what are "manly" cakes? This is not a new thing: in 1954, the Tested Recipe Institute published a booklet entitled *Cakes Men Like,* put forth as a collection of recipes for women who want to bake cakes for their husbands—although there is nothing particularly masculine about the cakes in the booklet. This idea was reintroduced in 1992, when another book was published with the same title. That book used vintage recipes to re-create the happy-homemaking baking nostalgia of the 1950s. Both books contain recipes for cakes we all can enjoy.

Today, bakers are still attempting to establish a genre of manly cakes. There are cupcake bakeries that apply a masculine aesthetic (think camouflage and houndstooth) to their presentation of this traditionally cute confection, and others that offer a selection of flavors just for men. Some people think that manly cakes have to be shaped like footballs or golf clubs or have to be adorned with a team logo. Others think they have to be filled with beer or booze. Is this because men and alcohol just naturally go together? And is barbecued cake considered more manly than other cakes because men and fire just naturally go together, too? My take on the whole idea is that men love cake, women love cake, and as long as the cake tastes good, it doesn't matter!

Crust

1½ cups graham cracker crumbs

3 tablespoons granulated sugar

½ cup sweetened flaked coconut, finely chopped

2 tablespoons unsalted butter, melted

Cake

1½ cups all-purpose flour

2 teaspoons baking powder

1 cup unsweetened cocoa powder

⅛ teaspoon salt

½ pound (2 sticks) unsalted butter, at room temperature

2 cups granulated sugar

1 tablespoon vanilla extract

4 large eggs

8 ounces chocolate chips

Chocolate Cream Filling

½ cup granulated sugar

¼ cup heavy cream

3 ounces unsweetened chocolate

1 teaspoon vanilla extract

Marshmallow Meringue

3 large egg whites

⅛ teaspoon salt

1 jar (7 ounces) marshmallow crème

Garnish

2 ounces semisweet chocolate chunks

S'mores Cakes

Makes eight 4-inch cakes

My birthday is in late August, and every year I spend the occasion somewhere deep in the woods, backpacking and, most years, celebrating with s'mores, my favorite campsite treat. As far as I'm concerned, my birthday lasts for the entire month, not just for one day, so throughout August, I re-create the outdoor experience with these cakes, which I would say are better than the real thing.

1. Preheat the oven to 350°F. Butter and flour eight extra-large muffin cups.

2. To make the crust, combine the cracker crumbs, sugar, coconut, and butter in a medium bowl until blended. Press the mixture into the bottom of the muffin cups and up the sides. Bake for 10 minutes, until lightly browned. Transfer to a rack to cool in the pans for 10 minutes.

3. To make the cake, combine the flour, baking powder, cocoa powder, and salt in a mixing bowl.

4. Beat the butter and sugar in a large mixing bowl with an electric mixer on medium speed until fluffy. Add the

vanilla and the eggs, one at a time, beating well after each addition.

5. Gradually add the flour mixture on low speed, then stir in the chocolate chips.

6. Pour the batter over the crusts and bake for 15–20 minutes, or until a tester inserted in the center comes out clean. Cool in the pans.

7. To make the filling, heat the sugar, heavy cream, and chocolate in a double boiler, stirring until the chocolate melts and the sugar dissolves. Stir in the vanilla.

8. To make the marshmallow meringue, in a clean bowl with clean beaters, beat the egg whites and salt until soft peaks form. Gradually add the marshmallow crème, continuing to beat until stiff peaks form.

9. Preheat the broiler. Line a baking sheet with foil. Spread the chocolate cream onto the cakes, then pipe with marshmallow meringue. Place on the baking sheet and broil for 1–2 minutes, until the meringue is lightly browned. Keep a close watch, as it can burn quickly. (Alternatively, you can toast the meringue with a kitchen torch.) Top with chocolate chunks and serve.

Cherry Dutch Oven Cake

Makes one 10-inch cake

Join the campfire baking revolution! This cherry-spiked cake, similar in texture to soda bread, can be made outdoors in a cast-iron Dutch oven, or indoors in a covered ceramic casserole. Once you get the cooking-over-coal technique down, you will want to bake everything over a campfire. No need to use the grill: the pot is placed directly on the coals.

1. Butter and flour a 10-inch Dutch oven. Place about 24 charcoal briquettes in your fire ring or barbecue and heat until they turn white.

2 cups all-purpose flour
1 teaspoon baking soda
⅛ teaspoon ground cinnamon
5⅓ tablespoons (⅔ stick) unsalted butter, at room temperature
1 cup granulated sugar
1 large egg
1 teaspoon vanilla extract
¾ cup buttermilk
3 cups Bing cherries, pitted
2 tablespoons confectioners' sugar for dusting

2. Combine the flour, baking soda, and cinnamon in a mixing bowl.

3. Beat the butter and sugar in a large mixing bowl with an electric mixer on medium speed until fluffy. Beat in the egg and vanilla.

4. Gradually add the flour mixture, alternating with the buttermilk, on low speed until blended. Fold in the cherries.

5. Pour the batter into the Dutch oven, cover with the lid, and set directly on the hot coals. Using barbecue tongs, place 13 hot coals on top of the closed lid, leaving 7 coals on the bottom and the remaining coals on the sides. Bake for 50–60 minutes, or until a tester inserted in the center comes out clean. Cool for 20 minutes, then dust with confectioners' sugar.

Variation

Indoor Cherry Cake: Pour the batter into a buttered and floured 10-inch ceramic casserole dish. Cover and bake at 350°F for 35 minutes. Remove the lid and bake for an additional 10–15 minutes to brown the top. Cool in the pan before dusting with confectioners' sugar.

Dutch Oven Baking Chart

When a Dutch oven is used to cook over briquettes on an outdoor barbecue, the coals must be applied to both the top and bottom of the pot to ensure even distribution of heat. Follow this chart to determine the number of briquettes needed to create the proper temperature. The general rule is to use the size of the pot as the basis for your calculations: subtract 3 to determine the number of coals that go on the bottom and add 3 to determine the number of coals that go on the top. For example, a 10-inch Dutch oven requires 7 coals on the bottom and 13 on the top to maintain a temperature of 325°F. Adding one additional briquette to the bottom and top will raise the temperature about 25 degrees.

	8-INCH		10-INCH		12-INCH		14-INCH		16-INCH	
	TOP	BOTTOM	TOP	BOTTOM	TOP	BOTTOM	TOP	BOTTOM	TOP	BOTTOM
300°	10	4	12	6	14	8	16	10	18	12
325°	11	5	13	7	15	9	17	11	19	13
350°	12	6	14	8	16	10	18	12	20	14
375°	13	7	15	9	17	11	19	13	21	15

Pineapple Upside-Down Cake

Makes one 8-inch cake

3 tablespoons unsalted butter

¼ cup firmly packed dark brown sugar

8 fresh or canned drained pineapple rings

8 maraschino cherries

6 large eggs

⅛ teaspoon salt

1 tablespoon vanilla extract

1 teaspoon grated orange zest

1 cup all-purpose flour

This cake's main claim to fame is the tempting fruit—pineapple rings and maraschino cherries—on top. Traditionally baked in a cast-iron skillet and then inverted onto a plate, upside-down cake can also be made in a cake pan. This recipe has no butter in the batter, so it is lower in fat than the traditional recipe. Serve it at your next tiki-inspired patio party.

1. Preheat the oven to 375°F. Line an 8-inch round pan with parchment paper and spray with cooking spray.

2. Melt the butter and 3 tablespoons of the sugar in a skillet over medium heat until bubbly. Add the pineapple rings and cook for about 5 minutes, flipping them over occasionally, or until lightly browned and the juices are released. Continue to cook over low heat until the juices are reduced to caramel, about 5 minutes longer. Arrange the pineapple rings in the prepared pan, add the caramel from the skillet, if any, then set the cherries in the center of each ring.

3. Beat the eggs, remaining sugar, and salt in a large mixing bowl with an electric mixer on medium speed until the mixture triples in volume. Beat in the vanilla and orange zest. Fold in the flour.

4. Pour the batter over the pineapple slices and bake for 35–40 minutes, or until a tester inserted in the center comes out clean. Cool in the pan. To serve, run a knife around the inside edge to loosen, then invert on to a serving plate. Replace any fruit that sticks to the pan.

Variations

Individual Pineapple Upside-Down Cakes: Arrange the pineapple rings in large muffin cups with a cherry in the center. Bake for 20–25 minutes.

Lavender Pineapple Upside-Down Cake: Add 1 teaspoon dried lavender to the batter with the flour. Serve garnished with lavender flowers.

Hawaiian Macadamia Nut Spice Cake

Makes one 5 x 9-inch loaf

Hawaiian-style parties are a favorite at our home. To make this cake sing, dress it up with lemon icing and tropical fruits. *Mahalo!*

2 cups all-purpose flour

½ cup sweetened flaked coconut

1½ cups macadamia nuts, toasted and chopped

½ cup granulated sugar

2 teaspoons baking powder

1 teaspoon salt

1 teaspoon ground allspice

1 teaspoon ground nutmeg

¼ teaspoon ground cloves

2 large eggs

½ cup coconut milk

½ cup (1 stick) unsalted butter, melted

1½ cups Lemon Icing (page 358)

2 sliced star fruits for garnish

6 whole kumquats for garnish

1 cup sliced assorted fresh tropical fruits, such as papaya, mango, and kiwifruit, for garnish

1. Preheat the oven to 350°F. Butter and flour a 5 x 9-inch loaf pan.

2. Combine the flour, coconut, nuts, sugar, baking powder, salt, allspice, nutmeg, and cloves in a mixing bowl.

3. Beat the eggs, coconut milk, and butter in a large mixing bowl with an electric mixer on medium speed until creamy.

4. Gradually add the flour mixture on low speed until blended.

5. Pour the batter into the pan and bake for 45–50 minutes, or until a knife inserted in the center comes out clean. Let cool in the pan for 20 minutes, then transfer to a rack to cool completely.

6. Place the loaf on a serving plate. Top with icing and tropical fruits.

DINNER PARTY CAKES

From the casual to the fancy, no matter what the tone of your party, these are the cakes that will pique your guests' taste buds and get them talking. I especially love the salty-and-sweet Bundts with new flavor combinations like bacon and chocolate, feta and apricot, and butterscotch and sea salt. For a summer soiree, you'll have trouble finding any cake more intriguing than chocolate-spice croutons topping cold strawberry soup. For parties where customization is key, look to the cheesecake selections and the dinner party slices. You can personalize each portion with warmth and style for your guests' palates and preferences.

Dinner Party Slices

I've always thought that the great appeal of an array of individual cakes is that it allows you to choose the one that reflects your mood or favorite flavors. That made me wonder: is there a way to apply that level of customization when preparing a larger layer cake? I tried it out when hosting a dinner party and this is what I came up with. By using a few simple batters, fillings, and frostings—and adding a few flavorings and mix-ins—I created eight different cakes. Present them on a large platter to highlight the variety.

Chocolate Mascarpone Cake

Makes 6 slices

Bake the cake in an 11½ x 17¼ x 1-inch jelly-roll pan for 25–30 minutes and cool according to the directions on page 76. Once cooled, cut the cake into four pieces. Stack the pieces on top of each other, spreading mascarpone cream between them, and spread chocolate ganache on top. Cut into slices and arrange on dessert plates. Using a pastry bag fitted with a medium round tip, pipe mascarpone cream on the ganache and garnish with white chocolate.

Lemon Cherry Cake

Makes 8 slices

Bake the cake in three 8 x 8-inch square pans for 20–25 minutes and cool according to the directions on page 69. Once cooled, place one

Opposite front to back, left: Chocolate Mascarpone Cake, Lemon Cherry Cake, Mocha Cake, Chocolate Raspberry Cake; right front to back: Chocolate Ganache Cake, Opera Cake, Black Forest Cake, Lemon Cake with White Chocolate Buttercream.

---

13 cups Devil's Food Cake batter (page 76)

2⅔ cups Lemon Mascarpone Cream (page 354)

1⅔ cups Chocolate Ganache (page 351)

1 ounce white chocolate, cut into pieces and decorated with an edible transfer, if desired

---

8 cups Lemon Cake batter (page
   70)
2½ cups Lemon Curd (page 353)
¾ cup cherry jam
2¼ cups Vanilla Buttercream
   (page 356)
Candied currants, candied orange
   peel, or candied lemon peel

2 teaspoons instant espresso powder
8 cups Devil's Food Cake batter
   (page 76)
5 cups Mocha Frosting (page
   351)
2 cups Chocolate Ganache (page
   351)
Candied currants

1¼ cups puréed fresh raspberries
8 cups Devil's Food Cake batter
   (page 76)
3½ cups Raspberry Mousse (page
   290)
2 cups Chocolate Ganache (page
   351)
Candied currants

layer of cake on a serving plate and spread with about half the lemon curd. Place a second layer of cake on top and spread with cherry jam. Place 1 cup of buttercream in a pastry bag fitted with a medium round tip and set aside. Spread a thin layer of the remaining buttercream over the jam. Top with a third layer of cake and a thicker layer of buttercream. Spread the remaining lemon curd on top and use a decorating comb to create lines. Cut into slices and arrange on dessert plates. Pipe a dot of buttercream on top of each slice and add a candied fruit in the center.

Mocha Cake

Makes 12 slices

Dissolve the espresso powder in ¼ cup hot water. Add to the cake batter and bake in a 9 x 13-inch pan for 30–35 minutes. Cool according to the directions on page 76. Once cooled, cut the cake in half horizontally. Place the bottom layer on a serving plate and spread with about half the mocha frosting. Top with the second layer of cake and the remaining mocha frosting. Add one-fourth of the ganache to a pastry bag fitted with a round tip and set aside. Spread the remaining ganache over the frosting and use a decorating comb to create lines. Cut into slices and arrange on dessert plates. Pipe ganache dots on top of each slice and garnish with candied currants.

Chocolate Raspberry Cake

Makes 12 slices

Add one-fourth of the puréed raspberries to the cake batter and bake in a 9 x 13-inch pan for 30–35 minutes. Cool according to the directions on page 76. Once cooled, cut the cake in half horizontally. Place the bottom layer on a serving plate and spread with the remaining puréed raspberries. Let them soak in for about 10 minutes, then spread with about half the raspberry mousse. Add the second layer of cake and the remaining mousse. Cover and chill for 3 hours. Make the ganache just before serving. Add half of it to a pastry bag fitted with a medium round tip and spread the rest over the mousse. Cut the cake into slices and arrange on dessert plates. Pipe ganache patterns on the slices. Top with candied currants.

8 cups Devil's Food Cake batter
(page 76)

2⅔ cups Chocolate Ganache (page
351)

1 cup confectioners' sugar

½ cup chocolate sprinkles

Maraschino cherries

1 ounce bittersweet chocolate,
decorated with an edible transfer,
if desired, and cut into leaves

---

7 cups Almond Marzipan Cake
batter (page 234)

4½ cups Coffee Buttercream (page
350)

1⅛ cups Coffee Syrup (page 352)

2 cups Chocolate Ganache (page
351)

½ cup pitted and chopped fresh
Bing cherries

8 cups Devil's Food Cake batter
(page 76)

2 tablespoons Kirsch

½ cup cherry jam

4½ cups Chocolate Buttercream
(page 350)

1 ounce dark (at least 70% cacao)
chocolate, melted

1½ cups Whipped Cream (page
359)

15 maraschino cherries

Chocolate Ganache Cake

Makes 12 slices

Bake the cake in a 9 x 13-inch pan for 30–35 minutes and cool according to the directions on page 76. Once cooled, cut the cake with a hexagonal cookie cutter. Line a baking sheet with parchment and set a wire rack on top. Set the cakes on the rack and pour the ganache over the cakes. Pour a second coat over the cakes, using some of the ganache that has settled on the baking sheet. Add confectioners' sugar to the remaining ganache to thicken it, and transfer to a pastry bag fitted with a medium round tip. Pipe a border around the base of the cakes. Sprinkle the piped borders with chocolate sprinkles and place the cakes on dessert plates. Top with cherries and candy.

Opera Cake

Makes 8 slices

Bake the cake in an 8 x 8-inch square pan for 35–40 minutes and cool according to the directions on page 351. Once cooled, cut the cake horizontally into three layers with a serrated knife. Place the bottom layer on a serving plate. Top with about one-fourth of the buttercream. Place a second layer on top, brush with half the coffee syrup, and then spread with about half the ganache and another one-fourth of the buttercream. Top with the remaining layer, brush with the remaining syrup, and spread with the remaining buttercream. Put one-fourth of the remaining ganache in a pastry bag fitted with a small writing tip. Then spread the remaining ganache over the buttercream. Cut into slices and arrange on dessert plates. Use the ganache in the pastry bag to pipe treble clefs on the top of each slice.

Black Forest Cake

Makes 12 slices

Add the fresh cherries to the cake batter and bake in a 9 x 13-inch pan for 30–35 minutes. Cool according to the directions on page 76. Once cooled, cut the cake in half horizontally. Place the bottom layer on a serving plate and brush with half the Kirsch. Spread with a thin layer of cherry jam, then with about half the buttercream. Repeat with a second layer of cake, Kirsch, jam, and buttercream, using an icing

7 cups Lemon Cake batter (page 70)

1¼ cups Lemon Curd (page 353)

3¾ cups White Chocolate Buttercream (page 350)

Yellow food coloring

18 lemon-flavored jelly candies

Crust

1½ cups graham cracker crumbs

2 tablespoons granulated sugar

4 tablespoons (½ stick) unsalted butter, melted

Cheesecake

4 boxes (8 ounces each) cream cheese, at room temperature

⅓ cup plus 3 tablespoons granulated sugar

4 large eggs

½ cup heavy cream

2 teaspoons vanilla extract

2 teaspoons grated lemon zest

⅛ teaspoon salt

1 cup crushed fresh raspberries

2 tablespoons water

Garnish

½ cup fresh raspberries

spatula to smooth the buttercream on top. Use a decorating comb to create lines in the buttercream. Drizzle melted chocolate over the cake. Cut into slices and arrange on dessert plates. Top with piped whipped cream and maraschino cherries.

Lemon Cake with White Chocolate Buttercream

Makes 12 slices

Bake the cake in an 8 x 12-inch pan for 30–35 minutes and cool according to the directions on page 69. Once cooled, level the cake, then cut the cake into two layers, making one layer slightly thicker. Place the thinner layer on a serving plate and top with lemon curd and about one-third of the buttercream. Place the thicker layer on top and spread with another one-third of the buttercream. Divide the remaining buttercream in half and color one batch yellow. Put each half in pastry bags fitted with a large tip and set aside. Cut the cake into slices and arrange on dessert plates. Pipe with buttercream patterns and top with lemon candies.

Raspberry Marble Cheesecakes

Makes 4 cakes

For your next dinner party, prepare a selection of cheesecakes so guests can pick their favorites—baking the cakes in miniature springform pans provides a reasonable portion for even the most ardent cheesecakeaholic. This marbleized raspberry cheesecake is my favorite and can be easily customized.

1. Preheat the oven to 350°F. Butter and flour four 4-inch springform pans and wrap the bottoms, sides, and outside in foil. Prepare a water bath large enough to fit the pans (see page 41) and set it in the oven on the middle rack.

2. To make the crust, combine the graham crackers, sugar, and butter in a mixing bowl until moistened. Press the crust into the pans.

3. To make cheesecake, beat the cream cheese and ⅓ cup of the sugar in a large mixing bowl with an electric

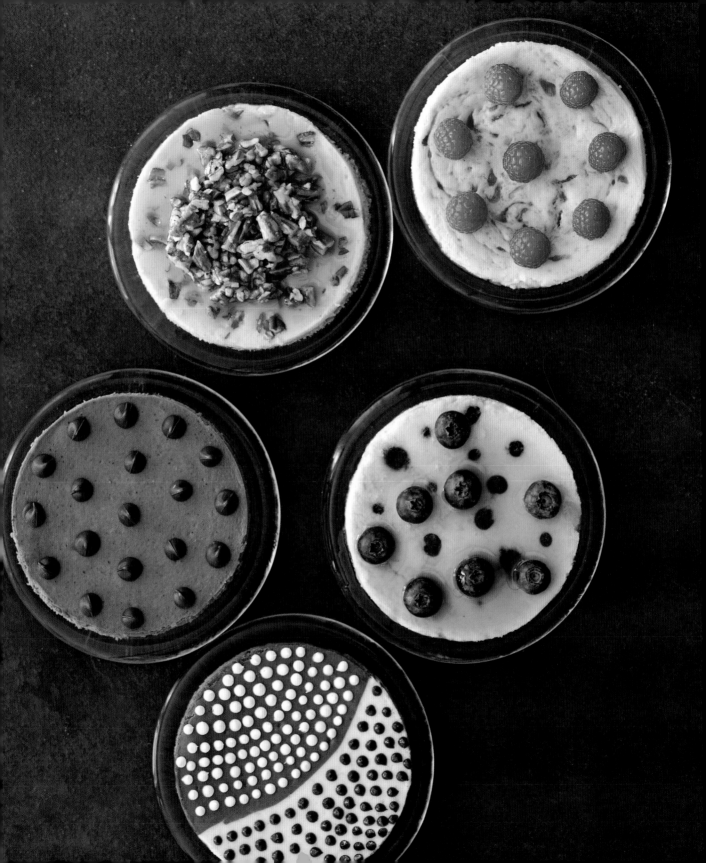

mixer on medium speed until fluffy. Add the eggs one at a time, beating well after each addition. Beat in the heavy cream, vanilla, lemon zest, and salt until smooth. Pour the batter into the pans.

4. Combine the crushed raspberries, water, and remaining 3 tablespoons sugar in a small saucepan over medium heat and stir until smooth. Drop spoonfuls of the raspberry mixture over the cake batter and use a knife to swirl.

5. Set the pans into the water bath and bake for 30–35 minutes, or until firm and a knife inserted in the center comes out clean. Cool in the pans on a rack for 1 hour, then cover and chill until ready to serve. Unmold the cakes and top with fresh raspberries.

Chocolate Cheesecakes

Makes 4 cheesecakes

1. Preheat the oven to 350°F. Butter and flour four 4-inch springform pans. Prepare a water bath large enough to fit the pans (see page 41) and set it in the oven on the middle rack.

2. To make the crust, combine the cookie crumbs, sugar, and butter in a mixing bowl until moistened. Press the crust into the pans.

3. To make the cheesecake, beat the cream cheese and sugar in a large mixing bowl with an electric mixer on medium speed until fluffy. Add the eggs one at a time, beating well after each addition. Beat in the chocolate, milk, sour cream, vanilla, and salt until smooth.

4. Pour the batter into the pans and set into the water bath. Bake for 30–35 minutes, or until firm and a knife inserted in the center comes out clean. Cool in the pans on a rack for 1 hour. Top with chocolate chips, then cover and chill until ready to serve.

Crust

1 cup finely crushed chocolate wafers

2 tablespoons granulated sugar

4 tablespoons (½ stick) unsalted butter, melted

Cheesecake

3 boxes (8 ounces each) cream cheese, at room temperature

¾ cup granulated sugar

3 large eggs

8 ounces bittersweet chocolate, melted and cooled

½ cup whole milk

½ cup sour cream

1 teaspoon vanilla extract

⅛ teaspoon salt

Garnish

¾ cup chocolate chips

Cheesecakes Galore

Both the Raspberry Marble Cheesecake batter and the Chocolate Cheesecake batter can be used as a canvas for a rainbow of different colors and flavors. Pictured in the photograph are, clockwise from top right: Raspberry Marble Cheesecake, Lemon Blueberry Cheesecake, White and Dark Chocolate Cheesecake, Chocolate Cheesecake, and Caramel Pecan Cheesecake. Find your favorites in the following variations.

Lemon Blueberry Cheesecakes: Prepare the graham cracker crust. Make the raspberry marble cheesecake batter, omitting the crushed raspberries and substituting 1 cup crushed fresh blueberries and ½ teaspoon lemon zest. Top with fresh blueberries.

Caramel Pecan Cheesecakes: Prepare the graham cracker crust, adding ¼ cup chopped pecans to the graham cracker crumbs. Make the raspberry marble cheesecake batter, omitting the crushed raspberries, water, and 3 tablespoons sugar, and add ½ cup chopped pecans to the batter before pouring in the pans. Top the cooled cheesecakes with additional chopped pecans and Caramel Glaze (page 350).

White and Dark Chocolate Cheesecakes: Prepare the chocolate cookie crust. Make the chocolate cheesecake batter, omitting the chocolate. Divide the batter in half. Add 4 ounces melted white chocolate to one batch and 4 ounces melted dark chocolate to the second. Fill each pan with half of the white chocolate batter and half of the dark chocolate batter. Once cooled, pipe alternating dark and white chocolate dots on top.

Chocolate Raspberry Cheesecakes: Prepare the chocolate cookie crust. Make the chocolate cheesecake batter, adding a mixture of 1 cup crushed fresh raspberries, 2 tablespoons water, and 3 tablespoons sugar before baking.

Apple Crumb Cheesecakes: Prepare the graham cracker crust. Make the raspberry marble cheesecake batter, omitting the crushed raspberries, water, and 3 tablespoons sugar, and add ¾ cup chopped fresh apples to the batter before pouring in the pans. Top with Streusel Topping (page 356).

Banana Cream Cheesecakes: Prepare the graham cracker crust. Make the raspberry marble cheesecake batter, omitting the crushed raspberries, water, and 3 tablespoons sugar. Mix 1 cup mashed bananas into the batter before pouring into the pans. Top with Whipped Cream (page 359).

Pineapple Mango Cheesecakes: Prepare the graham cracker crust. Make the raspberry marble cheesecake batter, omitting the crushed raspberries, water, and 3 tablespoons sugar. Add 1 cup drained canned pineapple chunks and ½ cup chopped fresh mango to the batter before pouring into the pans. Top the cooled cakes with pineapple rings, mango slices, and a maraschino cherry.

Dulce de Leche Cheesecakes: Prepare the graham cracker crust. Make the raspberry marble cheesecake batter, omitting the crushed raspberries, water, and 3 tablespoons sugar, and, after pouring it into the pans, divide ½ cup dulce de leche among the pans and swirl it with a knife before baking. Serve with additional dulce de leche and Whipped Cream (page 359).

Rocky Road Cheesecakes: Prepare the chocolate cookie crust. Add ½ cup chopped almonds, ½ cup miniature marshmallows, and ½ cup chopped chocolate to the chocolate cheesecake batter before pouring into the pans. Top the cooled cakes with Chocolate Glaze (page 351), miniature marshmallows, and almonds.

Chocolate Peanut Butter Cheesecakes: Prepare the chocolate cookie crust. Combine ½ cup peanut butter with ¼ cup confectioners' sugar. Make the chocolate cheesecake batter and, after pouring it into the pans, add spoonfuls of the peanut butter mixture and swirl it with a knife before baking. Top with Chocolate Glaze (page 351) and peanut butter chips.

Coconut Ginger Cream Cheesecakes: Prepare the gingersnap crust (page 182). Make the raspberry marble cheesecake batter, omitting the crushed raspberries, water, and 3 tablespoons sugar, and add 1 cup sweetened flaked coconut and ¹⁄₂ teaspoon ground ginger before pouring it into the pans. Top the cooled cakes with toasted flaked coconut (page 33), candied ginger, and Whipped Cream (page 359).

Coffee Cheesecakes: Prepare the chocolate cookie crust, adding ¹⁄₂ teaspoon ground espresso beans to the cookie crumbs. Add ¹⁄₄ cup double-strength brewed espresso to the chocolate cheesecake batter. Top the cooled cakes with chocolate-covered espresso beans.

Strawberry Soup

6 cups fresh strawberries, hulled
    and puréed

2 cups unsweetened apple juice

1 tablespoon freshly squeezed
    lemon juice

¹⁄₄ teaspoon ground cinnamon

¹⁄₄ teaspoon ground ginger

3 tablespoons heavy cream

Chocolate Spice Cake

1²⁄₃ cups all-purpose flour

1¹⁄₂ teaspoons baking powder

²⁄₃ cup unsweetened cocoa powder

¹⁄₄ teaspoon ground cinnamon

¹⁄₄ teaspoon ground ginger

³⁄₄ cup (1¹⁄₂ sticks) unsalted butter,
    at room temperature

¹⁄₂ cup granulated sugar

¹⁄₃ cup firmly packed light brown
    sugar

2 large eggs

¹⁄₂ cup orange juice

4 ounces dark chocolate chunks

Strawberry Soup with Cake Croutons

Makes 6–8 servings

Croutons made from chocolate spice cake accent a chilled strawberry soup for an elegant but not overly heavy first course or dessert. If you have a mini brownie pan—a pan with small individual cavities for each brownie, which allows every piece to have crispy, crunchy edges—use it to make this cake. Otherwise, simply make it in a square pan and cut the cake into cubes.

1. To make the soup, combine the puréed strawberries, apple juice, lemon juice, cinnamon, and ginger in a medium saucepan over medium heat. Cook for 10–12 minutes, or until the flavors blend. Remove from the heat and add the cream. Cover and chill for 2 hours.

2. To make the cake, preheat the oven to 325°F. Butter and flour a mini-brownie bar pan or an 8 x 8-inch square pan.

3. Combine the flour, baking powder, cocoa powder, cinnamon, and ginger in a mixing bowl.

4. Beat the butter and both sugars in a large mixing bowl with an electric mixer on medium speed until fluffy. Add the eggs one at a time, beating well after each addition.

5. Gradually add the flour mixture, alternating with the orange juice, on low speed until blended. Stir in half the chocolate chunks.

6. Pour the batter into the pan and scatter the remaining chocolate chunks on top. Bake for 12–16 minutes in a

mini brownie pan, or 30–35 minutes in an 8 x 8-inch pan, until a tester inserted in the center comes out clean. Cool completely in the pan before cutting into cubes.

7. To serve, ladle the soup into bowls and place the bowls on larger salad or dessert plates. Add a dollop of whipped cream to each plate. Thread the cake cubes onto skewers, reserving a few to garnish each bowl of soup. Dust the skewers with cocoa powder and set them on the plates.

Variations

Rosé Strawberry Soup: Replace 1 cup of the apple juice with 1 cup rosé wine.

Cake Parfait: Omit the soup. Layer the cake cubes in parfait glasses, a few at a time, with alternating layers of Vanilla and Chocolate

Pastry Cream (page 358). Top with Whipped Cream (page 359) and maraschino cherries.

Cake Fondue: Chocolate Spice Cake is perfect for dipping in a fondue. Try it with the Chocolate Glaze (page 351), or with Strawberry Sauce (page 127) or Pineapple Sauce (page 127). Make a triple batch of the recipe you choose for dipping and heat it in a fondue pot. Serve with Half-Whipped Cream (page 359) and nuts on the side for even more fun.

Phyllo Pastry Cake

Makes one 9 x 13-inch cake

The delicate nature of phyllo pastry is highlighted in this is baked custard cake soaked in a clear sugar syrup. The versatile dough can also be prepared in the manner of a French mille-feuille, in which the custard is added after the phyllo layers are baked.

2 cups granulated sugar

1½ cups semolina

3½ tablespoons cornstarch

¼ teaspoon salt

6 cups whole milk

1 teaspoon vanilla extract

6 large eggs

15 sheets frozen phyllo dough, thawed

¾ cup (1½ sticks) unsalted butter, melted

1 teaspoon freshly squeezed lemon juice

¾ cup of water

1. Preheat the oven to 350°F. Butter a 9 x 13-inch pan.

2. Combine 1 cup of the sugar, the semolina, cornstarch, and salt in a medium bowl.

3. Over medium heat, bring the milk to a boil in a large saucepan. Gradually add the sugar mixture, stirring until the sugar dissolves and the mixture thickens. Remove from the heat, add the vanilla, cover, and set aside.

4. Beat the eggs and ½ cup of the remaining sugar in a large mixing bowl with an electric mixer on medium speed until thick, about 7 minutes. Fold the egg mixture into the sugar mixture; set the custard aside.

5. One at a time, layer five sheets of phyllo in the pan, folding them to fit, if necessary, and brushing each one with butter after you set it in the pan. Spread half the custard over the phyllo. Cover with five more sheets of phyllo, brushing each with butter. Top with the remaining custard, then with the remaining phyllo and butter. Bake for 35–40 minutes, or until the phyllo is crisp and the custard has set. Let cool in the pan.Cover with foil if it begins to brown too much.

6. Combine the remaining ½ cup sugar and the lemon juice with water in a saucepan over low heat. Cook, stirring occasionally, until the sugar dissolves. Remove from heat and let cool to room temperature.

7. When the cake and syrup are at room temperature, brush the syrup on top of the cake, making sure to cover all the edges. Cool completely on a rack before serving.

Variation

Mille-Feuille: Prepare the custard; cover and refrigerate. Layer the phyllo and butter on two large baking sheets and bake for 20–25 minutes, or until browned. When the custard and phyllo have cooled to room temperature, assemble by layering the phyllo and custard, ending with the phyllo. Omit the syrup and dust the cake with confectioners' sugar.

Salty-Sweet Savory Bundts

Makes 8 mini Bundt cakes

2 cups all-purpose flour
1 teaspoon baking soda
1¼ teaspoons salt
¾ cup (1½ sticks) unsalted butter, at room temperature
1¼ cups granulated sugar
2 large eggs
3 large egg yolks
½ cup sour cream
1½ teaspoons vanilla extract
¾ cup whole milk

If you're intrigued by new tastes, these salty-sweet savory cakes are definitely "something different," and sure to get dinner conversation going. Salty-and-sweet combinations are all the rage in cooking nowadays, and these cakes take the synergy to the next level. Prepare the basic butter cake recipe and choose your flavors from page 264.

1. Preheat the oven to 350°F. Butter and flour eight 3½-inch mini Bundt pans.

2. Combine the flour, baking soda, and salt in a mixing bowl.

3. Beat the butter and sugar in a large mixing bowl with an electric mixer on medium speed until fluffy. One at a time, beat in the eggs and yolks, sour cream, and vanilla.

4. Gradually add the flour mixture, alternating with the milk, on low speed until blended. Stir in the salty and sweet additions (see page 264).

Salty-Sweet Savory Bundts, top and lower right of plate: Feta with honey and apricots; center: butterscotch and sea salt; left and right: blue cheese amd almonds; lower left: bacon and chocolate chunks.

5. Pour the batter into the pans and bake for 25–30 minutes, or until a knife inserted in the center comes out clean. Cool in the pans for 10 minutes, then transfer to a rack to cool completely.

6. Unmold the cakes onto dessert plates and sprinkle with the toppings.

Bundts Galore

Use the Salty-Sweet Savory Bundts batter (page 251) as a basis for these unique and delicious variations.

Bacon and Chocolate Chunk Bundts

12 strips cooked bacon, cut into small pieces
4 ounces dark (at least 60% cacao) chocolate chunks

Combine the bacon and chocolate in a small bowl. Reserve one-third of the mixture and stir the rest into the batter before baking. Top with the reserved bacon mixture when ready to serve.

Feta Apricot Bundts

¹/₄ cup clover honey
³/₄ cup crumbled feta cheese
1 cup pitted and chopped fresh apricots (about 4 medium)

Reduce the sugar to ³/₄ cup and add the honey to the batter. Combine the feta and apricots in a small bowl. Reserve one-third of the mixture and stir the rest into the batter before baking. Top with the reserved feta mixture when ready to serve.

Blue Cheese and Salted Almond Bundts

³/₄ cup whole salted almonds
1¹/₂ tablespoons chopped fresh tarragon
³/₄ cup crumbled blue cheese

Grind ¹/₂ cup of the nuts and add to the batter with the tarragon and ¹/₂ cup of the blue cheese. Combine the remaining whole nuts and remaining blue cheese in a small bowl. Top the cooled cakes with the mixture.

Butterscotch and Sea Salt Bundts

1 cup butterscotch chips
2 tablespoons sea salt
³/₄ cup Butterscotch Sauce (page 349)

Omit the table salt from the batter and replace it with the butterscotch chips and 1 tablespoon of the sea salt. Top the cooled cakes with the remaining sea salt and butterscotch sauce.

Parmesan Peach Bundts

³/₄ cup grated Parmesan cheese
1¹/₂ cups fresh peach slices
1 teaspoon grated lemon zest

Add ¹/₂ cup of the Parmesan, ³/₄ cup of the peaches, and the lemon zest to the batter after mixing. Top the cooled cakes with the remaining Parmesan and peaches.

Raspberry Napoleon Cake

Makes one 10-inch cake

18 sheets frozen phyllo dough, thawed

½ cup clarified butter (page 25), browned

6 cups Whipped Cream (page 359)

2 cups fresh raspberries

1 teaspoon confectioners' sugar

This recipe will make you a fan of the light and crispy texture of phyllo cakes. Raspberries and cream add sweetness to this classic flaky layered cake.

1. Preheat the oven to 375°F. Butter three 10 x 10-inch square pans.

2. Using scissors, cut the phyllo to fit the pans, then score the top sheet with a knife to indicate where you will make the slices (about 2½ x 3¼ inches each) when the cake is ready to eat. Cover the phyllo with a clean damp towel while you are working to keep it from drying out.

3. Layer five sheets of phyllo in each of two of the pans and eight sheets in the third pan, brushing each layer with clarified browned butter before adding the next sheet. Bake for 10–12 minutes, or until crisp. Cool in the pans on racks.

4. To assemble the cake, place one set of five phyllo sheets on a serving plate. Spread with half the whipped cream and top with another stack of five phyllo sheets. Add three-fourths of the raspberries and spread with the remaining whipped cream. Top with the set of eight sheets. Sprinkle with confectioners' sugar and top with remaining raspberries. Cut into slices to serve.

Variations

Chocolate Strawberry Napoleon: Replace the raspberries with sliced strawberries and the whipped cream with Chocolate Pastry Cream (page 358).

Peaches and Cream Napoleon: Make honey syrup by stirring together ¼ cup clover honey and 3 tablespoons water in a small bowl. Heat in the microwave for 40 seconds. Brush the top of the phyllo cakes with the honey syrup before baking. Replace the raspberries with 6 peeled, pitted, and sliced fresh peaches.

Kirsch Almond Pastry Cream

2 cups whole milk

4 large egg yolks

2 tablespoons cornstarch

½ cup granulated sugar

1 teaspoon vanilla extract

1 tablespoon Kirsch

⅓ cup ground almonds

Zinfandel Sour Cherry Filling

1 cup red Zinfandel wine

1 cinnamon stick

¼ teaspoon ground cloves

3 tablespoons clover honey

½ cup cherry jelly

1½ cups pitted fresh, drained
 canned, or thawed frozen sour
 cherries

Short Pastry

1 cup all-purpose flour

1 cup corn flour

1 teaspoon baking powder

¼ cup ground almonds

10 tablespoons (1¼ sticks) cold
 unsalted butter, cut into small
 pieces

1 large egg

2 large eggs, separated

1 cup confectioners' sugar

Basque Cake

Makes one 10-inch cake

The gâteau Basque is a specialty from the Basque country, a region that straddles Spain and France. Traditionally, the light, short pastry is filled with jam made from the sour black Itxassou cherries grown in the Basque country. Today, pastry cream alone or with cherry jam is also commonly used. It is a very impressive yet rustic dessert.

1. To make the pastry cream, beat ½ cup of the milk, the egg yolks, and cornstarch in a medium mixing bowl with an electric mixer on medium speed until smooth.

2. Bring the remaining milk and sugar to a boil in a large saucepan. Add one-fourth of the egg-yolk mixture, whisking briskly. Gradually add the remaining egg-yolk mixture, whisking until thick and smooth. Remove from the heat and whisk in the vanilla, Kirsch, and almonds. Transfer to a bowl, cover, and refrigerate until cool.

3. To make the filling, combine the wine, cinnamon, and cloves in a saucepan. Simmer over low heat for 10 minutes, or until the liquid is reduced by one-third. Add the honey and cherry jelly and stir until dissolved, then add the cherries. Reduce the heat to a simmer and cook until thickened. Remove from the heat, discard the cinnamon stick, and set aside to cool.

4. To make the pastry crust, combine both flours and the baking powder in a food processor or blender. Add the almonds and butter. Pulse several times until the mixture resembles coarse meal.

5. Whisk the egg, egg yolks, and sugar in a medium mixing bowl with an electric mixer on medium speed until smooth. Gradually add to the flour mixture and pulse until the mixture gathers into a ball. If the dough is too crumbly, add a bit of the egg white; if it is too sticky, add a bit more flour.

6. Divide the dough into two balls, one slightly larger than the other. Cover in plastic wrap and chill for 30 minutes.

7. Preheat the oven to 350°F. Butter and flour a 10-inch deep-dish pie pan (or a 10-inch round pan that's 2 inches deep).

8. Dust a work surface with flour. Roll out the larger ball of dough to an approximately 12-inch round that is ¼ inch thick. Fit the dough into the pan to cover the bottom and stretch up the sides, and bake for 5–7 minutes, or until lightly browned. Roll out the smaller ball to a 10-inch round. Using a fork, emboss the dough with a pattern of your choosing.

9. Pour half the pastry cream over the baked crust, then top with half the sour cherry filling. Add the remaining pastry cream and top with the 10-inch pastry, pinching around the edges to seal. Brush with the remaining egg whites and poke a few holes in the crust. Bake for 35–40 minutes, or until golden and set. Place the pan on a rack to cool completely.

10. Transfer the cake to a serving plate and serve with the remaining sour cherry filling.

Variations

Apricot Basque Cake: Replace the cherry jelly and sour cherries with equal amounts of apricot jam and fresh apricots. Replace the Zinfandel with Chardonnay and the Kirsch with brandy.

Hazelnut Basque Cake: Replace the almonds with an equal amount of ground hazelnuts. Replace the Zinfandel with Sauvignon Blanc and the Kirsch with hazelnut liqueur.

COCKTAIL PARTY CAKES

The cakes in this section have one thing in common: they all are flavored with alcoholic beverages, which give each cake a kick. They're perfect for a casual but swank dessert party or cocktail party. Keep in mind that, after about 15 minutes of baking, about 60 percent of the alcohol you use in a cake burns off; when baking time is increased to an hour, about 75 percent of the alcohol burns off. There is a fine line between adding enough alcohol to impart a subtle yet wonderful "boozy" flavor to a cake and adding not too much to overpower it. As I developed these recipes, I was intent on finding that line and figuring out which cakes and alcohols make killer combinations. I also wanted to devise designs that allow you to show off your skills and entertain in style. Enjoy the results!

Rum Cakes with Garnishes

Makes 4 cups batter, enough for about 12 servings

Boost your cocktail-party repertoire with cakes inspired by cocktail garnishes. Think of them as after-dinner appetizers. These were made in small silicone baking molds, but if you don't have any, you can use mini muffin tins or make the cake in a sheet pan and cut out the shapes with cookie cutters.

1½ cups all-purpose flour
½ teaspoon baking powder
¼ teaspoon salt
¾ cup (1½ sticks) unsalted butter, at room temperature
¾ cup granulated sugar
3 large eggs
¼ cup golden rum
1¾ cups *Rum Syrup* (page 355)
3 cups assorted fresh fruit and vegetable garnishes (such as grapes, kiwifruit slices, cucumber slices, lemon wedges, apple wedges, lemon peel, or Mandarin orange sections)

1. Preheat the oven to 350°F. Butter and flour 30 small (1¼ x ¾-inch or 2 x 1-inch) silicone molds in various shapes (or use mini muffin cups).

2. Combine the flour, baking powder, and salt.

3. Beat the butter and sugar in a large mixing bowl with an electric mixer on medium speed until fluffy. Add the eggs one at a time, beating well after each addition.

4. Gradually add the flour mixture, alternating with the rum, on low speed until blended.

5. Pour the batter into the molds and bake for 10–15 minutes, or until a tester inserted in the center comes out clean. Cool in the molds.

6. Unmold the cakes and brush with rum syrup. Thread 2–3 cakes onto each cocktail pick, alternating with the fruit and vegetable garnishes.

Coffee Liqueur Bundt Cake

Makes one 8-inch cake or eight 3½-inch cakes

3 cups all-purpose flour

½ cup unsweetened cocoa powder

1 tablespoon baking soda

½ teaspoon salt

¾ cup (1½ sticks) unsalted butter, at room temperature

1½ cups granulated sugar

1 teaspoon vanilla extract

3 large eggs, separated

3 ounces dark (at least 60% cacao) chocolate, melted

½ cup milk

¾ cup coffee liqueur

1½ cups Chocolate Ganache (page 351)

3 cups Whipped Cream (page 359)

Cake made with coffee liqueur has its own distinctive way of being the hit of a cocktail party. Chocolate ganache melts in the crevices, highlighting the chocolate in the cake. Whipped cream sits so nicely in the center and offers that coffee-and-cream flavor.

1. Preheat the oven to 350°F. Butter and flour an 8-inch Bundt pan or eight 3½-inch Bundt pans.

2. Combine the flour, cocoa powder, baking soda, and salt in a mixing bowl.

3. Cream the butter, 1 cup of the sugar, and vanilla in a large mixing bowl with an electric mixer on medium speed until light and fluffy. Beat in the egg yolks and chocolate.

4. Gradually add the flour mixture, alternating with the milk and liqueur, on low speed until blended.

5. In a clean bowl with clean beaters, beat the egg whites until soft peaks form. Gradually beat in the remaining sugar to make a meringue. Gently fold the egg whites into the batter with a rubber spatula.

6. Pour the batter into the pan or pans and bake for 50–55 minutes (for the 8-inch pan; bake 25–30 minutes in the smaller pans), or until a tester inserted in the center comes out clean. Cool in the pan for 10 minutes, then invert onto a rack to cool completely.

7. Place the cooled cake on a serving plate. For the large cake, top with ganache and spoon whipped cream on the side of each serving plate after slicing. If you are baking the miniature Bundt cakes, use a pastry bag fitted

with a large star-shaped tip to pipe whipped cream into the center of each cake.

Piña Colada Babas
Makes 12 cakes

The term "baba" means "grandma"—but this snazzy contemporary cake is anything but grandmotherly! Inspired by the famous rum-soaked cakes of France and Italy, these yeast cakes can be baked in baba molds if you have them, or in muffin tins if you don't.

1. To make the babas, butter and flour twelve 2 x 3½-inch baba molds, or line 12 large muffin cups with paper or foil liners.

2. Mix the yeast, water, and 1 teaspoon of the sugar in a small bowl and set aside for 7 to 10 minutes, or until foamy.

3. Combine the flour, coconut, and salt in a mixing bowl.

4. Beat the eggs and remaining sugar in a large mixing bowl with an electric mixer on medium speed until pale. Beat in the oil, butter, rum, and yeast mixture. Gradually add the flour mixture on low speed until blended.

5. Transfer the dough to a floured work surface and knead for 7–10 minutes, or until smooth. Roll the dough into a long log and cut into 12 pieces. Place in the molds and cover loosely with plastic. Let stand for 40–60 minutes, or until the dough has risen close to the top of each mold.

6. Preheat the oven to 350°F. Bake the babas for 13–16 minutes, or until light and golden. Transfer to a rack to cool completely.

7. Make a horizontal cut in the middle of the cooled babas, slicing about two-thirds of the way through the cake and leaving the top part attached. Brush on the syrup and let soak for 20 minutes.

Babas

2 packets (¼ ounce each) active dry yeast

¼ cup warm water

2 tablespoons granulated sugar

2⅓ cups all-purpose flour

½ cup sweetened flaked coconut

¼ teaspoon salt

5 large eggs

½ cup extra virgin olive oil

4 tablespoons (½ stick) unsalted butter, melted and cooled

2 teaspoons golden rum

1¾ cups Pineapple Rum Syrup (page 356)

Filling

2 cups heavy cream

¼ cup granulated sugar

1 teaspoon vanilla extract

¼ cup sweetened flaked coconut

¼ cup canned crushed pineapple, drained

Yellow food coloring

Garnish

12 fresh pineapple wedges

12 maraschino cherries, with stems

½ cup coconut curls, toasted (page 33)

8. To make the filling, beat the cream, sugar, and vanilla in a large mixing bowl with an electric mixer on medium speed until stiff peaks form. Transfer about half the whipped cream to a smaller bowl and add the coconut to it. Add the crushed pineapple and yellow food coloring to the large bowl.

9. To serve, place the babas on dessert plates. Carefully lift the top of each baba and, using a pastry bag fitted with a large round tip, pipe the pineapple cream into the middle. Using a large star-shaped tip, pipe the coconut cream on top. Thread a pineapple wedge and cherry onto each of 12 cocktail toothpicks or small skewers and place on top of the cakes. Sprinkle with coconut curls.

Peach Melba (and Cherries Jubilee)
Makes 12 servings

Peach Melba, and the similar cherries jubilee, are classic desserts attributed to the French chef Auguste Escoffier (1846–1935). Peach Melba is traditionally made from poached peaches, vanilla ice cream, and raspberry sauce. I've added peaches to the ice cream and liqueur to the raspberry sauce—and, of course, cake to the dessert itself. Even though I show it as a variation here, don't think that cherries jubilee comes in second in any way. Said to have been invented for Queen Victoria, this dessert is often flambéed and served with vanilla ice cream. I have added cherries to both the cake and the ice cream.

1. To make the ice cream, combine the egg yolks and milk in a double boiler. Add the sugar and salt. Beat with an electric mixer on medium speed until the mixture thickens and coats the back of a wooden spoon. Let cool to room temperature, then stir in the cream, almond extract, and peaches. Transfer to an ice cream maker and freeze according to the manufacturer's directions.

2. To make the cake, preheat oven to 350°F. Butter and flour 12 large muffin cups.

Peach Ice Cream
6 large egg yolks
2 cups whole milk
1 cup granulated sugar
½ teaspoon salt
2 cups heavy cream
1 teaspoon almond extract
2 cups peeled, pitted, and chopped fresh peaches (about 4 medium)

Peach Cake

1½ cups all-purpose flour

1 teaspoon baking powder

¼ teaspoon salt

½ cup (1 stick) unsalted butter, at
    room temperature

1¼ cups granulated sugar

3 large eggs

1 teaspoon vanilla extract

¾ cup whole milk

2 fresh peaches, peeled and diced

Raspberry Sauce

1 pound fresh or frozen raspberries

¾ cup granulated sugar

2 tablespoons freshly squeezed
    lemon juice

2 tablespoons raspberry liqueur

Garnish

4 fresh peaches, peeled, cut into
    wedges, and grilled (page 244)

3 cups fresh, thawed frozen, or
    drained canned black or sour
    cherries

½ cup cherry juice (reserved from
    canned cherries, if desired)

1 tablespoon granulated sugar

½ tablespoon cornstarch

¼ cup Kirsch

½ cup lemon zest

½ cup fresh mint leaves

3. Combine the flour, baking powder, and salt in a mixing bowl.

4. Cream the butter and sugar in a large mixing bowl with an electric mixer on medium speed until fluffy. Add the eggs one at a time, beating well after each addition. Beat in the vanilla.

5. Gradually add the flour mixture on low speed alternating with the milk, until blended, then fold in the peaches.

6. Pour the batter into the muffin cups, filling each about one-fourth full. Bake for 12–15 minutes, or until a tester inserted in the center comes out clean. Cool completely in the pans.

7. To make the raspberry sauce, purée the raspberries and press them through a sieve to remove the seeds. Combine the puréed raspberries, sugar, lemon juice, and liqueur in a food processor or blender and purée until smooth.

8. To serve, divide the ice cream, cakes, and grilled peaches among twelve dessert plates. Top with raspberry sauce.

Cherries Jubilee

1. Replace the peaches in the cake with 1 cup cherries and the peaches in the ice cream with 1 cup cherries. Bake the cakes in large muffin cups or small cake pans.

2. Omit the raspberry sauce. To make the cherry sauce, combine the cherry juice, sugar, and cornstarch in a saucepan. Heat until thickened, then stir in the remaining 1 cup cherries. Remove from the heat and stir in the Kirsch.

3. Serve the ice cream, cakes, and cherries in dessert bowls. Top with lemon zest and fresh mint.

Gelatin Layer

6 packets (¼ ounce each)
  unflavored gelatin

1 cup cold unsweetened apple juice

3 cups hot unsweetened apple juice

3 tablespoons clover honey

1 teaspoon amaretto liqueur

1½ cups slivered almonds

2 oranges, peeled and sliced lengthwise in ¼-inch-thick circles

1½ cups whole fresh strawberries,
  hulled

1 cup fresh blueberries

1 cup fresh blackberries

Cake

3 cups all-purpose flour

1 teaspoon baking powder

½ teaspoon salt

¾ pound (3 sticks) unsalted butter,
  at room temperature

1½ cups granulated sugar

6 large eggs

1 tablespoon grated orange zest

1 tablespoon orange juice

Garnish

½ cup Amaretto Syrup (page 356)

1½ cups sliced fresh strawberries

Jelly Fruitcake

Makes one 10-inch cake

Gelatin offers a wild and profound textural eating experience. It's been on trendy menus for a few years, but this cake brings it to a new, ultramodern level. For me, the best part of experimenting with gelatin is its transparency. Here I arranged fruits in a graphic pattern in a layer of gelatin, which I set over a sturdy orange pound cake. Soak the cake in amaretto syrup to make it a bit boozy and to help the layers stick together.

1. To make the gelatin layer, combine the gelatin and cold apple juice in a large mixing bowl and let sit for 1 minute. Stir in the hot apple juice, honey, and amaretto and let sit for 5 minutes longer.

2. Line a 10-inch springform pan with parchment paper. Spread the almonds in the pan. Cut the orange rounds in half so that they form half-moons. Starting with the smallest orange pieces, wrap 5–6 slices around each other in a circular pattern to create each rose. Place in the pan, then arrange the strawberries, blueberries, and blackberries so they radiate from the orange roses. Slowly and carefully pour in the gelatin mixture, cover, and refrigerate for 3–4 hours, or until set.

3. To make the cake, butter and flour a 10-inch round pan.

4. Combine the flour, baking powder, and salt in a mixing bowl.

5. Beat the butter and sugar in a large mixing bowl with an electric mixer on medium speed until creamy. Add the eggs one at a time, beating well after each addition. Beat in the orange zest and juice.

6. Gradually add the flour mixture on low speed until blended.

7. Pour the batter into the pan and bake for 45–55 minutes, or until a tester inserted in the center comes

out clean. Cool in the pan for 20 minutes, then transfer to a rack to cool completely.

8. Use a serrated knife to level the top of the cake. Place the cake on a serving plate. Brush the top with about half the amaretto syrup.

9. Carefully unmold the gelatin by inverting it onto a plate. Remove the parchment. Holding the plate, invert the gelatin on top of the cake and carefully remove the plate. Brush the strawberry slices with the remaining amaretto syrup and arrange at the base of the cake.

Irish Cream Cakes in Chocolate Cups

Makes 8 cakes

Flavored with Irish cream liqueur, coffee, chocolate, caramel, and vanilla, these decadently over-the-top cakes are served in chocolate cups for very impressive entertaining. The cups can be purchased ready-made from a baking-supplies store, or you can make them at home in any shape you like by experimenting with molds. Just be sure the mold for the cups is slightly larger than your muffin tins. Tempering the chocolate ensures that it will retain its shine.

1. To make the cake, preheat the oven to 350°F. Grease and flour eight medium muffin cups.

2. Combine the espresso and the Irish cream liqueur in one bowl and the flour, cocoa powder, baking soda, and salt in another.

3. Beat the butter, ½ cup sugar, and vanilla in a large mixing bowl with an electric mixer on medium speed until light and creamy. Add the egg yolks one at a time, beating well after each addition.

4. Gradually add the flour mixture, alternating with the espresso mixture, on low speed until blended.

5. In a clean bowl with clean beaters, beat the egg whites until soft peaks form. Gradually add the remaining ¼

Irish Cream Cakes

2 tablespoons double-strength
   brewed espresso
½ cup Irish cream liqueur
1⅓ cups all-purpose flour
¼ cup unsweetened cocoa powder
1½ teaspoons baking soda
¼ teaspoon salt
6 tablespoons (¾ stick) unsalted
   butter, at room temperature
¾ cup granulated sugar
1 tablespoon vanilla extract
2 large eggs, separated

Chocolate Cups

2½ pounds semisweet chocolate,
   tempered (see page 56)
Safflower oil, as needed

Irish Cream Whipped Cream

1½ cups heavy cream
1 teaspoon vanilla extract
1 tablespoon granulated sugar
¼ cup Irish cream liqueur

Caramel Sauce

¾ cup firmly packed light brown
   sugar
⅓ cup (about 5⅓ tablespoons)
   unsalted butter
⅓ cup heavy cream
1 teaspoon vanilla extract

Garnish

8 dark chocolate malted milk balls

cup sugar and beat until stiff peaks form. Gently fold the egg whites into the batter with a rubber spatula.

6. Pour the batter into the muffin cups, filling each 1 inch high. Bake for 15–20 minutes, or until knife inserted in the center comes out clean. Transfer to a rack to cool completely.

7. To make the chocolate cups, fill eight 3½-inch-diameter plastic or paper cups or dome-shaped silicone molds with water and place in the freezer. After 20–30 minutes, or when the water has begun to freeze, place a wooden stick or spoon in the center. Freeze for about 3 hours, or until the ice is solid, checking periodically to make sure that the stick remains upright.

8. Line a baking sheet with wax paper and draw fifteen 3-inch circles on the paper. When the ice is solid (which should take about 3 hours, depending on the size of the container and your freezer), melt the chocolate in a double boiler and keep warm; add a little safflower oil as needed if it begins to harden. Using a tablespoon, spoon ⅓ of the chocolate onto the wax paper circles and let harden. The circles should be about ¼ inch thick. Reserve the remaining chocolate over very low heat.

9. Remove the ice from the cups (tear off paper cups; flex the silicone molds to pop out the ice; or let plastic cups stand for 5 minutes to melt slightly). Wipe off all the moisture from one of the ice rounds—it should be as dry as possible. Do not drip any water into the reserved melted chocolate or it will lose the desired texture. Holding the ice by the stick, put it into the melted chocolate and coat. Remove quickly and allow the chocolate to harden (less than 1 minute). Once hardened, the chocolate should slide off of the ice easily. Set the cups on another baking sheet lined with wax paper. Wipe the block of ice to remove any chocolate and dry. Repeat to make the desired number of cups. Use additional ice molds if necessary.

10. Attach the chocolate circles to the bottom of the chocolate cups with the remaining melted chocolate and let set. Refrigerate until ready to use.

11. To make the Irish cream whipped cream, beat the heavy cream, vanilla, sugar, and Irish cream in a large mixing bowl with an electric mixer on medium speed until soft peaks form and the cream is smooth and satiny. Refrigerate until needed.

12. To make the caramel sauce, bring the brown sugar, butter, and cream to a boil in a saucepan over medium heat. Reduce the heat to a simmer and continue to cook, stirring, for 5 minutes. Remove from the heat and stir in the vanilla.

13. To assemble, place the chocolate cups on dessert plates or a serving plate. Pipe or spoon about ¼ cup of the whipped cream into each cup, so that it reaches the top. Place a cake in each cup, anchoring it in the whipped cream on the diagonal. Drizzle with caramel sauce and garnish with malted milk balls. Serve with a fork.

Variation

Irish Cream Bundt Cake: Prepare the cake in a 9-inch Bundt pan and bake for 40–50 minutes. Top with Chocolate Sauce (page 352) in addition to the Irish cream whipped cream and caramel sauce.

Blackberry Whiskey Cake

Makes one 8-inch cake

Irish whiskey and berries are a perfect match in this cake. This version is made with blackberries, although both the cake and sauce can also be made with blueberries or raspberries.

1. Preheat the oven to 350°F. Butter and flour an 8-inch round pan.

2. Combine the flour, baking powder, and salt in a mixing bowl.

3. Beat the butter, sugar, and whiskey in a large mixing bowl with an electric mixer on medium speed until creamy. Add the eggs one at a time, beating well after each addition.

4. Gradually add the flour mixture, alternating with the milk, on low speed until just blended. Fold in the blackberries.

5. Pour the batter into the pan and bake for 40–50 minutes, or until a knife inserted in the center comes out clean. Cool in the pan for 30 minutes, then transfer to a rack to cool completely.

6. To make the blackberry sauce, combine the sugar and water in saucepan over medium heat, stirring until dissolved. Remove from the heat and stir in the berries and whiskey. Cool slightly, then transfer to a bowl, cover, and refrigerate for 1 hour.

7. Place the cooled cake on a serving plate and pour over the sauce.

Whiskey Cake

2 cups all-purpose flour

1 tablespoon baking powder

1 teaspoon salt

½ cup (1 stick) unsalted butter, at room temperature

2 teaspoons Irish whiskey

2 large eggs

¾ cup whole milk

1 cup granulated sugar

¾ cup fresh blackberries

Blackberry Sauce

¼ cup granulated sugar

¼ cup water

3 tablespoons Irish whiskey

2 cups fresh blackberries

Chapter 6

Holiday Cakes

NEW YEAR'S EVE CAKES

The Gregorian New Year is the most widely celebrated holiday throughout the world—and can you believe there is not one international cake recipe that we all agree is perfect for the occasion? So here I submit a few recipes for consideration. When I think of New Year's, I think of Champagne—with chocolate and grapes. The chocolate orange checkerboard roll is inspired by and suitable for the most impressive black-tie affairs. And espresso cake is great for people like me, who love coffee and don't like to stay up late. Let me know your vote.

Chocolate Orange Checkerboard Roll

Makes one 9-inch rolled cake

For years, I coveted a 1930s checkerboard cake pan so I could make a vintage-style black-and-white cake. Others kept outbidding me on eBay (as they do almost all the time), so I never won, and finally I got fed up. I came up with my own checkerboard cake-in-a-roll recipe that is easy to make without the special pan. This recipe makes more chocolate-covered candied orange peel than is needed to top the cake, so either serve the excess alongside the cake or save it for snacking. After the peel is cooled, it can be pressed flat between two cutting boards or naturally formed into curls by just placing it on a rack to dry.

Chocolate-Covered Candied Orange Peel

½ cup granulated sugar

¼ cup water

1 tablespoon corn syrup

Peel of 3 oranges, cut into very thin strips

4 ounces bittersweet chocolate

Cake

⅓ cup all-purpose flour

⅓ cup unsweetened cocoa powder

3 ounces bittersweet chocolate

4 tablespoons (½ stick) unsalted butter

2 teaspoons vanilla extract

4 large eggs

½ cup granulated sugar

10 cups Lavender Orange Cake batter (page 112), made without lavender

Orange food coloring

¼ cup unsweetened cocoa powder

3 cups Whipped Cream (page 359)

Topping

½ cup Orange Glaze (page 354)

¾ cup Mandarin orange segments

1. To make the chocolate-covered candied orange peel, bring the sugar, water, and corn syrup to a boil in a saucepan over medium-high heat. Add the orange peel and boil for 20 minutes, stirring occasionally. Remove from heat and, using tongs, place the peel on a wire rack. Dry the peel for 6 hours or overnight.

2. Cover a baking sheet with wax paper. Melt the chocolate in a double boiler. Dip the peel into the chocolate and place on the baking sheet. Let set for 1½ hours to harden at room temperature, or place in the refrigerator to harden quickly.

3. To make the cake, preheat the oven to 375°F. Line a 9 x 12¼-inch jelly-roll pan with parchment paper.

4. Combine the flour and cocoa powder in a mixing bowl; set aside.

5. Melt the chocolate and butter in a double boiler over medium heat and stir in the vanilla until smooth. Remove from heat and let cool.

6. Beat the eggs and sugar in a large mixing bowl with an electric mixer on medium speed until thick and pale.

7. Gradually add the flour mixture on low speed until blended. Pour in the chocolate mixture and gently stir, being careful not to deflate the batter.

8. Spread the batter in the pan and bake for 15–18 minutes, or until the cake springs back when touched and a toothpick inserted in the center comes out clean.

9. Dust a clean towel with confectioners' sugar. Turn the cake onto the towel and remove the parchment. Roll the cake from the long side and let sit for 1 minute, then unroll and let sit for 2 minutes. Roll again and let cool completely.

10. Meanwhile, butter and flour a 9 x 13-inch pan. Divide the lavender orange cake batter among three bowls, adding the food coloring to one and the cocoa powder

to the second, and leaving the third plain. Pour the batters next to each other in the pan in horizontal stripes, keeping the batters separate.

11. Bake for 35–40 minutes, or until a tester inserted in the center comes out clean. Cool in the pan for 10 minutes, then transfer to a rack to cool completely.

12. Cut the cooled cake horizontally into six 1½–2 x 9-inch strips, slicing where the colors divide. You should have two plain, two orange, and two brown strips. Using one brown strip as a base, cover it on the top and sides with whipped cream. Stack an orange strip on top of it, then cover the orange strip on the top and sides with whipped cream. Stack a plain strip on top of the orange strip and cover the top and sides with whipped cream. Then make a second stack of three next to the first stack, starting with the plain strip, putting the orange strip in the middle and the brown strip on top, and covering the top and sides with whipped cream as you go. The six stacks together should make a checkerboard pattern when viewed from the ends.

13. Unroll the chocolate cake and spread with whipped cream. Place the checkerboard in the center, matching up the 9-inch sides, and wrap the chocolate cake around the checkerboard. Place on a serving plate, seam side down. Top with orange glaze, Mandarin orange segments, and chocolate-covered orange peel.

Espresso "Cup" Cakes
Makes 6 cakes

When you dig your spoon into these "cup" cakes, you will get the espresso jolt needed to stay up super late on New Year's Eve. I definitely need this, since my normal bedtime is way before midnight! For a party, I make the whole shebang—this recipe and both variations, as well as the whipped cream, coffee, *and* mocha frostings— but for a casual modern coffee klatch, I make only one variety.

Espresso Cake

1 cup all-purpose flour
1½ cups granulated sugar
2 tablespoons finely ground
   espresso beans
½ teaspoon salt
12 large egg whites (cold)
¼ cup double-strength brewed
   espresso
1 teaspoon cream of tartar
1 teaspoon vanilla extract

Frosting

¼ cup double-strength brewed
   espresso
1 teaspoon vanilla extract
¾ pound (3 sticks) unsalted butter,
   at room temperature
3½ cups confectioners' sugar
2 teaspoons finely ground espresso
   beans

Garnish

3 cups Whipped Cream (page
   359)
Chocolate shavings
Cocoa powder

1. Preheat the oven to 350°F. Spray six 2½–3-inch round by 3½–4-inch tall paper baking cups with nonstick cooking spray.

2. Combine the flour, ¾ cup of the sugar, ground espresso, and salt in a mixing bowl.

3. Beat the egg whites, brewed espresso, cream of tartar, and vanilla in a large mixing bowl with an electric mixer on medium speed until foamy with tiny bubbles. Gradually add the remaining ¾ cup sugar until the foam is creamy white but before soft peaks form. Gently fold the flour mixture into the egg whites, mixing until completely integrated.

4. Pour the batter into the cups and bake for 25–30 minutes, or until a tester inserted in the center comes out clean. Cool in the cups.

5. To make the frosting, combine the brewed espresso and vanilla in a small bowl.

6. Cream the butter and 1 cup of the sugar in a large mixing bowl with an electric mixer on medium speed until blended. Beat in the espresso mixture. Gradually add the remaining sugar until the frosting reaches a piping consistency. Stir in the ground espresso.

7. Transfer the frosting to a pastry bag fitted with a large star-shaped tip and pipe it onto the cakes—or simply dollop the frosting on with a spoon. Top with whipped cream chocolate shavings, and cocoa powder.

Variations

Mocha "Cup" Cakes: Add 3 ounces melted semisweet chocolate to the cake batter after it is fully mixed. To make mocha frosting, add ¼ cup unsweetened cocoa powder to the frosting batter with the sugar.

Hazelnut "Cup" Cakes: Add ¼ cup ground hazelnuts to the cake batter after it is fully mixed. Top with semisweet chocolate shavings, whipped cream, and chopped hazelnuts.

Chocolate Champagne Cake with Grape Topping

Makes one 10-inch two-layer cake

Serious Champagne fans bring in the New Year with bubbly in every form imaginable—including cake. Similar to a traditional Champagne cake, this version is filled with pastry cream, but nothing else in it is standard. The chocolate and grapes offer a fresh taste to savor and add a luxurious note to the night. Choose a sweet, fairly inexpensive Champagne or sparkling white wine for the cake and save the vintage bottle for your midnight toast. Use a variety of grapes in assorted colors to make a jewel-like topping. For a simpler cake, make the glazed Bundt variation.

1. To make the topping, soak the grapes in 1¾ cups of the Champagne in a large bowl for at least 1 hour. Drain the liquid from the grapes. Combine the remaining ¼ cup Champagne, cornstarch, and sugar in a medium saucepan and bring to a boil. Reduce the heat to low, add the grapes, and cook, stirring occasionally—being careful to keep most of the grapes whole—until the mixture thickens, about 5 minutes. Transfer to a large bowl, pouring off any excess liquid, and refrigerate until ready to use.

2. To make the cake, preheat the oven to 350°F. Butter and flour two 10-inch fluted round pans.

3. Combine the flour, cocoa powder, baking powder, and salt in a mixing bowl.

4. Beat the butter and sugar in a large mixing bowl with an electric mixer on medium speed until light and fluffy. Gradually add the flour mixture, alternating with the Champagne, on low speed until blended.

5. In a clean bowl with clean beaters, beat the egg whites until stiff peaks form. Gently fold the egg whites into the batter with a rubber spatula.

6. Pour the batter into the pans and bake for 30–35 minutes, or until a tester inserted in the center comes

out clean. Cool in the pans for 10 minutes, then transfer to a rack to cool completely.

7. To make the frosting, beat the butter, Champagne, and food coloring in a large mixing bowl with an electric mixer on medium speed. Gradually add the confectioners' sugar until it reaches a thick spreading consistency.

8. Place one cake on a serving plate. Level the top with a serrated knife and top with the pastry cream and one-third of the grape topping. Level the top of the other cake, place it over the grapes, and spread the frosting on the top and sides of both cakes. Top with the remaining grape topping.

Variation

Glazed Champagne-Soaked Bundt Cake: Bake the cake in a 10-inch Bundt pan for 45–50 minutes. Omit the grape topping, champagne frosting, and pastry cream. Combine ⅓ cup Champagne with 3 cups confectioners' sugar (or more if needed) until the mixture reaches the consistency of a glaze. Pour over the cake and let harden before serving.

VALENTINE'S DAY CAKES

I met my husband, Brian, at a lonely-hearts Valentine's Day party, so February 14 is an extra-special day for us—both as an anniversary and as a day for cake. Every year for the occasion, I make Brian a new type of cake, and this section features our greatest hits: playfully decorated chocolate truffle cakes; a purple rose cake that symbolizes love; velvet cakes in colors beyond red, which marry favorite flavors with favorite colors; and the aphrodisiac cake, which I don't need to explain. And although the outcome is not a mystery for me and Brian, I still love the "loves me, loves me not" cake as an homage to the game. These love tokens in cake form are just as welcome at anniversaries, weddings, bridal showers, or a beloved's birthday party as they are on Valentine's Day.

Chocolate Truffle Cakes

Makes 10 cakes

These blast-to-decorate cakes are based on everybody's favorite chocolate confection—truffles. This recipe calls for a raspberry mousse filling, but you can use an equal amount of blueberries or strawberries to suit your preference. If nuts are more to your liking, try one of the variations. I like to leave the contents of the fruit-filled cakes a mystery, concealing the fillings just as they would be hidden in a sampler box of candy, but I identify the cakes that contain nuts by using nuts as part of the decoration, so those with allergies will know which ones to avoid. Serve these bonbons on a heart-shaped plate, or set them in paper liners and package them in a gift box.

1. To make the mousse, beat the egg yolks and 2 tablespoons of the lemon juice in a double boiler until blended. Cook over low heat, stirring, until it coats the back of a metal spoon or reaches 160°F on an instant-read thermometer. Set aside to cool.

2. Combine the gelatin and remaining 2 tablespoons lemon juice in a large bowl, stirring until dissolved.

Raspberry Mousse

2 large eggs, separated

¼ cup freshly squeezed lemon juice

1 packet (¼ ounce) unflavored gelatin

1 pound fresh or thawed frozen raspberries, puréed and seeded

½ cup granulated sugar

1 cup water

1⅓ cups heavy cream

½ teaspoon cream of tartar

Opposite: Raspberry Truffle Cakes, Almond Truffle Cakes, Hazelnut Truffle Cakes, White Chocolate Pistachio Cakes.

Cake

2½ cups all-purpose flour

2 teaspoons baking soda

¼ teaspoon salt

1½ cups unsweetened cocoa powder

1 cup water

10 tablespoons (1¼ sticks) unsalted butter, at room temperature

1⅓ cups granulated sugar

1⅓ cups firmly packed light brown
  sugar

3 large eggs

1 tablespoon vanilla extract

1¼ cups buttermilk

3 ounces dark (at least 60%
  cacao) chocolate, melted

Garnish

8 ounces white chocolate, chopped

8 ounces milk chocolate, chopped

8 ounces dark (at least 60%
  cacao) chocolate, chopped

3. Add the raspberries and ¼ cup of the sugar to the gelatin mixture. Beat with an electric mixer on medium speed until smooth, then add the cream and beat until stiff.

4. In a medium saucepan over medium heat, with clean beaters, beat the egg whites, remaining ¼ cup sugar, water, and cream of tartar until the mixture reaches 160°F. Remove from the heat, transfer to a bowl, and continue to beat until stiff peaks form. Fold the cream and raspberry mixture into the egg yolks until blended. Cover and refrigerate for 2–3 hours, until thickened.

5. To make the cakes, preheat the oven to 325°F. Butter and flour ten 2½–3-inch round, square, oval, and rectangular baking molds, or 10 medium muffin cups.

6. Combine the flour, baking soda, and salt in a mixing bowl. Combine the cocoa powder and water in another bowl, stirring to dissolve.

7. Beat the butter and both sugars in a large mixing bowl with an electric mixer on medium speed until light and fluffy. Add the eggs one at a time, beating well after each addition, then add the vanilla.

8. Gradually add the flour mixture, alternating with the buttermilk, on low speed until blended. Stir in the melted chocolate.

9. Pour the batter into the molds and bake for 18–22 minutes, or until a tester inserted in the center comes out clean. Transfer to a rack to cool completely.

10. Line three baking sheets with parchment paper and place a cooling rack over each. Cut the cooled cakes in half horizontally. Scoop out a hole about 1½ inches in diameter and ¼ inch deep from the top and the bottom halves. Fill both halves with mousse, then press the tops onto the bottoms. Place the assembled cakes on the cooling racks.

11. Melt the chopped chocolates separately, one at a time, in a double boiler. Pour the chocolate over the cakes, covering some with white, others with milk, and others with dark chocolate. Allow the chocolate to drip onto the parchment, then pour the drippings back into the double boiler and keep warm. Once the chocolate on the cakes has set, add an additional layer if necessary to achieve a smooth finish. Let dry completely.

12. Melt the chocolates again and transfer to pastry bags fitted with your choice of tips. Pipe patterns and designs in the different chocolates onto the cakes.

Variations

Almond Truffle Cakes: Omit the raspberry mousse. Fill the cakes with Marzipan (page 354). After the cakes are assembled, press whole almonds into the cakes to make a pattern. Pour chocolate over the nuts. Top with additional almonds.

Hazelnut Truffle Cakes: Omit the raspberry mousse. Fill the cakes with Hazelnut Buttercream (page 350). After the cakes are assembled, press whole hazelnuts into the cakes to make a pattern. Pour chocolate over the nuts. Top with additional hazelnuts.

White Chocolate Pistachio Cakes: Omit the raspberry mousse. Fill the cakes with Pistachio Mousse (page 232). Omit the milk and dark chocolates and use 24 ounces of melted white chocolate to top the cakes. After the cakes are assembled, press whole pistachios into the cakes to make a pattern. Pour chocolate over the nuts. Top with additional pistachios.

Aphrodisiac Cake

Makes one 7-inch three-layer cake

Figs, dates, and chocolate are all considered aphrodisiacs in different cultures around the globe. I combined them all in this triple-layer cake to create a triple dose of power. Melt the very best dark chocolate you can find and serve the cake with one of the suggested wines on page 292. For other cake-and-wine pairings, swap the melted chocolate called for in the recipe for your personal favorite, and match it with an appropriate wine.

Cake

⅓ cup unsweetened cocoa powder

1⅓ cups boiling water

4 ounces bittersweet (at least 80% cacao) chocolate, coarsely chopped

1⅓ cups all-purpose flour

1 teaspoon baking soda

⅛ teaspoon salt

½ pound (2 sticks) unsalted butter, at room temperature

1 cup granulated sugar

3 large eggs

1 teaspoon vanilla extract

⅔ cup plain yogurt, at room temperature

1. Preheat the oven to 350°F. Butter and flour three 7-inch round pans.

2. Place the cocoa in a small bowl. Pour in the boiling water and whisk until all lumps are dissolved. Mix in the bittersweet chocolate, whisking until melted and smooth. Set aside to cool.

3. Combine the flour, baking soda, and salt in a mixing bowl.

4. Beat the butter and sugar in a large mixing bowl with an electric mixer on medium speed until fluffy. Add the eggs one at a time, and beat well after each addition. Beat in the vanilla.

5. Add half the flour mixture on low speed until blended. Blend in the yogurt, then add the remaining flour mixture and blend. Add the chocolate mixture on low speed just until blended. Do not overmix.

6. Pour the batter into the pans and bake for 25–30 minutes, or until a tester inserted in the center comes

Wine and Chocolate

When pairing chocolate cake and wine, the general rule is that delicately flavored chocolates work better with light-bodied wines and intensely flavored chocolates work with full-bodied wines. The lightness or deepness of flavor has nothing to do with color: a dark chocolate can have a light flavor or a white chocolate can have an intense flavor. Chocolate and wine that have the same types of flavors (nutty or fruity) can be eaten together or contrasted—it is all a matter of personal taste.

White chocolate has a creamy, buttery, honey flavor. It goes well with sherry, Moscato d'Asti, Orange Muscat, white Zinfandel, Riesling, and Champagne.

Milk chocolate (about 34 percent cacao) has less chocolate and more sugar than semisweet, bittersweet, or dark chocolate. Its sweeter taste needs a sweeter wine. Pair it with Pinot Noir, Merlot, tawny port, dessert wines, rosé Champagne, and muscatel.

Semisweet chocolate (55–70 percent cacao) has nutty, spicy, and fruity nuances that many wines can pick up beautifully. In addition to the wines suggested for bittersweet chocolate, try semisweet chocolate with red Zinfandel, drier Rieslings, and ruby port.

Bittersweet chocolate (70–100 percent cacao) has a bold, bitter flavor that needs a strong wine with fruity notes. Serve with Cabernet Sauvignon, Pinot Noir, Shiraz, Bordeaux, Marsala, or Beaujolais-Villages.

Filling

5–6 medium fresh figs, unpeeled

1 cup medjool dates

3 tablespoons orange juice

2 teaspoons granulated sugar

Topping

1⅓ cups Chocolate Ganache (page 351)

Garnish

1½ cups medjool dates

1 teaspoon freshly squeezed lemon juice

¼ cup sweetened flaked coconut

¼ cup blanched almonds

6 large fresh figs

out clean. Cool in the pans for 20 minutes, then transfer to a rack to cool completely.

7. To make the filling, cut the figs in quarters and purée them in a food processor. You should have 1 cup purée. Add the dates, orange juice, and sugar.

8. Place one cooled cake layer on a work surface and spread with half the filling. Place a second cake layer on top and spread with the remaining filling. Transfer one-fourth of the ganache to a pastry bag fitted with a medium star-shaped tip and pour the rest over the cake. Transfer the cake to a serving plate and pipe the chocolate ganache around the bottom of the cake.

9. To make the garnish, combine the dates and lemon juice in a blender and pulse to chop. Press chopped dates into twelve ¾ x 2-inch logs and roll in coconut. Press a blanched almond into each log.

10. Top the cake with the date logs and whole and halved figs. Serve with additional figs and date logs on the side.

Variations

Semisweet Chocolate Chocolate Chip Cake: Replace the chopped bittersweet chocolate with 4 ounces chopped semisweet chocolate. Add 4 ounces semisweet chocolate chips after the batter is mixed. Prepare the ganache with semisweet chocolate.

White Chocolate Raspberry Cake: Replace the bittersweet chocolate with 7 ounces white chocolate. Add 2 cups fresh or thawed frozen raspberries to the batter after it is mixed. Prepare the ganache with white chocolate. Replace the filling with raspberry jam. Top with fresh raspberries.

Milk Chocolate Cake: Replace the bittersweet chocolate with 6 ounces milk chocolate. Prepare the ganache with milk chocolate. Replace the filling with milk chocolate ganache.

Purple Rose of Cake

Makes one 9-inch cake

The best part about baking in my rose-shaped Bundt pan is that I get to play around with the color of the cake to convey different meanings for different occasions. For example, a purple rose, which symbolizes enchantment, elegance, and grandeur, is my favorite choice for Valentine's Day—although you might want to use other colors to convey other types of love (see page 297). Even before you take a bite of this cake, you'll "taste" its shape, and the aroma of the rosewater icing drizzled in the crevices will enchant you. Surround the cake with crystallized edible flowers.

1. To make the sugared roses, lightly beat the egg white in a small bowl. Using a small brush, lightly coat the entire blossom—including the tops and bottoms of the petals, but not the stem—with the egg white, then sprinkle with the sugar. Place the flowers on wax paper or parchment paper and let dry for about 1 hour, or until firm.

2. To make the cake, preheat the oven to 350°F. Generously butter and flour a 9-inch rose-shaped Bundt pan.

3. Combine flour, baking powder, and salt in a mixing bowl.

4. Beat the butter and sugar in a large mixing bowl with an electric mixer on medium speed until light and fluffy. Add the eggs one at a time, beating well after each addition. Beat in the rose water and orange zest.

5. Gradually add the flour mixture, alternating with the milk, on low speed until smooth. Stir in the food coloring.

6. Pour the batter into the pan and bake for 50–60 minutes, or until a tester inserted in the center comes out clean. Cool in the pan for 20 minutes, then invert onto a rack to cool completely.

7. To make the icing, beat the sugar, rose water, and orange juice in a large mixing bowl with an electric mixer on medium speed until blended. Add more confectioners' sugar or orange juice as needed for the icing to reach drizzling consistency.

8. Place the cooled cake on a serving plate. Drizzle the icing on the tips of the cake "petals" and sprinkle with purple and pink sugar.

Variation

Fondant Rose Cake: Bake the cake in a traditional Bundt pan. Top with
fondant roses (page 196).

7 cups Lemon Chiffon Cake batter
  (page 74)
4½ cups Vanilla Buttercream
  (page 356)
Green and yellow food coloring
3 cups Fondant (page 353)

Loves Me, Loves Me Not Cake

Makes one 6-inch two-layer cake

The fondant daisies atop this lemon-and-buttercream cake are
inspired by the tradition of plucking the petals from flowers one
by one to determine if a love is true. This petite cake is a nice
treat if it's just the two of you—or if you're by yourself—for the
holiday. Otherwise, you can prepare a larger sheet cake (make
it in a 9 x 13-inch pan, with double the amount of batter) for a
Valentine's Day party.

1. Bake the cake in two 6-inch round pans for 30–35
   minutes. Cool completely on a rack.

2. Leave about three-fourths of the buttercream in one
   bowl; divide the remainder between two smaller bowls.
   Tint the large bowl a light sage green and one of the
   smaller bowls yellow; leave the second small batch
   white. Place the white frosting in a pastry bag fitted
   with a medium round tip and the yellow frosting in a
   pastry bag fitted with a small round tip.

3. Place one cooled cake layer on a serving plate and top with about one-third of the green frosting. Place the second layer on top and spread the top and sides with the remaining green frosting. Pipe white dots around the bottom of the cake and overpipe with yellow dots.

4. Leave about three-fourths of the fondant white and tint the remaining one-fourth yellow. Roll out the fondant and, using a utility knife, cut two sets of white petals for each flower. Rather than cutting a separate piece of fondant for each petal, leave the petals connected so that they remain in a circle, attached to each other by the white center. The circles should be about 1 inch, 2 inches, 2½ inches, and 3 inches in diameter. Using the utility knife, cut out one round yellow center for each flower. To assemble, attach the two sets of petals to each other with frosting, making sure to rotate the top set of petals so that the spaces in between the bottom set of petals are filled in. Cut off some of the petals, then attach the yellow centers with frosting. Place the flowers and petals—including the loose, cut-off single petals—on the cake and pipe "Loves me" and "Loves me not" in yellow frosting.

Velvet Cake

Makes one 8-inch two-layer cake

Velvet cakes—chocolate enhanced with the sour flavors of vinegar and buttermilk and topped with cream cheese frosting—are all the rage. Although red velvet is the best-known variety, and perhaps the most obvious choice for Valentine's Day, I prefer to make a blue velvet cake for my husband, Brian, and me, because it's our favorite color. For Valentine's parties with a large crowd, I make velvet cakes in a selection of different colors (blue, red, green, and orange) and shapes (loaves, Bundts, and cupcakes) so each person can choose his or her own favorite.

1. To make the cake, preheat the oven to 350°F. Butter and flour two 8-inch round pans.

Crafty Cake Stands

I made the cake stands shown below from my collection of vintage vases, candleholders, and plates. Scour thrift stores and garage sales for plates without large rims and for weighty candleholders and vases. Just attach them with epoxy glue and let dry.

Cake

2¼ cups all-purpose flour

1 teaspoon baking soda

¾ cup unsweetened cocoa powder

1½ cups granulated sugar

2 large eggs

1¼ cups canola oil

1 teaspoon cider vinegar

1 bottle (1 ounce) blue food coloring

1 teaspoon vanilla extract

1¼ cups buttermilk

Frosting

¾ cup (1½ sticks) unsalted butter, at room temperature

1½ boxes (8 ounces each) cream cheese, at room temperature

1 teaspoon vanilla extract

2 tablespoons whole milk

4 cups confectioners' sugar

2. Combine the flour, baking soda, and cocoa powder in a mixing bowl.

3. Beat the sugar and eggs in a large mixing bowl with an electric mixer on medium speed until fluffy. Beat in the oil, vinegar, food coloring, and vanilla.

4. Gradually add the flour mixture, alternating with the buttermilk, on low speed until blended.

5. Pour the batter into the pans and bake for 25–30 minutes, or until a tester inserted near the center comes out clean. Cool in the pans for 10 minutes, then transfer to a rack to cool completely.

6. To make the frosting, beat the butter, cream cheese, vanilla, and milk in a large mixing bowl with an electric mixer on medium speed until fluffy. Add the confectioners' sugar until the frosting reaches spreading consistency.

7. Place a cooled cake on a serving plate and level the top. Top with half the frosting. Place the second cake on top and frost, leaving the sides exposed so the color is visible.

Variations

Pecan Blueberry Blue Velvet Cake: After frosting each layer, top with ¾ cup fresh blueberries and ¼ cup pecan halves.

Green Velvet Loaf Cake: Replace the blue food coloring with green and bake in two 8-inch loaf pans for 40–45 minutes. Once cooled, level the tops with a serrated knife. Place one loaf on a plate and frost. Invert the second loaf over it and frost the top.

Red (or Orange) Velvet Bundts: Replace the blue food coloring with red or orange and bake in one 8-inch Bundt pan for 45–55 minutes or in eight small Bundt pans for 25–30 minutes. Omit the frosting and dust the cakes with confectioners' sugar.

Velvet Cupcakes: Divide the batter among four bowls. Add blue, green, red, and orange food coloring to each bowl. Pour batter into 24 muffin cups lined with paper or foil liners and bake for 20–25 minutes. Let cupcakes cool. Using a pastry bag fitted with a large star-shaped tip, pipe the frosting in a swooping spiral on top.

EASTER CAKES

Traditionally, Easter desserts consist of flavorful, yeast-risen, bready fruit cakes such as White Fruitcake (page 304), which is perfect for a pre- or post-church breakfast. Bunny- and egg-shaped cakes symbolize new beginnings and offer a universal celebration of spring. But for me, the flavor standout of the holiday—the too-good-to-be-true overabundance—is epitomized in the Meringue Layers with Marshmallow Filling (page 302), which reminds me of my favorite Easter marshmallow candies.

Bunny Cakes

Makes 8 bunny cakes

14 cups Devil's Food Cake batter
  (page 76)
5 cups Chocolate Frosting (page
  351), thinned with ¼ cup whole
  milk
3 cups Vanilla Frosting (page
  357), thinned with ¼ cup whole
  milk
Colored sprinkles
Crystal sugar

Come spring, I have a particular fondness for chocolate Easter bunnies and eggs . . . especially those made of cake! I like to make the eggs (see the variation on page 302) and the oval bunny heads in my eight-cavity egg-shaped pan, or in my dome-shaped baking pans, but if you don't have those, pour the batter into large muffin cups. Then, once the cakes have cooled, you can shape them into eggs and bunny heads by cutting and rounding off the edges with a serrated knife.

1. Pour two-thirds of the batter in eight 3-inch-diameter dome-shaped pans and the remainder in an 8 x 8-inch square pan. Bake the cakes for 25–30 minutes. Cool completely in pans.

2. Divide the frosting into one large and one smaller batch each.

3. Line a baking sheet with parchment paper and place a rack on top. To make the bunnies, cut out ears from the square cake and attach to the tops of each dome with frosting. Set the bunnies on the rack and let harden.

4. Pour the larger batch of chocolate frosting over 5 of the dome-shaped cakes, covering them on all sides. Pour the larger batch of vanilla frosting over 3 of the dome-shaped cakes, covering them on all sides. Spoon the coconut, sprinkles, and crystal sugar over the bunnies.

5. Thicken the remaining smaller batches of frosting by adding more confectioners' sugar and, using a pastry bag fitted with a small round tip, pipe frosting on the faces and in the ears. To make the noses, pipe a dot of frosting in the center of the face and press crystal sugar into the frosting. Sprinkle with sugars in complementary colors.

Variation

Easter Egg Cakes: Bake the batter in 16 dome-shaped pans and attach the domes to each other with frosting to form 8 egg shapes. Frost the eggs and roll in remaining toppings to cover.

Meringue Layers with Marshmallow Filling

Makes 3 three-layer cakes

I created these cakes in the spirit of Peeps, those sugar-coated bunny- and chick-shaped marshmallow candies found during the springtime. These all-grown-up meringue cakes are light and fluffy, yet they evoke the taste of the creamy, kitschy originals at the same time.

6 large egg whites

½ teaspoon cream of tartar

⅓ cup granulated sugar

2 teaspoons vanilla extract

2 tablespoons red crystal sugar

2 tablespoons green crystal sugar

2 tablespoons purple crystal sugar

4 cups Marshmallow Frosting
(page 345)

1. Preheat the oven to 150°F. Line a baking sheet with parchment paper. Using a pencil, draw nine 4-inch circles on the parchment. Flip the paper over and put it on the baking sheet. You should see the lines through the paper; if you don't, darken them.

2. Beat the eggs whites and cream of tartar in a large mixing bowl with an electric mixer on medium speed until soft peaks form. Gradually beat in the sugar and vanilla until stiff peaks form. Place the meringue in a pastry bag fitted with a star-shaped tip.

3. Pipe the meringue in spirals to fill the circles on the parchment and bake for 1 hour, or until the surface is hard to the touch. Turn off the oven and let the meringues cool in the oven for 2 hours. Transfer the meringues from the parchment to a rack to cool completely.

4. Place one cooled meringue on a dessert plate and top with one-sixth of the marshmallow cream. Place a second meringue on top and spread with another one-sixth of the marshmallow cream, then top with a third meringue. Repeat with remaining meringues and marshmallow cream. Dust the meringues with colored sugars.

Variation

Lemon Meringue Sandwiches: Rather than nine 4-inch meringues, make twelve 3-inch meringues, and bake them for 50 minutes. Replace the marshmallow filling with Lemon Filling (page 354) and use it to top 6 of the cooled meringue layers. Place the other 6 layers on top of the filled layers to make 6 sandwiches.

White Fruitcake

Makes one 13-inch round cake

¼ cup dried apricots, chopped

⅓ cup golden raisins

⅓ cup dried pineapple, chopped

½ cup light rum

5 strands saffron

2 cups warm whole milk

1 packet (¼ ounce) active dry
    yeast

6 cups bread flour

1 teaspoon ground cardamom

½ teaspoon salt

½ cup (1 stick) unsalted butter, at
    room temperature

⅔ cup granulated sugar

2 large eggs

2 tablespoons grated orange zest

½ cup slivered almonds, chopped

2 ounces almond paste

½ cup candied ginger, chopped

1 large egg, lightly beaten

2 teaspoons yellow crystal sugar

From the first bite of this white fruitcake, you can distinguish the flavor of each ingredient, but at the same time, the flavors are laced together in a delicate but delicious harmony. White fruitcakes are made from lighter—in both color and flavor—fruits, nuts, and spices than are used in regular fruitcake. Here I used apricots, golden raisins, saffron, and cardamom. I form the yeast dough into a spiral and bake it on a baking sheet, but it can also be braided, baked in a ring pan, or formed into loaves.

1. Combine the apricots, raisins, pineapple, and rum in a medium bowl. Let plump overnight.

2. Combine the saffron and warm milk in a small bowl. Let sit for 20 minutes. Add the yeast and let sit for 10 minutes, or until foamy.

3. Combine the flour, cardamom, and salt in a medium bowl.

4. Beat the butter and sugar in a large mixing bowl with an electric mixer on medium speed until light and fluffy. Mix in the eggs, zest, almonds, almond paste, and ginger. Drain the dried fruits and add them to the batter.

5. Gradually add the flour mixture, alternating with the saffron mixture, on low speed until a soft dough forms.

6. Transfer the dough to a floured work surface and knead for 8–10 minutes, or until smooth and stretchy. If the dough is sticky, add additional flour. Place the dough in a floured bowl, cover loosely, and let rise for about 2 hours, or until doubled in volume.

7. Transfer the dough back to the floured work surface and punch it to deflate. Roll the dough into a log about 18–20 inches in length. Transfer to a 14 x 17-inch baking sheet covered with parchment paper and, starting from the center, curl the log into a spiral. Cover again and let rise for 45–60 minutes, or until doubled in volume.

8. Preheat the oven to 325°F. Brush the dough with the beaten egg and sprinkle with sugar. Bake for 45–55 minutes, or until golden and the cake sounds hollow when tapped. Cool on the pan.

Variation

Loaf Fruitcake: Roll the dough into a log about 14 inches in length. Coat a 4 x 16-inch loaf pan with cooking spray, line the bottom with parchment, and bake the fruitcake for 45–55 minutes. Top with Rum Syrup (page 355) and Orange Icing (page 358) after cooling.

CAKES FOR JEWISH HOLIDAYS

Many of my friends know about my fascination with the crossover between culinary and cultural history, especially the role that baked goods play in worldwide celebrations and traditions. That is why, although I am not Jewish, I appreciate the meanings behind the cakes in this section—not to mention their flavors. Each one of these selections stands out on its own as a delicious treat, and each can be enjoyed anytime and anyplace, regardless of the occasion.

Jelly Doughnuts

Makes 10–12 doughnuts

Oil is central to the Hanukkah story: an oil lamp used to rededicate the Temple in Jerusalem in the second century BCE had enough oil to burn for only one day, but it lasted for eight days, and the Festival of Lights began. Food fried in oil became symbolic of the holiday, and the sweet jelly on the inside of the *sufganiyah* (jelly doughnut) became essential to the celebration of this festival. These doughnuts are coated with a glaze and then dusted with confectioners' sugar. If you would like to enjoy them warm, skip the glaze and simply sprinkle the doughnuts with sugar.

1. Mix the yeast and milk in a small bowl. Let sit for 10 minutes, or until foamy.

2. Combine the flour, sugar, salt, and eggs in a large mixing bowl with an electric mixer on medium speed. Add the yeast mixture on low speed until blended.

3. Transfer the dough to a floured work surface and knead for 7–10 minutes, or until smooth.

4. Beat the butter in a medium mixing bowl with an electric mixer on medium speed until creamy. Knead the butter into the dough until mixed. Place the dough in a buttered bowl and cover with a clean, dry towel. Let rise until doubled in bulk, about 1–1½ hours.

Doughnuts

1 packet (¼ ounce) active dry yeast

1 cup warm whole milk

4½ cups all-purpose flour

¾ cup granulated sugar

½ teaspoon salt

2 large eggs

½ cup (1 stick) unsalted butter, at room temperature

1½ cups cherry jelly

3½ cups vegetable oil

Glaze

¼ cup whole milk

1 teaspoon vanilla extract

2 cups confectioners' sugar

5. Roll out the dough on a floured work surface to ½ inch thick. Cut out an even number of circles with a 3½–4-inch cutter. Top half the circles with 1 tablespoon jelly each, then set the remaining circles on top, pressing the edges together to seal. Sprinkle with flour, cover with a towel, and let rise on a baking sheet for 30 minutes.

6. Heat the oil in a large deep saucepan until it reaches 365°F on a deep-fat thermometer. Test the heat with a small bit of batter to see if it browns, then fry one doughnut for 2–3 minutes on each side, or until golden. Cut to see if the dough is cooked all the way through and adjust the cooking time accordingly. Fry the doughnuts, three at a time, then transfer to plates lined with paper towels to drain.

7. To make the glaze, heat the milk and vanilla in a small saucepan. Sift in all but 2 tablespoons of the confectioners' sugar and stir until blended. Remove from the heat and dip the doughnuts into the glaze. Set on a cooling rack to harden, dusting with the remaining confectioners' sugar.

Coconut Sandwiches

Makes 12 sandwiches

Just this year I learned that many of my more liberal Jewish friends bake during Passover. Their rabbis say it is okay for them to use nonkosher ingredients as long as they are bought and opened before Passover begins. This opened up a whole world of cakes that I could create for my friends for this holiday. These coconut macaroon sandwich cakes are inspired by colorful French macaroon cookies and are in keeping with Passover's traditional flavors. If you still would like to follow more conservative kosher rules, try making these cakes at another time.

1. To make the macaroons, preheat the oven to 350°F. Butter and flour 12 medium muffin-top cups.

2. Combine the flour, coconut, baking powder, and salt in a mixing bowl.

Macaroons

1½ cups all-purpose flour

1½ cups sweetened flaked coconut

2 teaspoons baking powder

½ teaspoon salt

½ cup (1 stick) unsalted butter, at room temperature

½ cup granulated sugar

1 teaspoon vanilla extract

4 large egg yolks

1 cup whole milk

Red, green, and purple food coloring

Filling

3½ cups Coconut Cream Filling (page 358)

Garnish

½ cup sweetened flaked coconut

3. Beat the butter, sugar, and vanilla in a large mixing bowl with an electric mixer on medium speed until light and fluffy. Add the eggs one at a time, beating well after each addition.

4. Gradually add the flour mixture, alternating with the milk, on low speed until blended.

5. Divide the batter among three bowls and color each with food coloring. Pour into the muffin-top cups, making an even number of each color. Bake for 20–25 minutes, or until a tester inserted in the center comes out clean. Transfer to a rack to cool completely.

6. Make the sandwiches by spreading 3¼ cups of the coconut cream filling on half the muffin tops and topping them with the remaining muffin tops. Roll the edges of the sandwiches in coconut. Drop a small amount of the remaining ¼ cup coconut cream filling on the top of each sandwich. Sprinkle the remaining coconut on the top of each dollop of filling.

Passover Wine Cake

Makes one 9-inch cake

Some modern Jews add kosher wine to recipes prepared for the Passover Seder to help fulfill their obligation to drink four cups of wine during the meal. For this recipe, I've taken liberties with a plain Israeli cake and updated it with a wine taste. Reducing the wine before baking gives a more intense flavor to this cake. Knowing that Passover is the feast of unleavened bread, I was a bit concerned when I began developing this cake that I might be breaking Passover law by adding baking soda. I soon learned that, unlike yeast, which causes rising through fermentation and is strictly forbidden, baking soda and baking powder are considered chemical leaveners and are kosher for Passover.

1. To make the cake, preheat the oven to 350°F. Butter a 9-inch angel food pan.

Cake

2¼ cups kosher Concord grape
  wine
2½ cups kosher-for-Passover cake
  meal
¼ teaspoon sea salt
2½ teaspoons baking soda
½ teaspoon ground cinnamon
1 large egg
1 cup granulated sugar
1 cup firmly packed light brown
  sugar
½ cup canola oil
1 tablespoon vanilla extract
4 large egg whites

Wine Icing

½ cup (1 stick) unsalted butter, at
  room temperature
1 cup confectioners' sugar
¼ cup kosher Concord grape wine
1 teaspoon vanilla extract

2. Heat the wine in a small saucepan over low heat and boil until reduced to 1 cup. Remove from the heat and cool.

3. Combine the cake meal, salt, baking soda, and cinnamon in a mixing bowl.

4. Beat the egg, both sugars, oil, and vanilla in a large mixing bowl with an electric mixer on medium speed until creamy.

5. Gradually add the flour mixture, alternating with the wine, on low speed until blended.

6. In a clean bowl with clean beaters, beat the egg whites until stiff peaks form. Gently fold the egg whites into the batter with a rubber spatula.

7. Pour the batter into the pan and bake for 40–50 minutes, or until a knife inserted in the center comes out clean. Let cool in the pan for 15 minutes, then transfer to a rack to cool completely.

8. To make the icing, beat the butter and sugar in a medium mixing bowl with an electric mixer on medium speed until blended. Stir in the wine and vanilla, adding more sugar or wine to reach the desired glazing consistency.

9. Place the cooled cake on a serving plate and pour the glaze on top.

Variations

White Wine Cake: Replace the Concord grape wine in the cake and the icing with Chardonnay.

Chocolate Chip Wine Cake: Add 1 cup semisweet chocolate chips to the batter before the egg whites are folded in. Replace the wine icing with Chocolate Glaze (page 351).

1 packet (¼ ounce) active dry
  yeast
¾ cup warm whole milk
1 cup plus 1 tablespoon granulated
  sugar
3 cups all-purpose flour
⅛ teaspoon salt
½ cup (1 stick) unsalted butter, at
  room temperature
2 large egg yolks
¾ cup clover honey
1 tablespoon grated orange zest
½ cup golden raisins
½ cup dark raisins
½ cup chopped almonds
¼ cup candied orange peel
1 cup water
1 large egg, lightly beaten
1 orange, cut into ¼-inch rounds
¼ cup confectioners' sugar
2 cups Vanilla Frosting (page
  357)
¼ cup slivered almonds

Rosh Hashanah Fruitcake

Makes one 5 x 9-inch loaf

Honey is part of a traditional meal on Rosh Hashanah, as it symbol-izes sweetness and new beginnings for the coming year. This cake's cool shape came from my ribbed cylindrical loaf pan, but any loaf pan or ring pan will also produce impressive results. Candied orange slices and vanilla frosting put the cake over the top. In case you are not a fruitcake fan, try the honey almond cake recipe on page 313.

1. To make the cake, butter and flour a 5 x 9-inch ribbed or plain loaf pan.

2. Combine the yeast, milk, and 1 tablespoon of the sugar in a small bowl. Set aside for 10 minutes, or until foamy.

3. Combine the flour, salt, and yeast mixture in a large mixing bowl with an electric mixer on medium speed until blended. Transfer to a floured work surface and knead for 7–10 minutes, or until smooth.

4. Cover loosely and let rise for 1½ hours, or until doubled in size.

5. Beat the butter in a medium mixing bowl with an electric mixer on medium speed until light and fluffy. Beat in the egg yolks, ½ cup of the honey, and orange zest. Transfer the dough to a floured work surface and work the butter mixture into the dough with your hands, kneading until smooth, and adding more flour if the dough becomes sticky. Knead in the raisins, almonds, and candied orange peel. Transfer the dough to the pan, cover loosely, and let sit for 1 hour, or until it increases in volume by about 50 percent.

6. Preheat the oven to 350°F. When the dough is ready, remove it from the pan and roll the cake into a log to fit the pan. Brush with the beaten egg, put back in the pan, and bake for 45–55 minutes, or until golden and a tester inserted in the center comes out clean. Cool completely in the pan.

7. Combine the remaining 1 cup sugar with 1 cup water and the remaining ¼ cup honey in a saucepan. Bring to a gentle boil and simmer 5 minutes. Add the orange slices and simmer another 5 minutes, making sure the fruit becomes soft but does not fall apart. Using a slotted spoon, transfer the orange slices to wax paper to cool.

8. Dust the cake with confectioners' sugar. Pipe five mounds of frosting on the cake to support the orange slices. Place an orange slice on each mound and pipe another mound on top in the center and add an almond to each. Serve with the remaining orange slices and almonds on the side.

Honey Almond Cake

Makes one 8-inch cake

Honey is all the rage today as a replacement for sugar, but it has been the sweetener of choice for thousands of years in Jewish baking. This is a simple honey-sweetened butter cake with a touch of almond flavor. For more about baking with honey, see page 28.

2 cups all-purpose flour
1 tablespoon baking powder
½ teaspoon salt
½ cup (1 stick) unsalted butter, at room temperature
½ cup granulated sugar
2 large eggs
½ cup clover honey
¾ cup whole milk
½ cup slivered almonds, chopped
2 tablespoons confectioners' sugar for dusting

1. Preheat the oven to 350°F. Butter and flour an 8-inch round pan that's 3 inches high.

2. Combine the flour, baking powder, and salt in a mixing bowl.

3. Beat the butter and sugar in a large mixing bowl with an electric mixer on medium speed until light. Add the eggs one at a time, beating well after each addition, until fluffy.

4. Add the honey, pouring in a thin, steady stream, and beat until mixed. Gradually add the flour mixture, alternating with the milk, on low speed until blended. Stir in the almonds.

5. Pour the batter into the pan and bake for 50–60 minutes, or until a knife inserted in the center comes out clean. Cool in the pan for 10 minutes, then invert onto a rack to cool completely. Dust with confectioners' sugar.

Left: Rosh Hashanah Fruitcake.

FOURTH OF JULY CAKES

On this patriotic holiday, isn't it convenient that that the best fruits of the season happen to be red and blue? Topping or filling Fourth of July cakes with blueberries, blackberries, raspberries, cherries, and strawberries, over a layer of white vanilla cream or whipped cream, blends the flavors of season with the patriotic colors of the day.

American Flag Cake with Raspberries and Blueberries
Makes one 7 x 13-inch cake

Not all patriotically themed cakes are made to look like flags—but this one is! Choux pastry dough forms part of the stripes, and the colors are provided by pastry cream, raspberries, and blueberries. To add a note of true white to the cake, you can replace the pastry cream with whipped cream.

2 cups all-purpose flour

4 teaspoons granulated sugar

⅛ teaspoon salt

2 cups water

½ pound (2 sticks) unsalted butter, at room temperature

8 large eggs

3 cups Vanilla Pastry Cream (page 358)

1½ cups fresh blueberries

1½ cups fresh raspberries

2 teaspoons confectioners' sugar

1. Preheat the oven to 350°F. Place a piece of parchment paper on a 14 x 17-inch baking sheet. Using a pencil, draw a dark 7 x 13-inch rectangle on the parchment. Flip the paper over and put it on the baking sheet. You should see the rectangle through the paper; if you don't, darken it.

2. Combine the flour, sugar, and salt in a small bowl.

3. Bring the water to a boil in a medium saucepan, then reduce the heat to low. Add the butter and stir until melted. Remove from the heat and immediately add the flour mixture, stirring vigorously with a wooden spoon, until it pulls away from the sides of the pan.

4. Transfer the dough to a bowl. Add the eggs one at a time, beating well after each addition, until the dough is shiny and falls from the spoon. Transfer the dough to a pastry bag fitted with a large round tip. Pipe the dough in six horizontal lines within the parchment rectangle. Spritz the dough with water from a spray bottle.

5. Bake for 25–30 minutes, then remove from the oven and cool completely in the pan.

2 cups all-purpose flour

1 tablespoon baking powder

1 tablespoon granulated sugar

¼ cup ground hazelnuts

½ teaspoon salt

5 tablespoons (about ⅔ stick) cold unsalted butter, cubed

¾ cup heavy cream

¼ cup chopped pitted fresh Bing cherries

1 egg white

2 tablespoons crystal sugar

6 cups Whipped Cream (page 359)

3 cups fresh Bing cherries, pitted and halved

8 whole fresh Bing cherries, pitted, for garnish

8 fresh blueberries for garnish

6. Using a pastry bag fitted with a large round tip, pipe the pastry cream in lines over cake. Top with the blueberries and raspberries, then dust with confectioners' sugar.

Cherry Hazelnut Shortcakes

Makes 8 shortcakes

If red, white, and blue had a taste, it would be cherries, blueberries, and whipped cream. In the spirit of the American shortcake, these desserts are the perfect picnic pick.

1. Preheat the oven to 425°F. Cover a baking sheet with parchment paper.

2. Combine the flour, baking powder, granulated sugar, hazelnuts, and salt in a food processor. Add the butter and pulse until the mixture resembles coarse meal.

3. Add the cream and pulse until the dough forms a ball. Transfer to a floured work surface and knead in the chopped cherries. Roll out the dough to ¾ inch thick.

4. Cut out 8 circles with a 3½-inch cookie cutter and place on the baking sheet 1½ inches apart. Brush with egg white and dust with crystal sugar. Bake for 15–18 minutes, or until golden. Transfer to a rack to cool completely.

5. When ready to serve, slice the cakes in half horizontally and fill with whipped cream and halved cherries. Top each cake with a cherry and blueberry and an American flag.

Variation

Blueberry Almond Shortcakes: Replace the ground hazelnuts with ground almonds and the chopped and sliced cherries with blueberries.

HALLOWEEN AND DAY OF THE DEAD CAKES

I have given in to the will of the people and have "officially" declared the period from October 31 to November 2 a three-day holiday for baking. Even though Halloween, celebrated on October 31, and the Day of the Dead, celebrated on November 2, are two separate holidays, they are thematically related, and that's good enough for me. Over the years, the Day of the Dead has grown from a Latin American holiday popular in the Southwest to a more common celebration throughout all regions of the United States—just as Halloween has become more and more popular around the world. So what's to stop us from making playfully decorated Day of the Dead skull cakes for Halloween? And why not make the pumpkin or the caramel apple cakes for yourself and your ancestors on the Day of the Dead? I am sure they will love them, too.

Day of the Dead Skull Cake

Makes one 7-inch cake

6 cups White Cake batter (page 75)

3 cups Vanilla Icing (page 358)

3 cups Vanilla Frosting (page 357)

2½ cups Chocolate Frosting (page 351)

Red, green, yellow, blue, and orange food coloring

Over the years, November 2—the Day of the Dead—has become my favorite cake-decorating day. The observance is even more meaningful when I bake this cake in honor of departed loved ones. Although any flavor or color of cake can be used, I bake a white cake so that the skull looks more realistic. A skull-shaped pan does the forming for you, allowing you time to bake and decorate additional "skulls." If you don't have a skull-shaped pan, bake the cake in a square or round cake pan and cut a skull shape out of the center, continuing the pattern with piped borders of frosting around the edges. Of course, this cake could also be prepared for our homegrown holiday, Halloween.

1. Preheat the oven to 350°F. Butter and flour a 7-inch skull-shaped pan. Pour the batter into the pan and bake for 30–35 minutes, or until a knife inserted in the center comes out clean. Cool completely on a rack.

2. Place a piece of parchment paper on a baking sheet and put a rack on top. Prepare the icing in a glass measuring

cup with a spout, adding enough water to achieve a thin, pourable consistency, and pour over the cake to cover completely. Let the extra icing flow onto the parchment, and return it to the measuring cup. Cover the cup to keep the icing from drying out. Let the icing on the cake dry, then pour on a second coat. Repeat if necessary until the cake is covered with a smooth finish. Let dry completely, then transfer to a serving plate.

3. Divide the vanilla frosting among 5 small bowls and color each with food coloring. Spread the chocolate frosting onto the cake with an icing spatula to make big shapes such as the eyes. Use one-fourth of the red frosting for the heart. Pipe tiny chocolate-frosting flowers using a pastry bag fitted with a pansy tip. Let dry.

4. To make a rose, use a pastry bag fitted with a flat tip and red frosting. Pipe a mound onto the cake to act as the base. Starting at the center, pipe petals that stand straight up, making a circle around the center in overlapping segments as you go. To make other kinds of roses, vary the size of the segments, making them small in the center and larger toward the perimeter. To make leaves, use green frosting and a flat tip, radiating the frosting outward from the flower. The leaves can surround the entire flower or you can add just a few.

5. Using pastry bags fitted with small round tips, pipe the remaining frosting as dots, lines, and detailed designs around and over the large shapes in different colors.

Caramel Apple Cake

Makes one 8-inch two-layer cake

If you spend all year looking forward to the caramel apple flavors of fall, this is the cake for you. Here, I use this classic Halloween combination in a light apple cake packed with apple filling and topped with gooey caramel.

Apple Cake

2¾ cups all-purpose flour

1¼ cups granulated sugar

1 teaspoon baking powder

½ teaspoon baking soda

½ teaspoon salt

3 large eggs

½ cup vegetable oil

½ cup unsweetened apple juice

1 teaspoon vanilla extract

1 tablespoon freshly squeezed
 lemon juice

Apple Filling

2 teaspoons unsalted butter

4 Gala apples, peeled, cored, and
 cubed

¼ cup unsweetened apple juice

¼ teaspoon cornstarch

¼ teaspoon ground cinnamon

Topping

2¼ cups Caramel Topping (page
 350)

1. To make the cake, preheat the oven to 350°F. Butter and flour two 8-inch square pans.

2. Combine the flour, sugar, baking powder, baking soda, and salt in a mixing bowl.

3. Combine the eggs, oil, apple juice, vanilla, and lemon juice in a large mixing bowl and beat with an electric mixer on medium speed.

4. Gradually add the flour mixture on low speed until blended.

5. Pour the batter into the pans and bake for 30–35 minutes, or until a tester inserted in the center comes out clean. Cool in the pans for 20 minutes, then transfer to a rack to cool completely.

6. To make the filling, melt the butter in a saucepan. Add the apples and sauté until lightly browned. Stir in the apple juice, cornstarch, and cinnamon. Continue to cook, stirring occasionally, until the apples have softened and the mixture has thickened. Cool in the saucepan for about 30 minutes.

7. Place one cooled cake layer on a serving plate and top with the apple filling. Place the second cake on top. Pour the caramel topping over the cake, then cut the cake into triangles.

Variations

Salty Caramel Cake: Add ¾ teaspoon sea salt to the caramel topping.

Caramel Spice Cake: Add 1 teaspoon ground cinnamon, ⅛ teaspoon ground nutmeg, and ¼ teaspoon ground cloves to the flour mixture.

Peanut Caramel Cake: Add ¼ cup ground unsalted peanuts to the cake batter before pouring in the pans, and sprinkle the caramel topping with chopped salted peanuts.

Pumpkin Rum Cakes

Makes 12 cakes

2 cups all-purpose flour
2 teaspoons baking powder
¼ teaspoon baking soda
1 teaspoon ground cinnamon
1 teaspoon ground ginger
½ teaspoon ground nutmeg
⅛ teaspoon ground cloves
¼ teaspoon ground allspice
½ cup (1 stick) unsalted butter, at
  room temperature
1⅓ cups firmly packed light brown
  sugar
2 large eggs
½ teaspoon salt
½ cup buttermilk
1¼ cups canned pumpkin purée
1 teaspoon vanilla extract
½ cup golden rum
2 cups Fondant (page 353)
Brown and green food coloring
3½ cups Rum Cream Cheese Frosting (page 352)

A friendly reminder of fall, these pumpkin cakes have a sweet surprise inside—rum-spiked cream cheese frosting. I make these in small pumpkin-shaped Bundt pans. Mine have twelve cavities and make six cakes each (the tops and bottoms are different), but you can get a similar shape by pressing two small Bundt cakes together.

1. To make the cake, preheat the oven to 350°F. Butter and flour two 12-cavity 3½-inch pumpkin-shaped pans or 24 miniature Bundt pans.

2. Combine the flour, baking powder, baking soda, cinnamon, ginger, nutmeg, cloves, and salt in a small bowl.

3. Beat the butter and sugar in a large mixing bowl with an electric mixer on medium speed until fluffy. Add the eggs one at a time, beating well after each addition.

4. Gradually add the flour mixture, alternating with the buttermilk, on low speed until blended. Add the pumpkin, vanilla, and rum and beat until smooth.

5. Fill pans three-fourths full (if there is extra batter, refrigerate and save for another use) and bake for 25–30 minutes, or until a tester inserted in the center comes out clean. Cool on a rack.

6. To make the fondant leaves, color some of the fondant green. Roll out to ⅟₁₆ inch thick and cut leaf shapes with a utility knife. Emboss veins with a toothpick. Curve the leaves and let dry. Color additional fondant brown and form stalk shapes. Let set to dry.

7. Using a serrated knife, level the cakes so they fit together. Scoop out a teaspoonful of cake from the center of the top and bottom halves. Spread the frosting in the holes and between the top and bottom layers, leaving ¼ inch around the edges. Press the cakes

together and set on a serving plate. Attach the leaves
and stalks with frosting.

Variation

Pumpkin Loaf: Prepare the cake in two 4 x 8-inch loaf pans. Top with
Vanilla Buttercream (page 356) and roasted pumpkin seeds.

THANKSGIVING CAKES

I find it unbelievable that Thanksgiving, the biggest American harvest festival and the one holiday that centers primarily around food, does not have a traditional cake. I set out to fix this and created several cakes that use ingredients native to the New World.

Cranberry Orange Chiffon Cakes with Cranberry Sauce
Makes eight 4-inch cakes

Chiffon cakes use oil instead of butter, and since it is hard to beat air into oil, foamy egg whites are added to give these cakes a fluffy texture. Prepare them in individual serving dishes and serve with cranberry sauce on the side or on top.

1. To make the cake, preheat the oven to 350°F. Butter and flour eight 4-inch oven-safe bowls or ramekins.

2. Combine the flour, sugar, baking powder, and salt in a large bowl. Using an electric mixer on medium speed, beat in the oil, egg yolks, orange zest, orange juice, and vanilla. Fold in the cranberries.

3. In a clean bowl with clean beaters, beat the egg whites and cream of tartar until soft peaks form. Gently fold the egg whites into the batter with a rubber spatula, being careful not to deflate the batter.

4. Pour the batter into the bowls and bake for 30–35 minutes, or until a tester inserted in the center comes out clean. Cool in the bowls.

5. To make the cranberry sauce, combine the cranberries, sugar, water, and orange zest in a saucepan and bring to a boil. Lower the heat and cook for 10 minutes, stirring occasionally, until thickened. Remove from the heat and let cool. Serve the cakes in the bowls with the sauce alongside, or spoon the sauce over the top of the cakes in the bowls.

Cake
2¼ cups all-purpose flour
1½ cups granulated sugar
1½ teaspoons baking powder
½ teaspoon salt
½ cup vegetable oil
6 large eggs, separated
2 teaspoons grated orange zest
¾ cup freshly squeezed orange juice
1 teaspoon vanilla extract
1½ cups whole fresh cranberries
½ teaspoon cream of tartar

Cranberry Sauce
2 cups whole fresh cranberries
1 cup granulated sugar
1 cup water
½ teaspoon grated orange zest

Variations

Chocolate Cranberry Cakes: Add 1 cup chocolate chips to the batter with the cranberries. Replace the cranberry sauce with Chocolate Sauce (page 352).

Cranberry Chiffon Tube Cake: Bake the cake in a 10-inch tube pan for 50–60 minutes. Cool completely in the pan, then invert onto a rack and drizzle with Orange Glaze (page 354). Serve the cranberry sauce on top or on the side.

Chocolate Chip Cranberry Roll

Makes one 12¼-inch cake

⅓ cup all-purpose flour

⅓ cup cornstarch

5 large eggs, separated

⅓ cup granulated sugar

1 teaspoon vanilla extract

½ teaspoon salt

½ cup semisweet miniature chocolate chips

Confectioners' sugar for dusting

1½ cups Cranberry Sauce (page 324)

3 cups Whipped Cream (page 359)

1½ cups Chocolate Glaze (page 351)

Recently, I read a scientific study in which it was revealed that chocolate is a stress reliever. How great is that? It's especially good news around the holidays, which are filled with so much stress. Chocolate isn't a traditional Thanksgiving flavor, but now we know that, by adding a little chocolate to our cranberry dishes, we can enjoy the taste of relaxing bliss whenever we feel the need.

1. Preheat the oven to 375°F. Butter a 9 x 12¼-inch jelly-roll pan and cover with parchment paper. Butter and flour the parchment.

2. Combine the flour and cornstarch in a small bowl; set aside.

3. Beat the egg yolks, half the sugar, and the vanilla in a large bowl until the sugar is dissolved and the mixture forms a ribbon when the beaters are lifted from the bowl.

4. In a clean bowl with clean beaters, beat the egg whites until foamy. Add the salt and continue to beat until soft peaks form. Gradually add the remaining sugar and continue beating until stiff peaks form.

5. Gently fold the egg whites into the yolk mixture with a rubber spatula. Sprinkle the flour mixture and chocolate chips over the egg mixture and fold until blended.

6. Spread the batter in the pan and bake for 10–12 minutes, or until springy to the touch.

7. Dust a clean towel with confectioners' sugar. Turn the cake onto the towel and remove the parchment. Roll the cake from the long side and let sit for 1 minute, then unroll and let sit for 2 minutes. Roll again and cool completely while rolled in the towel.

8. Unroll the cake and spread with the cranberry sauce and whipped cream. Roll the cake again and place it seam side down on a serving plate. Top with chocolate glaze and fresh cranberries.

Sweet Potato Cake

Makes about 7 cups, enough for one 9 x 12-inch cake

Here I've taken the liberty of turning a popular Thanksgiving flavor combination into a dessert that can also be eaten as a sweet side dish. For a milder cake, use white instead of orange sweet potatoes. The cake can also be baked in a 4-quart casserole dish instead of a baking pan. Top it with a bit of confectioners' sugar instead of marshmallows and you will have a cake close to the authentic, puddinglike sweet potato cakes of early America.

1. To make the cake, preheat the oven to 350°F. Butter and flour a 9 x 12-inch baking dish.

2. Combine the flour, salt, baking powder, nutmeg, cinnamon, ginger, and allspice in a mixing bowl.

3. Beat the butter and dark brown sugar in a large mixing bowl with an electric mixer on medium speed until creamy. Add the eggs one at a time, beating well after each addition. Add the potatoes, lime zest, lime juice, and maple syrup, beating well.

4. Gradually add the flour mixture, alternating with the milk, until well blended. Stir in the pecans.

5. Pour the batter into the pan and bake for 40–50 minutes, or until a tester inserted in center comes out clean. Turn on the broiler.

Cake

1½ cups all-purpose flour

¼ teaspoon salt

2 teaspoons baking powder

½ teaspoon ground nutmeg

1 teaspoon ground cinnamon

½ teaspoon ground ginger

½ teaspoon ground allspice

½ cup (1 stick) unsalted butter, at room temperature

¾ cup firmly packed dark brown sugar

2 large eggs

2 cups mashed cooked sweet potatoes, cooled

1 tablespoon grated lime zest

1 tablespoon freshly squeezed lime juice

2 tablespoons pure maple syrup

½ cup whole milk

1 cup chopped pecans

Topping

3 cups miniature marshmallows

½ cup pecan halves

1 tablespoon clover honey

1 tablespoon firmly packed dark or light brown sugar

6. Top the cake with the marshmallows and broil for about 1 minute, or until the marshmallows are lightly toasted. Keep a close eye on them and remove from the oven when ready.

7. To make the topping, combine the pecans, honey, and brown sugar in a small saucepan over low heat. Stir until the sugar dissolves, then remove from heat and cool for 20 minutes. Spread over the cooled cake.

Variation

Rum Sweet Potato Cake: Add ¼ cup golden rum to the batter with the pecans and replace the brown sugar with muscovado sugar. Top with Rum Syrup (page 355) instead of the pecan mixture.

Walnut Cakes

Makes 36 cakes

Although this recipe tastes wonderful made with the common English walnut, it tastes even more special with black walnuts.

2½ cups all-purpose flour
1 teaspoon baking soda
1 teaspoon baking powder
½ teaspoon salt
1½ teaspoons ground cinnamon
1½ teaspoons ground allspice
1½ teaspoons ground nutmeg
½ pound (2 sticks) unsalted butter, at room temperature
½ cup granulated sugar
½ cup unsulfured molasses
3 large eggs
1 teaspoon vanilla extract
1 cup buttermilk
1 cup walnut halves, chopped
3 tablespoons pure maple syrup
36 walnut halves for garnish

1. Preheat the oven to 350°F. Butter and flour 36 mini muffin cups.

2. Combine the flour, baking soda, baking powder, salt, cinnamon, allspice, and nutmeg in a mixing bowl.

3. Beat the butter and sugar in a large mixing bowl with an electric mixer on medium speed until light and fluffy. Beat in the molasses, eggs, and vanilla.

4. Gradually add the flour mixture, alternating with the buttermilk, on low speed until blended. Fold in the chopped walnuts.

5. Pour the batter into the muffin cups and bake for 15–20 minutes, or until a tester inserted in the center comes out clean. Cool in the pan for 5 minutes, then transfer to a rack to cool completely.

6. Dab the maple syrup on the cakes and top each with a walnut half.

Acorn Cakes

Makes 24 cakes

1 cup all-purpose flour

1¼ cups acorn flour

½ teaspoon baking powder

½ teaspoon salt

½ cup olive oil

½ cup granulated sugar

¼ cup clover honey

3 large egg yolks

½ cup whole milk

¼ cup walnut pieces

1¼ cups Lemon Curd (page 353)

Native Americans ground acorns into flour, but today you can just buy acorn flour at gourmet markets or at supermarkets that sell organic flours and grains. These Thanksgiving-appropriate cakes are based on an Italian cake called *castagnaccio*, which uses chestnut flour. Bake them in a pan that makes small acorn-shaped cakes, or use mini muffin tins instead.

1. Preheat the oven to 375°F. Butter and flour 24 acorn-shaped cups or mini muffin cups.

2. Combine both flours, the baking powder, and salt in a mixing bowl.

3. Beat the olive oil, sugar, honey, and egg yolks in a large mixing bowl with an electric mixer on medium speed until blended.

4. Gradually add the flour mixture, alternating with the milk, on low speed until blended. Stir in the walnut pieces.

5. Pour the batter into the cups and bake for 12–15 minutes, or until a tester inserted in the center comes out clean. Cool completely in the pans. Spoon the lemon curd onto serving plates and set the cooled cakes on top. Serve with a fork.

Pecan Cake

2½ cups all-purpose flour

1 cup finely ground cornmeal

2 teaspoons baking powder

½ teaspoon salt

1½ teaspoons ground cinnamon

½ teaspoon ground nutmeg

½ teaspoon ground allspice

2¼ cups pecans, chopped

¾ cup (1½ sticks) unsalted butter,
   at room temperature

1¼ cups granulated sugar

1 cup firmly packed light brown
   sugar

6 large eggs

½ cup bourbon

½ cup pure maple syrup

1 cup unsweetened apple juice

Pecan Cake

Makes one 12-inch round cake

Pecan cake is a great choice for Thanksgiving. Fill it with cranberry and pumpkin ice creams to pack even more festive flavors into the holiday.

1. To make the cake, preheat the oven to 375°F. Butter and flour a 12-inch ring pan that's 3 inches high.

2. Combine the flour, cornmeal, baking powder, salt, cinnamon, nutmeg, allspice, and pecans in a mixing bowl.

Pecan Apple Topping

3 tablespoons unsalted butter

2 medium Fuji or Gala apples, peeled, cored, and thinly sliced (about 1½ cups)

1½ cups pecans, chopped

½ teaspoon ground cinnamon

¼ cup raisins

3 tablespoons freshly squeezed lemon juice

3 tablespoons firmly packed light brown sugar

Bourbon Spiced Whipped Cream

1½ cups heavy cream

1 tablespoon bourbon

½ teaspoon ground cinnamon

Garnish

Pumpkin Ice Cream (page 357)

Cranberry Ice Cream (page 357)

3. Cream the butter and both sugars in a large mixing bowl with an electric mixer on medium speed until fluffy. Add the eggs one at a time, beating well after each addition. Beat in the bourbon, maple syrup, and apple juice. Gradually add the flour mixture on low speed; do not overmix.

4. Pour the batter into the pan and bake for 50–60 minutes, or until a knife inserted in the center comes out clean. Cool in the pan for 20 minutes, then transfer to a rack to cool completely.

5. To make the topping, melt the butter in a skillet over medium heat. Add the apples, pecans, and cinnamon and sauté until the apples are lightly brown. Remove from the heat and add the raisins, lemon juice, and brown sugar, mixing well.

6. To make the whipped cream, combine the heavy cream, bourbon, and cinnamon in a medium bowl. Whip according to directions for Whipped Cream (page 359).

7. Place the cake on a serving plate. Mound scoops of the ice creams into the center. Spoon the topping over the ice cream and cake and serve with the bourbon whipped cream alongside.

Variation

Pecan Bourbon Layer Cake: Prepare the batter in two 9-inch round pans. Spread the topping between the layers and spread the top and sides with Cream Cheese Frosting (page 352) flavored with maple syrup (page 29).

CHRISTMAS CAKES

Whether you like your Christmas season filled with traditional desserts or are looking for playful creativity in your cakes, you'll find plenty of both in this section. With just one of these cakes you can host an instant holiday party, or try several for a dessert buffet. My favorite thinking-outside-the-box cake is the Christmas cactus trifle with cactus jam, but the chocolate fruitcakes, Yule log, and peppermint cakes also provide a delicious and modern spin on classic holiday flavors.

Holiday Ginger Cakes

Makes 8–10 cakes

¾ cup vegetable oil
¼ cup unsulfured molasses
2 tablespoons unsalted butter, melted
¼ cup firmly packed dark brown sugar
3¼ cups all-purpose flour
½ teaspoon salt
1 teaspoon minced fresh ginger
1 teaspoon ground cinnamon
½ teaspoon freshly grated or ground nutmeg
½ teaspoon ground allspice
1 tablespoon baking powder
½ teaspoon baking soda
2 large egg whites
3½ cups Royal Icing (page 355)
Green, red, blue, pink, yellow, black, and orange food coloring

If you're looking for an alternative to crispy gingerbread cookies, try these flat gingerbread cakes, inspired by the delicately decorated heart-shaped cookie necklaces sold in Germany during Oktoberfest. The rich flavor comes from freshly ground ginger and nutmeg. For me, these cakes provide a similar experience for creative decoration as the gingerbread "men" we so often see around Christmastime. I use a round cookie cutter with scalloped edges, but you can cut the dough into any shape you like. The sturdy royal icing ensures that the decorations have staying power.

1. Preheat the oven to 375°F. Line two baking sheets with parchment paper.

2. Beat the oil, molasses, butter, and brown sugar in a medium mixing bowl with an electric mixer on medium speed until combined.

3. Combine the flour, salt, ginger, cinnamon, nutmeg, allspice, baking powder, and baking soda in a large bowl, making a well in the center. Add the oil mixture to the well, and mix on low speed of an electric mixer until the dough forms a ball. The dough should be soft. If it is sticky, add a few tablespoons more flour; if it is dry, add a few tablespoons of milk.

4. Roll out the dough on a floured work surface to about ⅜ inch thick. Using cookie cutters or a knife, cut

dough into 8–10 five-inch shapes. Reroll scraps and cut additional shapes, if desired.

5. Transfer to the baking sheets and brush with the egg white. Bake for 18–22 minutes, or until lightly browned. Cool on the pans.

6. Divide the icing among eight bowls. Add desired colors of food coloring to seven of the bowls, and leave one bowl white. Decorate the cakes and let sit to harden before serving.

Christmas Cactus Trifle with Cactus Jam

Makes one 10-inch display

8 cups Golden Yellow Cake batter (page 69)
1 cup cactus jelly or strawberry preserves
3 cups Vanilla Pastry Cream (page 358)
5 cups cookie crumbs (use pizzelle, graham crackers, or vanilla wafers)
4 cups Fondant (page 353)
1½ cups Vanilla Frosting (page 357)
1 cup chocolate rock candy
White rock candy balls
Orange sprinkles
Yellow and rainbow crystal sugar

When I'm not baking, I enjoy tending the cacti and succulents in my rock garden, and I wanted to combine those two passions somehow in this book. I pondered where in the book a cactus-shaped cake would fit best, and then I remembered how much I love my Christmas cactus, which blooms every year around the holidays. So I came up with the idea of making a fondant trifle holiday centerpiece based on my blooming Christmas cactus. I decided that a creamy trifle would be the best form for this cake because it allows you to dig in with a big spoon to scoop up the cake, cream, crunchy cookies, and fondant cacti all in one bite. I chose prickly pear cactus jelly to spread between the layers; prickly pear grows like a weed on the hillside behind my house, and what better place to use the jars of it that I put up every year than in a cactus trifle? If you want to go easy on the effort, though, you can use store-bought cactus jelly, or choose another flavor. You'll also need a clear glass container, such as a terrarium or fishbowl, measuring about 10 inches in diameter with an 8-inch opening, to act as your trifle dish (*see photo*, page 336).

1. Preheat the oven to 350°F. Butter and flour two 7-inch round cake pans, 4 large muffin cups, and 7 mini muffin cups. Pour in the batter and bake the 7-inch cakes for 30–35 minutes, the large cupcakes for 25–30 minutes,

and the mini cupcakes for 12–15 minutes. Cool in the pans for 10 minutes, then transfer to racks to cool completely.

2. Cut the 7-inch cakes in half to make 4 layers. Spread the cactus jelly on one layer, then place it in the glass container and cover with vanilla pastry cream, Repeat with more jelly and the remaining layers and cream. This trifle will act as the base, or "soil," for the cacti blooming above it in the bowl.

3. Sprinkle half the cookie crumbs around the cake to form "sand," filling the space on the side of the bowl and sprinkling some on top of the cake. Decorate the cupcakes as cacti, following the instructions on page 336. Arrange the cacti in the "garden" with the layered cake, setting the fondant Christmas cactus in the center. Sprinkle the remaining cookie crumbs around the cacti, then top with rock candy, sprinkles, and crystal sugar.

Cacti Cake How-To

Those who know me well know I am just as crazy about cacti as I am about cakes. Here's how to make one of each cactus pictured in the photograph on page 336, but feel free to come up with your own miniature terrarium landscape—the arrangement is all up to you. You can also create an assortment of cacti and place them in individual serving dishes. This is desert dessert at its best.

Nestled in the large container in the photo on page 336 are, a large flowering cactus, carrion plant, miniature saguaro, Christmas cactus, aloe, and a small flowering cactus. The small container holds a single column cactus.

Christmas cactus: Form green fondant into 25 oval disks about 1 inch long. Wrap five disks around each of 5 black licorice laces—two of which should be 5 inches long, two of which should be 6 inches long, and one of which should be 7 inches long. Flatten the disks and press them around the licorice, leaving $1/2$ inch on one end and 1 inch on the other end of each piece. Form red fondant into 5 three-pointed flowers. Add one to the short end of each piece of licorice. Cover one mini cupcake with green fondant and poke holes into the cake with a skewer. Add some vanilla frosting to each hole and insert the long end of the licorice, pressing it into the frosting. Attach the cupcake to the trifle layer cake in the garden with vanilla frosting. Repeat with the 4 remaining pieces and 4 more mini cupcakes.

Small flowering cactus: Color the fondant with a two-tone green pattern. Wrap the fondant around a mini cupcake and press grooves into the sides with the back of a knife. Press orange sprinkles into the sides to make spines. Form purple fondant into small petals for each flower. Add a

dot of blue fondant to the center to make a flower. Press into the top of the cupcake.

Large flowering cactus: Stack two large cupcakes, one inverted on top of the other, to make a tall rounded cactus. Cover with dark green fondant. With red fondant, make 18 spiky petals 1–1½ inches long and build a flower. With yellow fondant, make eight ⅛-inch dots in the center.

Aloe: Roll out green fondant to ¼ inch thick. Cut eight spiky spines ranging from 1 inch to 4 inches in length. Attach the spines to each other with vanilla frosting and press into a mini cupcake. Curve the spines and add vanilla-frosting stripes to the center of each.

Miniature saguaro: Wrap green fondant around a mini cupcake and use additional fondant to shape into a 2-inch-tall cactus with a stub on one side. Add some vanilla frosting to the top and four ½-inch fondant petals for the flower. Cover the exposed frosting with yellow sugar. Press large coarse rainbow crystal sugar into the fondant.

Carrion plant: Stack two large cupcakes, one inverted on top of the other, to make a tall rounded cactus. Trim the sides with a serrated knife to form a rounded obelisk shape. Marbleize light green and white fondant, roll it out to ⅛ inch thick, and use it to cover the cake. Add stripes of vanilla frosting to the sides and attach white rock candy balls. Add a pool of frosting to the top center of the cactus. Form purple fondant into five ½-inch petals for the flower and attach to the top center. Add orange sprinkles to the frosting at the center of the flower.

Column cactus: Form a small rounded column out of light green fondant to make the smallest cactus. Wrap light green fondant around a mini cupcake to make the medium cactus. Stack two mini cupcakes, one inverted on top of the other, to make the tallest cactus. Wrap the stack in light green fondant. Place all three cacti in the container and add spikes to each with vanilla frosting.

White Chocolate Pepper-
mint Bark

1 pound white chocolate

1½ teaspoons vegetable shortening

*½ cup coarsely crushed peppermint
candies*

Cake

3 cups all-purpose flour

1 teaspoon baking soda

½ teaspoon salt

*½ pound (2 sticks) unsalted butter,
at room temperature*

2 cups granulated sugar

4 large eggs

1 teaspoon peppermint extract

1 cup whole milk

*⅛ ounce (½ packet) unflavored
gelatin*

1 cup water

Red food coloring

*2¼ cups White Chocolate But-
tercream (page 350)*

½ cup ground peppermint candies

Topping

Red-hot cinnamon candies

Peppermint candies

Magic Peppermint White Forest Cake

Makes one 8-inch three-layer cake

Black Forest cake is named for a mountain range in Germany, but
I've still always thought there should also be a white forest cake.
This is how I envision it: a holiday peppermint cake made with
several layers of white chocolate buttercream, peppermint bark,
and a touch of cinnamon candy. Magical, fresh, and delicious.

1. To make the peppermint bark, line a baking sheet with
   parchment paper and butter the parchment. Combine
   the chocolate and shortening in a double boiler and stir
   until melted. Pour half the chocolate into 12 leaf-shaped
   plastic or silicone molds and let set.

2. Stir ¼ cup of the peppermint candy into the remaining
   chocolate, then pour onto the parchment, spreading ¼
   inch thick. Sprinkle with the remaining candy and any
   peppermint dust. Let set for 3 hours to cool, then break
   the candy into bark.

3. To make the cake, preheat the oven to 325°F. Butter and
   flour three 8 x 8-inch square pans.

4. Combine the flour, baking soda, and salt in a mixing
   bowl.

5. Cream the butter and sugar in a large mixing bowl with
   an electric mixer on medium speed until fluffy. Add the
   eggs one at a time, beating well after each addition. Beat
   in the peppermint extract.

6. Gradually add the flour mixture, alternating with the
   milk, on low speed until blended.

7. Pour the batter into the pans and bake for 25–30
   minutes, or until a toothpick inserted in the center
   comes out clean. Cool in the pans.

8. Combine the unflavored gelatin with water and 2 drops
   of red food coloring. Let sit until the mixture is thick
   and smooth but still pourable.

9. Reserve 1 cup of the white chocolate buttercream. Add the ground candies and 1 drop of red food coloring to the remainder.

10. Place one cooled cake layer on a serving plate and spread with one-third of the colored buttercream. Place a second layer on top and spread with another one-third of the colored buttercream, then repeat with the third layer and remaining colored buttercream. Pour the gelatin mixture onto the center of the cake and smooth it to the perimeter. Place in refrigerator for 2 hours to set.

11. Divide the reserved buttercream in half; color one batch green and leave the other white. Place the white buttercream in a pastry bag fitted with a medium star-shaped tip and the green buttercream in a pastry bag fitted with a leaf tip. Pipe white designs and green leaves on the cake. Decorate the top of the cake with peppermint bark, white chocolate leaves, and peppermint and cinnamon candies.

Eggnog Fudge Cupcakes

Makes 24 cupcakes

This recipe is essentially Boston cream pie reinvented as a holiday cupcake. The batter is flavored with eggnog; the cupcakes are filled with eggnog cream and covered with rum fudge. For a bit of an Italian flair, try the variation for the spicy eggnog cake with pine nuts.

Eggnog Cream

½ cup granulated sugar

¼ cup cornstarch

2 large egg yolks

2 cups eggnog

½ teaspoon vanilla extract

Cupcakes

3 cups all-purpose flour

1 teaspoon baking powder

½ teaspoon salt

¾ pound (3 sticks) unsalted butter,
    at room temperature

2 cups granulated sugar

4 large eggs

1 teaspoon vanilla extract

½ teaspoon almond extract

2 tablespoons golden rum

1 cup eggnog

1 cup Rum Syrup (page 355)

Rum Fudge Frosting

¼ cup heavy cream

½ tablespoon light corn syrup

½ cup granulated sugar

1½ tablespoons unsalted butter

2 teaspoons golden rum

3 ounces semisweet chocolate

Garnish

2 ounces white chocolate, melted

2 tablespoons red-hot cinnamon
    candies

2 tablespoons white sprinkles

1. To make the eggnog cream, mix ¼ cup of the sugar and cornstarch in a heatproof medium bowl. Add the egg yolks and stir to form a paste, then stir in ½ cup eggnog.

2. Combine the remaining eggnog and remaining sugar in a saucepan and bring to a boil over medium heat. Pour into the paste mixture and beat well.

3. Pour the mixture back into the saucepan and cook, stirring occasionally, over medium heat for 7–10 minutes, or until thick and smooth. Remove from the heat, stir in the vanilla, and continue to stir for 1 more minute. Transfer to a bowl, cover, and chill for 2 hours, or until thickened.

4. To make the cupcakes, preheat the oven to 350°F. Line 24 medium muffin cups with paper or foil liners.

5. Combine the flour, baking powder, and salt in a mixing bowl.

6. Cream the butter and sugar in a large bowl with an electric mixer on medium speed until fluffy. Add the eggs one at a time, beating well after each addition. Beat in the vanilla and almond extracts and the rum.

7. Gradually add the flour mixture, alternating with the eggnog, on low speed until blended.

8. Pour the batter into the liners, filling each three-fourths full. Bake for 15–20 minutes, or until a tester inserted in the center comes out clean. While the cupcakes are still warm, brush rum syrup on top.

9. To make the frosting, combine the cream, corn syrup, and sugar in a small saucepan over medium heat. Bring to a boil and remove from the heat. Add the butter, rum, and semisweet chocolate to the pan, stirring until melted and smooth. Set aside to cool slightly.

10. Scoop out about 2 teaspoons of cake from the center of each cupcake (a grapefruit spoon is an ideal tool if you have one). Using a pastry bag fitted with a large round tip, pipe the eggnog cream into the holes, then frost the cupcakes. Change to a small round tip, then pipe the white chocolate in stripes over the frosting. Top with cinnamon candies and white sprinkles.

Variation

Spicy Eggnog Cupcakes: Replace the rum with amaretto in the cake and frosting. Add ½ teaspoon ground nutmeg, ½ teaspoon cinnamon, and ½ cup pine nuts to the cake batter with the extracts.

Strawberry Pistachio Yule Log Slices

Makes 8 slices

Yule logs are my favorite Christmas cakes. They provide so many opportunities for flavor combinations—what with the batter, frosting, fillings, and toppings—and just as many opportunities for creative decorating. Ever since I saw a holiday window display at Bloomingdale's in New York City as a teenager, pink

1½ cups cake flour

1½ teaspoons baking powder

½ teaspoon salt

4 large eggs

2 teaspoons vanilla extract

1½ cups granulated sugar

3 drops red food coloring

1 cup fresh strawberries, hulled and
  finely chopped

3 tablespoons brandy

4½ cups Pistachio Buttercream
  (page 356)

1 cup chopped pistachio nuts

and pistachio green have been a favorite Christmas color combination of mine. I had just attended a graphic design class that featured a lecture on color, and seeing how the window designer had forgone the traditional bright red and forest green in favor of fresher, more playful colors—still in the same family and still in keeping with the spirit of the holiday—really got me thinking.

Every year, I develop a Yule log recipe in a new flavor combination and devise a presentation to match. This strawberry and pistachio cake was inspired by that display in the Bloomingdale's window, and each slice is presented as though it were a miniature window display—albeit one that's edible. The log can also be served whole, with the fondant sculptures and strawberry Santas placed on top and around the log.

Fondant Christmas Decorations

4 cups Fondant (page 353)
1½ cups Vanilla Frosting (page 357)
6 whole strawberries
6 miniature marshmallows
6 cinnamon candies
Black, green, and red food coloring

Strawberry Santa: Remove the stem from a strawberry. Cut ½-inch tip from the small end of the strawberry to form Santa's hat. Place a miniature marshmallow between the tip and the body to make Santa's head. Draw the face with a toothpick dipped in black food coloring. Using a pastry bag fitted with a small star-shaped tip, pipe vanilla frosting on the figure to make the beard and buttons. Use the frosting to attach a cinnamon candy to the top of the hat.

Holly leaves and berries: Divide the fondant into a large ball and a small ball. Color the large ball green and small ball red. Roll out the green to ¹⁄₁₆ inch thick and cut out leaf shapes. Use a knife to press vein indentations into the leaves. Drape the leaves over a curved surface and let sit to dry. Roll the red fondant into small berries and let dry.

Mushrooms: Divide the fondant into a large ball and a small ball. Leave the large ball white and color the small ball red. Shape the white ball into mushroom stems and tiny dots. Shape the red ball into mushroom caps and press the dots on top. Attach the caps to the stems with a little water, pressing to secure. Let dry.

House: Divide the fondant into a large ball and a small ball. Color the large ball red and leave the other ball white. Shape the red ball into a house, then shape the white ball into a roof and a chimney to fit. Attach the roof with a little water, pressing to secure. Let dry. Draw the door and window with a toothpick dipped in food coloring.

Christmas trees: Color the fondant green. Shape into cones and use scissors to snip outlines of branches into each.

Snowman: Divide the fondant into one large ball and two small balls. Leave the large ball white, color one of the small balls black, and color the other small ball red. Create two balls out of the white fondant, one slightly smaller than the other. Place the smaller ball on top of the larger ball, sticking them together with a little water and pressing to secure. Roll out the red fondant to ⅛ inch thick and cut into the shape of a scarf. Wrap the scarf around the snowman. Shape the black fondant into a top hat. Attach with a little water, pressing to secure. Let dry. Draw the face and buttons with a toothpick dipped in food coloring.

1. Preheat the oven to 350°F. Line a 9 x 12¼-inch jelly-roll pan with parchment paper and butter the parchment.

2. Combine the flour, baking powder, and salt in a mixing bowl.

3. Beat the eggs, vanilla, sugar, and food coloring in a large mixing bowl with an electric mixer on medium speed until creamy.

4. Gradually add the flour mixture on low speed until blended. Fold in the strawberries.

Cake

½ cup raisins

⅓ cup chopped dates

¼ cup brandy

2 cups all-purpose flour

2 teaspoons baking powder

½ teaspoon salt

2 teaspoons ground cinnamon

¼ teaspoon ground nutmeg

½ teaspoon ground cloves

3 ounces unsweetened chocolate

½ cup (1 stick) unsalted butter, at
   room temperature

1¼ cups granulated sugar

2 large eggs

1 teaspoon vanilla extract

1 container (8 ounces) sour cream

½ cup milk

¼ cup green candied cherries

¼ cup red candied cherries

½ cup pecans, chopped

White Fudge Frosting

2 tablespoons unsalted butter

3 cups granulated sugar

1 cup whole milk

¼ teaspoon salt

1 teaspoon vanilla extract

Topping

¼ cup red or green candied cherries

5. Spread the batter evenly into the pan, covering the entire surface. Bake for 20–25 minutes, or until the cake springs back when touched.

6. Dust a clean towel with confectioners' sugar. Turn the cake onto the towel and remove the parchment. Roll the cake from the long side and let sit for 1 minute, then unroll the cake, brush with brandy, and let sit for 2 minutes. Roll again and let cool completely.

7. Unroll the cake, spread with a thin layer of buttercream, and sprinkle with ½ cup pistachios. Roll the cake again and cover the surface with the remaining buttercream and pistachios. Cut 8 slices and arrange on plates with fondant decorations (see page 344).

Chocolate Cherry Fruitcakes

Makes about 10 cups batter, enough for two 4¼ x 8½-inch loaves

Who says fruitcakes should be an object of ridicule? Not me! I love baking fruitcakes in pretty bakeware and passing them out as holiday gifts, and my friends and family love eating them—or so they say. With this recipe, it's the chocolate that does it for them. When you add in brandy, candied cherries, dates, raisins, and pecans, this hefty, sweet cake is irresistible. Dolled up with white fudge frosting, it is definitely a cake to win the fruitcake debate.

1. Soak the raisins and dates in the brandy for 3 hours.

2. Preheat the oven to 350°F. Butter and flour two 4¼ x 8½-inch loaf pans.

3. Combine the flour, baking powder, salt, cinnamon, nutmeg, and cloves in a mixing bowl; set aside.

4. Melt the chocolate in a double boiler. Remove from the heat and let cool.

5. Beat the butter and sugar in a large mixing bowl with the mixer on medium until light and fluffy. Beat in eggs and vanilla, then beat in the sour cream and milk.

6. Gradually add the flour mixture on low speed until blended, then stir in the raisins, dates, and brandy, the red and green cherries, and the pecans.

7. Pour the batter into the pans and bake for 40–50 minutes, or until a knife inserted in the center comes out clean. Cool in the pans for 10 minutes, then transfer to a rack to cool completely.

8. To make the frosting, combine the butter, sugar, milk, and salt in a saucepan. Heat, stirring constantly, until the mixture reaches 234°F on a candy thermometer. Let cool completely and add the vanilla. Beat with an electric mixer on medium speed until the frosting reaches a spreading consistency.

9. Using a pastry bag fitted with a large round tip, pipe the frosting down the center of the loaf and top with candied cherries.

Variation

Christmas Tree Fruitcakes: Bake the cake batter in four 4-inch tree-shaped pans for 35–40 minutes. After piping with the frosting in a garland-like pattern, top with silver dragées (for ornaments) and maraschino cherries (as the toppers).

Colored Coconut

Red and green food coloring

3 cups sweetened flaked coconut

Coconut Cake

3 cups all-purpose flour

1¼ cups granulated sugar

½ cup firmly packed brown sugar

1½ tablespoons baking powder

4 large eggs

2 teaspoons vanilla extract

½ pound (2 sticks) unsalted butter, melted

½ cup whole milk

2½ cups sweetened flaked coconut

1 cup raspberry jam

Marshmallow Frosting

1 tablespoon whole milk

3 tablespoons granulated sugar

1 bag (10½ ounces) miniature marshmallows

1 tablespoon boiling water

½ teaspoon vanilla extract

Coconut Snowballs

Makes 6 snowballs

A big part of the fun of holiday baking is making cookies and candies and goodies with different textures, and these miniature coconut cakes should be on your list. Frosted with marshmallow and rolled in coconut, they're gooey and chewy at the same time. If your favorite part of baking is decorating, try the fondant-covered variation.

1. To make the colored coconut, combine a few drops of water and a few drops of red food coloring in a small plastic container. Add 1 cup of the coconut. Cover and shake well, until the coconut is coated. In another small plastic container, combine a few drops of water and a few drops of green food coloring. Add 1 cup of the coconut. Cover and shake well, until the coconut is coated. Spread the colored coconut onto splatter screens and let air dry for 6 hours, or toast in a 120°F oven for 20–30 minutes, and keep an eye on it. When dry, place the white coconut and tinted coconut in separate small deep bowls.

2. To make the cake, preheat the oven to 375°F. Butter and flour twelve 3-inch dome-shaped pans.

3. Combine the flour, both sugars, and baking powder in a mixing bowl.

4. Beat the eggs in a large mixing bowl with an electric mixer on medium speed until smooth. Add the vanilla and the melted butter.

5. Gradually add flour mixture, alternating with the milk, on low speed until blended. Stir in the coconut.

6. Pour the batter into the pans and bake for 18–22 minutes, or until a knife inserted in the center comes out clean. Transfer to a rack to cool completely. If necessary, level the flat ends of the cooled cakes so that they will

fit together perfectly. Spread jam on the flat side of each dome, then press the flat sides together, making 6 balls.

7. To make the frosting, combine the milk and sugar in a medium saucepan over low heat for 2 minutes, or until warm. Keep over low heat.

8. Heat the marshmallows in a double boiler. When they are very soft, add the boiling water, stirring until smooth. Remove from the heat and add the vanilla, then beat in the warm sugar mixture. Continue to beat until slightly cool and the frosting is thick and spreadable. Add 1 tablespoon more water if necessary.

9. Dip the balls into the frosting to coat, and then roll immediately in the colored or the white coconut. Place the snowballs on wax paper to set.

Variation

Fondant Snowballs: After pressing the cakes together, coat with a thin layer of Lemon Icing (page 358) and set on a rack to harden. Cover the remaining icing with plastic wrap. Make Fondant (page 353) and divide into thirds. Color one part red and one part dark green, and divide the third into five smaller batches and color them light green, black, pink, and blue, leaving one white. Cover the small batches of fondant in plastic wrap until ready to use. Dust a work surface with confectioners' sugar and roll out the red and dark green fondant to $\frac{1}{16}$ inch thick. Cut out 5-inch circles and wrap them around the cakes, smoothing with your fingers or a fondant smoother to seal the seams. Roll out the smaller batches of fondant to $\frac{1}{8}$ inch. Use cookie cutters to cut out a snowman, Santa, Christmas tree, snowflake, and holly leaves. Add details to each element with the remaining fondant. Attach to the snowballs with reserved icing.

Chapter 7

Toppings and Fillings

Apricot Filling

Makes 3½ cups

3 cups fresh apricots, peeled, pitted, and diced

2½ cups granulated sugar

¼ cup freshly squeezed lemon juice

2 tablespoons water

Combine all the ingredients in a saucepan and bring to a boil, stirring occasionally, until the sugar has dissolved and the mixture has thickened. Remove from the heat and refrigerate to cool.

Butterscotch

Makes 1⅓ cups

6 tablespoons (¾ stick) unsalted butter

¼ cup firmly packed dark brown sugar

¼ cup granulated sugar

2 tablespoons water

¼ cup light corn syrup

5 tablespoons heavy cream

Combine all the ingredients in a saucepan over medium heat and cook, stirring occasionally, until melted. Continue to cook, stirring, for 2–3 minutes to thicken. Remove from the heat and let cool.

Caramel Glaze

Makes ⅔ cup

Combine the butter, sugar, and corn syrup in a medium saucepan over medium heat, stirring until the sugar is dissolved. Increase the heat and boil for 1 minute. Remove from the heat and stir in the cream. Cool in the pan until the caramel reaches the desired consistency.

Caramel Topping

Makes 1⅛ cups

Combine the caramels and evaporated milk in a small saucepan over medium-low heat, stirring occasionally, until melted and smooth. The topping will thicken as it cools, so use while still warm and fluid.

Chocolate Buttercream

Makes 2¼ cups

1. Combine the milk and cocoa powder in a medium bowl, stirring until smooth. Let cool.

2. Add the remaining ingredients and beat until smooth and fluffy.

Variations

White Chocolate Buttercream: Omit the cocoa powder. Use 4 ounces white chocolate instead of the semisweet chocolate.

Coffee Buttercream: Omit the semisweet chocolate. Replace the cocoa powder with 2 teaspoons instant coffee granules dissolved in 2 teaspoons hot whole milk.

Hazelnut Chocolate Buttercream: Add ⅓ cup ground hazelnuts to the batter with the sugar. Replace the vanilla extract with 1 tablespoon hazelnut syrup.

Storage for Topping and Fillings

The rule of thumb for storing baked goods is that toppings and fillings made with perishable ingredients like butter, eggs, milk, or cream cheese should be refrigerated for safety. Wrap tightly in plastic wrap or store in a cake keeper to preserve moisture, since baked goods dry out when refrigerated. Unfrosted or unfilled cakes, or those whose toppings and fillings aren't perishable, can be kept at room temperature to prevent drying out.

Chocolate Frosting

Makes 5 cups

14 ounces semisweet chocolate

2 tablespoons vanilla extract

5 cups confectioners' sugar

¾ cup unsweetened cocoa powder

¾ cup (1½ sticks) unsalted butter, melted and cooled

⅓ cup whole milk

1. Melt the chocolate in a double boiler. Remove from the heat and stir in the vanilla. Let cool.

2. Combine the confectioners' sugar and cocoa powder in a mixing bowl.

3. Beat the butter and milk in a large mixing bowl with an electric mixer on medium speed until combined. Beat in the chocolate. Gradually add the sugar mixture on low speed until the frosting is thick.

Variations

Dark Chocolate Frosting: Replace the semisweet chocolate with dark (at least 70% cacao) chocolate.

Milk Chocolate Frosting: Replace the semisweet chocolate with milk chocolate.

Coffee Frosting: Omit the chocolate and cocoa powder. Dissolve 2 teaspoons instant coffee granules in 2 teaspoons hot whole milk. Let cool, then beat in with the butter and ⅓ cup milk.

Mocha Frosting: Dissolve 2 teaspoons instant coffee granules in 2 teaspoons hot whole milk. Add an additional ½ cup confectioners' sugar with the ⅓ cup milk.

Chocolate Ganache

Makes 2⅔ cups

12 ounces chocolate (white or dark), chopped

1½ cups heavy cream

Place the chocolate in a heatproof bowl. Bring the cream to a boil in a small saucepan. Pour over the chocolate and stir until the chocolate is melted. Let cool to room temperature.

Chocolate Glaze

Makes 3 cups

¾ cup heavy cream

6 ounces bittersweet chocolate, chopped

1½ teaspoons light corn syrup

1 teaspoon vanilla extract

Heat the cream in a saucepan until scalding. Remove from the heat and add the chocolate, corn syrup, and vanilla, stirring until melted. Set aside for 20–30 minutes to cool.

Chocolate Sauce

4 ounces unsweetened chocolate

2 tablespoons unsalted butter

¼ cup granulated sugar

1¼ cups heavy cream

Makes 2⅛ cups

Melt the chocolate and butter in a double boiler. Stir in the sugar and cream and lower the heat. Continue to cook, stirring occasionally, for about 10 minutes longer, or until thick.

Cinnamon Sugar

1 teaspoon ground cinnamon

2 tablespoons granulated sugar

Makes 2⅓ tablespoons

Combine the cinnamon and sugar in a small bowl.

Coffee Syrup

¾ cup double-strength brewed espresso

½ cup granulated sugar

Makes 1⅛ cups

Combine the espresso and sugar in a small saucepan over medium-high heat. Cook for 5 minutes, or until the sugar is dissolved and the syrup has thickened slightly.

Cream Cheese Frosting

1 box (8 ounces) cream cheese, at room temperature

¾ cup (1½ sticks) unsalted butter, at room temperature

2 teaspoons vanilla extract

4 cups confectioners' sugar

Makes 3½ cups

Beat the cream cheese, butter, and vanilla in a large mixing bowl with an electric mixer on medium speed until creamy. Gradually add the confectioners' sugar on low speed until thick.

Variations

Cream Cheese Chocolate Chip Frosting: Add 4 ounces of melted and cooled semisweet chocolate to the butter and cream cheese. Use 5 cups confectioners' sugar and add ¼ cup finely chopped semisweet chocolate with the sugar.

Lemon Cream Cheese Frosting: Replace the vanilla with 3 tablespoons freshly squeezed lemon juice. Add 1 teaspoon grated lemon zest with the confectioners' sugar.

Coconut Cream Cheese Frosting: Add ½ cup sweetened flaked coconut to the butter mixture.

Rum Cream Cheese Frosting: Replace the vanilla with 3 tablespoons dark rum. Use 4½ cups confectioners' sugar.

Fondant

Makes 4 cups (about 2 pounds)

¼ cup water

1 packet (¼ ounce) unflavored gelatin

½ cup light corn syrup

1½ tablespoons glycerin

1½ tablespoons vanilla extract

2 pounds confectioners' sugar, plus more as needed

Food coloring (optional)

1. Combine the water and gelatin in a small saucepan. Heat for about 5 minutes, or until the gelatin is dissolved and clear. Remove from the heat and stir in the corn syrup, glycerin, and vanilla until blended.

2. Put the sugar in a very large bowl and make a well in the center. Pour the gelatin mixture into the well and mix with an electric mixer on low speed until blended.

3. Dust a work surface with additional confectioners' sugar. Turn out the fondant and knead for about 5 minutes, or until smooth and pliable. If the mixture is sticky, add more confectioners' sugar until smooth. Wrap the fondant in plastic and let sit at room temperature for several hours, or overnight if possible. Do not refrigerate. The fondant will stay fresh at room temperature for 2 days.

4. When ready to use, knead in the food coloring as desired. Add more sugar if sticky or water if dry.

Variation

Chocolate Fondant: Add 2 ounces melted dark (at least 70% cacao) chocolate and 2 tablespoons unsweetened cocoa powder to the corn syrup mixture. Add additional confectioners' sugar to achieve a smooth consistency.

Key Lime Curd

Makes 1¼ cups

4 tablespoons (½ stick) unsalted butter

⅓ cup granulated sugar

2 large eggs

½ teaspoon grated Key lime zest

½ cup fresh Key lime juice or ¼ cup Key lime concentrate

Melt the butter in a saucepan. Add the sugar, eggs, lime zest, and lime juice and stir constantly over very low heat until the mixture forms a custard. Allow to cool, then pour into a jar and refrigerate for 3 hours. The curd will thicken while cooling.

Variation

Lemon Curd: Replace the lime juice and zest with lemon juice and zest.

Lemon Filling

Makes 4 cups

4 large egg yolks

1½ cups granulated sugar

1 teaspoon grated lemon zest

⅓ cup freshly squeezed lemon juice

⅛ teaspoon salt

¼ cup cornstarch

2½ cups warm water

1. Beat the egg yolks, sugar, lemon zest, lemon juice, and salt in a medium mixing bowl with an electric mixer on medium speed. In a separate bowl, stir the cornstarch into the water, then beat into the egg mixture.

2. Transfer to a double boiler and cook, stirring occasionally, until thickened. Cool slightly, then pour into a bowl, cover, and chill.

Lemon Mascarpone Cream

Makes 3 cups

¼ cup granulated sugar

4 tablespoons freshly squeezed lemon juice

2 cups heavy cream

½ cup mascarpone

2 teaspoons vanilla extract

Beat all the ingredients in a large mixing bowl with an electric mixer on medium speed until stiff.

Marzipan

Makes 3¾ cups (about 1½ pounds)

3 cups ground almonds

1½ cups confectioners' sugar, plus more for dusting

¾ cup superfine sugar

1½ teaspoons freshly squeezed lemon juice

1 teaspoon almond extract

1 large egg, beaten

1. Combine the almonds and both sugars in a mixing bowl and mix with a wooden spoon. Add the lemon juice and almond extract, then add enough of the egg to make a soft, firm dough. Gather to form a ball.

2. Dust a work surface with additional confectioners' sugar. Turn out the marzipan and knead for about 5 minutes, until smooth and pliable. Wrap in plastic until ready to use. The marzipan should be eaten within 24 hours.

Orange Glaze

Makes ¾ cup

1 cup confectioners' sugar

2 tablespoons unsalted butter, melted

2½ tablespoons orange juice

Combine all the ingredients in a mixing bowl and beat with an electric mixer on low speed until thick.

Root Beer Frosting

Makes 1¾ cups

2½ cups confectioners' sugar

4 tablespoons (½ stick) unsalted butter, at room temperature

⅓ cup root beer

½ teaspoon vanilla extract

Beat the confectioners' sugar and butter in a medium mixing bowl with an electric mixer on medium speed until well mixed. Add the root beer and vanilla.

Royal Icing

Makes 1¾ cups

2 large egg whites

½ teaspoon cream of tartar

2 teaspoons water

1 pound confectioners' sugar, plus more if necessary

Combine all the ingredients in a large bowl and beat with an electric mixer on medium speed until stiff peaks form. If necessary, add a bit more sugar to stiffen. Cover the icing with plastic wrap until your cakes are ready to frost.

Rum Buttercream

Makes 3 cups

¾ cup water

1 cup granulated sugar

½ pound (2 sticks) unsalted butter, at room temperature

6 large egg yolks

3 tablespoons golden rum

1. Combine the water and sugar in a small saucepan over medium heat, stirring until dissolved. Remove from the heat and let cool.

2. Beat the butter in a medium mixing bowl with an electric mixer on medium speed until light; set aside.

3. Beat the egg yolks in a large mixing bowl with an electric mixer on medium speed until light and fluffy. Gradually beat in the cooled syrup until the mixture thickens. Beat in the rum. Gradually add the butter, and continue to beat until thick. Cover and refrigerate to thicken.

Rum Syrup

Makes 1¾ cups

1 cup water

2 tablespoons freshly squeezed lemon juice

¾ cup granulated sugar

¼ cup dark rum

Combine the water, lemon juice, and sugar in a saucepan over medium-high heat. Cook, stirring occasionally, for 10 minutes, or until the sugar is dissolved and the syrup has thickened slightly. Remove from the heat and stir in the rum. Cool in the pan. Syrup should be used while it's still warm.

Variations

Amaretto Syrup: Replace the rum with amaretto.

Pineapple Rum Syrup: Replace the water with 1 cup pineapple juice.

Rum Honey Sauce: Replace the lemon juice with 2 tablespoons clover honey.

Streusel Topping

Makes 2¼ cups

Combine all ingredients in a bowl. Blend well.

> ½ cup light brown sugar, firmly packed
>
> ⅓ cup granulated sugar
>
> 1½ teaspoons ground cinnamon
>
> 1½ cups chopped walnuts

Vanilla Buttercream

Makes 2¼ cups

Beat the butter and vanilla in a large bowl with an electric mixer on medium speed until fluffy, then add the sugar until blended. Gradually add the water until the frosting reaches spreading consistency.

> 1⅓ cups (2⅔ sticks) unsalted butter, at room temperature
>
> 1 teaspoon vanilla extract
>
> 1½ cups confectioners' sugar
>
> ¼ cup water

Variation

Pistachio Buttercream: After the frosting reaches spreading consistency, add ¾ cup ground pistachios and 1 drop of green food coloring to the buttercream.

Vanilla Custard

Makes 2 cups

> 4 large eggs
>
> ¼ cup granulated sugar
>
> 2 tablespoons cornstarch
>
> 1½ cups hot whole milk
>
> 2 tablespoons unsalted butter
>
> 1 teaspoon vanilla extract

1. Beat the eggs and sugar in a large mixing bowl with an electric mixer on medium speed until blended. Add the cornstarch and whisk until smooth. Add the hot milk and stir until smooth.

2. Pour into a saucepan and cook over medium heat, stirring constantly, for 2–3 minutes, or until mixture thickens. Transfer mixture to a heatproof bowl. Beat in the butter and vanilla until melted and combined. Let cool slightly, then cover and refrigerate for 2 hours.

Vanilla Frosting

Makes 3 cups

Combine the butter, sugar, milk, and salt in a medium saucepan over medium heat. Bring to a boil and cook, stirring, until the mixture reaches 234°F on a candy thermometer. Remove from the heat and add the vanilla. Let cool, then beat until the frosting reaches a spreading consistency.

2 tablespoons unsalted butter
3 cups granulated sugar
1 cup whole milk
¼ teaspoon salt
2 teaspoons vanilla extract

Vanilla Ice Cream

Makes 4½ cups

6 large egg yolks
1 cup granulated sugar
⅛ teaspoon salt
2 cups heavy cream
1½ cups milk
1 tablespoon vanilla extract

1. Beat the egg yolks, sugar, and salt in a medium mixing bowl with an electric mixer on medium speed until the mixture forms ribbons when the beaters are lifted from the bowl.

2. Combine the cream and milk in a saucepan over medium heat until scalding. Slowly whisk in the egg mixture and cook, stirring constantly, until the custard coats the back of a wooden spoon, about 5 minutes.

3. Return the mixture to the bowl and stir in the vanilla. Place the bowl over a larger bowl half full of ice water (the top bowl should touch the ice water) and let cool, stirring occasionally. Cover and refrigerate for 1 hour.

4. Transfer to an ice cream maker and freeze according to manufacturer's directions.

Variations

Pumpkin Ice Cream: Stir one 15-ounce can (about 1½ cups) puréed pumpkin, 1 teaspoon pumpkin pie spice, and 3 drops orange food coloring into the mixture when you set it over the ice water.

Cranberry Ice Cream: Make cranberry purée by combining 2 cups fresh cranberries with 1 cup sugar in a saucepan and heating until sugar dissolves and berries just begin to pop. Purée the mixture in a blender until smooth. Stir 1 cup cranberry purée and 3 drops dark red food coloring into the ice cream mixture when you set it over the ice water.

Mint Chocolate Chip Ice Cream: Replace the vanilla with ½ teaspoon peppermint extract. Stir 1½ cups chopped semisweet chocolate and 3 drops green food coloring into the mixture when you set it over the ice water.

Vanilla Icing

Makes 1½ cups

3 cups confectioners' sugar, plus more if necessary
3 tablespoons warm water
2 teaspoons vanilla extract

Put the sugar in a medium bowl and gradually beat in the water until smooth. Beat in the vanilla. Add more sugar to thicken, if necessary.

Variations

Lemon Icing: Replace the vanilla with freshly squeezed lemon juice.
Almond Icing: Replace the vanilla with 1 teaspoon almond extract.
Cherry Icing: Replace the water with cherry juice.
Orange Icing: Replace the water with orange juice.

Vanilla Pastry Cream

Makes 3 cups

5 large egg yolks
⅔ cup granulated sugar
2 cups whole milk
⅛ teaspoon salt
1 teaspoon vanilla extract
⅓ cup all-purpose flour

1. Beat the egg yolks and sugar in a large mixing bowl with an electric mixer on medium speed until pale and thick.

2. Combine the milk, salt, and vanilla in a medium saucepan and bring to a boil. Stir in the flour. Stir about ¼ cup of the milk mixture into the egg mixture. Add the egg mixture to the saucepan and cook over low heat, stirring constantly, for 6–8 minutes, or until it coats the back of a wooden spoon and registers 160°F on an instant-read thermometer. Remove from the heat and let cool for 20 minutes. Cover with plastic wrap and refrigerate until ready to use.

Variations

Chocolate Pastry Cream: Reduce the flour to ¼ cup and add ¼ cup unsweetened cocoa powder.
Coconut Cream Filling: Reduce the milk to 1 cup and add 1 cup coconut milk. Add ½ cup sweetened flaked coconut after the mixture has cooled.

Whipped Cream

1½ cups heavy cream
1 teaspoon vanilla extract
1 tablespoon granulated sugar

Makes 3 cups

Beat all the ingredients in a large mixing bowl with an electric mixer on medium speed until soft peaks form and the cream is smooth and satiny. Stop before it becomes stiff, or you will end up with butter.

Variations

Half-Whipped Cream: Beat the ingredients until the cream starts to become thick and hold its shape, but not long enough to allow soft peaks to form. This is the best consistency when you're serving the cream alongside a cake.

White Chocolate Whipped Cream: Fold in 6 ounces finely chopped white chocolate to the cream after the soft-peak stage.

Berry Cream: Fold in 1 cup puréed fresh seeded raspberries, blackberries, or blueberries to the cream after the soft-peak stage.

Liquid Ingredients

This chart can also be used for small amounts of dry ingredients, like salt and baking powder.

U.S. QUANTITY	METRIC EQUIVALENT
¼ teaspoon	1 ml
½ teaspoon	2.5 ml
¾ teaspoon	4 ml
1 teaspoon	5 ml
1¼ teaspoons	6 ml
1½ teaspoons	7.5 ml
1¾ teaspoons	8.5 ml
2 teaspoons	10 ml
1 tablespoon	15 ml
2 tablespoons	30 ml
⅛ cup	30 ml
¼ cup (2 fluid ounces)	60 ml
⅓ cup	80 ml
½ cup (4 fluid ounces)	120 ml
⅔ cup	160 ml
¾ cup (6 fluid ounces)	180 ml
1 cup (8 fluid ounces)	240 ml
1½ cups (12 fluid ounces)	350 ml
2 cups (1 pint, or 16 fluid ounces)	475 ml
3 cups	700 ml
4 cups (1 quart)	950 ml (.95 liter)

Dry Ingredients

INGREDIENT	1 CUP	¾ CUP	⅔ CUP	½ CUP	⅓ CUP	¼ CUP	2 TBSP
All-purpose flour	120 g	90 g	80 g	60 g	40 g	30 g	15 g
Granulated sugar	200 g	150 g	130 g	100 g	65 g	50 g	25 g
Confectioners' sugar	100 g	75 g	70 g	50 g	35 g	25 g	13 g
Brown sugar, firmly packed	180 g	135 g	120 g	90 g	60 g	45 g	23 g
Cornmeal	160 g	120 g	100 g	80 g	50 g	40 g	20 g
Cornstarch	120 g	90 g	80 g	60 g	40 g	30 g	15 g
Butter	240 g	180 g	160 g	120 g	80 g	60 g	30 g
Shortening	190 g	140 g	125 g	95 g	65 g	48 g	24 g
Chopped fruits and vegetables	150 g	110 g	100 g	75 g	50 g	40 g	20 g
Chopped nuts	150 g	110 g	100 g	75 g	50 g	40 g	20 g
Ground nuts	120 g	90 g	80 g	60 g	40 g	30 g	15 g

Index

Note: Page numbers in *italics* indicate recipe variations.